CIPS STUDY MATTERS

DIPLOMA IN PURCHASING AND SUPPLY

COURSE BOOK

Managing contracts and relationships in procurement and supply

i

Printed and distributed by:

The Chartered Institute of Procurement & Supply, Easton House, Easton on the Hill, Stamford,
Lincolnshire PE9 3NZ
Tel: +44 (0) 1780 756 777
Fax: +44 (0) 1780 751 610
Email: info@cips.org
Website: www.cips.org

First edition September 2012
Reprinted with minor amendments June 2016

Contents

Preface

Welcome to your new Study Pack.

For each subject you have to study, your Study Pack consists of two elements.

- A **Course Book** (the current volume). This provides detailed coverage of all topics specified in the unit content.
- A small-format volume of **Revision Notes**. Use your Revision Notes in the weeks leading up to your exam.

For a full explanation of how to use your new Study Pack, turn now to page xi. And good luck in your exams!

A note on style

Throughout your Study Packs you will find that we use the masculine form of personal pronouns. This convention is adopted purely for the sake of stylistic convenience – we just don't like saying 'he/she' all the time. Please don't think this reflects any kind of bias or prejudice.

The Office of Government Commerce

The Course Book refers several times to the UK's Office of Government Commerce (OGC). The OGC no longer functions in its original form and its responsibilities have been allocated to different areas within the UK Government, principally the Crown Commercial Service (CCS). However, the OGC's publications remain an authoritative source of guidance on best practice in procurement and definitions of terminology. It is perfectly valid to cite the work of the OGC in these areas when answering exam questions.

June 2016

Managing Contracts and Relationships in Procurement and Supply

The Unit Content

The unit content is reproduced below, together with reference to the chapter in this Course Book where each topic is covered.

Unit purpose and aims

On completion of this unit, candidates will be able to apply methods to improve supplier performance, recognising the need for a structured approach when dealing with performance and relationship issues.

This unit concentrates on approaches to contract and supplier relationship management involving stakeholders in these processes. Personnel involved in creating contracts and relationships with external organisations need to ensure outcomes that achieve organisational requirements including costs, quality, risk management and timing.

Upon completion of this unit, candidates will be capable of applying methods to improve supplier performance, recognising the need for a structured approach when dealing with performance and relationship issues.

Learning outcomes, assessment criteria and indicative content

Chapter

1.0 Understand the dynamics of relationships in supply chains

1.1 Classify types of commercial relationships in supply chains

- Internal and external relationships   1
- The relationship spectrum   1
- The relationship lifecycle   1

1.2 Apply portfolio analysis techniques to assess relationships in supply chains

- Probability and impact assessment of risks   2
- Matrices to identify supply, supplier and purchaser positioning   2
- Developing action plans   2

1.3 Classify the competitive forces that impact on relationships in supply chains

- Sources of competitive advantage   3
- Competitive forces: sources of competitive rivalry, bargaining power of buyers and suppliers, threat of new entrants and potential substitutes   3
- STEEPLE factors that impact on supply chains (social, technological, economic, environmental, political, legislative and ethical)   3

1.4 Analyse the sources of added value that can be achieved through supply chain relationships

- The link between relationships as a process and the achievement of added value outcomes   4
- Sources of added value: pricing and cost management, improving quality, timescales, quantities and place considerations in procurements from external suppliers   4
- The link between organisations in supply networks   4

How to Use Your Study Pack

Organising your study

'Organising' is the key word: unless you are a very exceptional student, you will find a haphazard approach is insufficient, particularly if you are having to combine study with the demands of a full-time job.

A good starting point is to timetable your studies, in broad terms, between now and the date of the examination. How many subjects are you attempting? How many chapters are there in the Course Book for each subject? Now do the sums: how many days/weeks do you have for each chapter to be studied?

Remember:

*   Not every week can be regarded as a study week – you may be going on holiday, for example, or there may be weeks when the demands of your job are particularly heavy. If these can be foreseen, you should allow for them in your timetabling.
*   You also need a period leading up to the exam in which you will revise and practise what you have learned.

Once you have done the calculations, make a week-by-week timetable for yourself for each paper, allowing for study and revision of the entire unit content between now and the date of the exams.

Getting started

Aim to find a quiet and undisturbed location for your study, and plan as far as possible to use the same period each day. Getting into a routine helps avoid wasting time. Make sure you have all the materials you need before you begin – keep interruptions to a minimum.

Using the Course Book

You should refer to the Course Book to the extent that you need it.

*   If you are a newcomer to the subject, you will probably need to read through the Course Book quite thoroughly. This will be the case for most students.
*   If some areas are already familiar to you – either through earlier studies or through your practical work experience – you may choose to skip sections of the Course Book.

The content of the Course Book

This Course Book has been designed to give detailed coverage of every topic in the unit content. As you will see from pages vii–ix, each topic mentioned in the unit content is dealt with in a chapter of the Course Book. For the most part the order of the Course Book follows the order of the unit content closely, though departures from this principle have occasionally been made in the interest of a logical learning order.

Each chapter begins with a reference to the assessment criteria and indicative content to be covered in the chapter. Each chapter is divided into sections, listed in the introduction to the chapter, and for the most part being actual captions from the unit content.

All of this enables you to monitor your progress through the unit content very easily and provides reassurance that you are tackling every subject that is examinable.

Each chapter contains the following features.

- Introduction, setting out the main topics to be covered
- Clear coverage of each topic in a concise and approachable format
- A chapter summary
- Self-test questions

The study phase

For each chapter you should begin by glancing at the main headings (listed at the start of the chapter). Then read fairly rapidly through the body of the text to absorb the main points. If it's there in the text, you can be sure it's there for a reason, so try not to skip unless the topic is one you are familiar with already.

Then return to the beginning of the chapter to start a more careful reading. You may want to take brief notes as you go along, but bear in mind that you already have your Revision Notes – there is no point in duplicating what you can find there.

Test your recall and understanding of the material by attempting the self-test questions. These are accompanied by cross-references to paragraphs where you can check your answers and refresh your memory.

The revision phase

Your approach to revision should be methodical and you should aim to tackle each main area of the unit content in turn. Read carefully through your Revision Notes. Check back to your Course Book if there are areas where you cannot recall the subject matter clearly. Then do some question practice. The CIPS website contains many past exam questions. You should aim to identify those that are suitable for the unit you are studying.

Additional reading

Your Study Pack provides you with the key information needed for each module but CIPS strongly advocates reading as widely as possible to augment and reinforce your understanding. CIPS produces an official reading list of books, which can be downloaded from the bookshop area of the CIPS website.

To help you, we have identified one essential textbook for each subject. We recommend that you read this for additional information.

The essential textbook for this unit is *Purchasing and Supply Chain Management* by Kenneth Lysons and Brian Farrington.

Examination

This subject is assessed by completion of four exam questions, each worth 25 marks, in three hours. Each exam question tests a different learning outcome.

CHAPTER 1

Commercial Relationships

Assessment criteria and indicative content

 Classify types of commercial relationships in supply chains

- Internal and external relationships
- The relationship spectrum
- The relationship lifecycle

Section headings

1 The nature of commercial relationships
2 Internal and external relationships
3 The relationship spectrum
4 Which type of relationship is best?
5 The relationship lifecycle

Introduction

The first section of the syllabus is designed to give you an overview of the nature of commercial relationships, and the role and importance of managing such relationships in order to achieve competitive advantage and added value for the organisation and the supply chain.

In this chapter, we begin by exploring some of the major concepts in supplier relationship management. We start with the concept of 'relationship' itself: in what sense can organisations enter into 'relationships', and how do inter-organisational or commercial relationships differ from inter-personal relationships? Next, we consider the differing nature of external and internal relationships within the supply chain, and highlight some of the key internal relationships for the procurement function.

In Sections 3–5, we consider two major theoretical frameworks for understanding and classifying relationships: the relationship 'spectrum' (that is, the range of possible relationship types, on a continuum from distant or adversarial to close or collaborative) and the relationship 'lifecycle' (that is, how relationships change and develop over time, from their 'birth' or formation to their 'death' or termination).

1 The nature of commercial relationships

1.1 Can organisations really have 'relationships' in the way that people do? Most writers would acknowledge that organisational relationships aren't really the same as interpersonal relationships. Many commercial dealings are one-sided and emotionless: what kind of 'bond' do you really feel with your supermarket or bus service? Buyers need to be careful about claiming that they have 'relationships' with their suppliers, and marketers with their customers, when all they really have are a series of impersonal exchanges or transactions. (Even repeat business doesn't necessarily imply 'loyalty' or 'commitment': merely, the satisfactory fulfilment of a repeated need…)

1.2 However, there are certain basic features of relationships that are the same for people and organisations, and this enables us to use the concept of relationship to describe certain types of exchanges or interactions between organisations and other parties.

1.3   Relationships imply **longevity**. They may be defined as 'the pattern of interactions and the mutual conditioning of behaviours *over time*, between a company and a customer, a supplier or another organisation' (Ford, Gadde, Håkansson and Snehota, *Managing Business Relationships*, 2003). This is a key difference between a relationship and a *transaction*: a single exchange between an organisation and another party, such as a single purchase (goods exchanged for money) or exchange of information.

1.4   Much business activity, including procurement, is focused on single transactions: seeking to maximise short-term gains for the organisation from *this* exchange, without necessarily considering future contacts – or the effect of this transaction on the potential for future contacts. *Relationships* only develop when the focus shifts to **plans for future interaction**: repeated contacts over time, with the potential for increasing co-operation, and perhaps deepening mutual commitment and loyalty.

1.5   Relationships also imply some kind of meaningful *links or ties* between the parties. These may take various forms, which have been given technical names in network theory (Håkansson and Snehota, *Developing Relationships in Business Marketing*, 1995).

- *Actor bonds*: recurring contacts, interactions and communication between individuals in each firm. The development and use of personal contacts is common in business-to-business dealings and business networking, for example.
- *Activity links*: doing things together. This may take the form of commercial transactions, co-ordination of plans, collaboration (working together) or data-sharing, for example.
- *Resource ties*: the investment of resources, such as time or finance, in the relationship. Close relationships often result when one or both parties invest in adaptations made especially for the other party, such as the integration of supplier and buyer information systems. Such adaptations create mutual dependency: it is more difficult, and costly, to switch suppliers if your systems and processes are tailored to the ones you have.

1.6   Relationships imply some kind of **commitment** from both parties. This may also be reflected in a number of ways, such as:

- Recognition of the relationship's status: that is, both parties acknowledge that it isn't merely a one-off transaction or occasional contact
- The development of mutuality or 'reciprocity': that is, it is not a one-sided relationship. The risks, costs, benefits and gains of the relationship are shared, more or less fairly over time. There may perhaps be a degree of inter-dependency. Loyalty and co-operation 'go both ways'
- The development of trust (willingness to rely on the other party)
- The development of transparency (willingness to share information)
- A programme of frequent, regular, meaningful interaction and communication
- Efforts made to overcome sources of *distance* (such as cultural differences) and *barriers* (such as conflicting interests) between the parties.

Relationship drivers

1.7   Relationship drivers are key qualities or values which build relationships. They include: quality of interaction, trust, transparency, commitment, co-operation and mutuality.

1.8   **Quality of interaction** in customer relationships is represented by customer service encounters: the relationship depends on the supplier's ability consistently to fulfil customer expectations and to create a positive experience of doing business, at every encounter and touch point with the organisation. Similarly, in supplier relationships, each contact and transaction may represent a positive or negative episode, which will build or undermine trust, create goodwill or conflict, enhance or impede co-operation – and, over time, make each party more or less 'desirable' to do business with.

1.9   **Trust** is central to the success of supply chain relationships. It reduces the risk of doing business together, and supports mutual investment in the relationship. If suppliers distrust a buyer, for example, they are unlikely to share confidential information, put effort into proposals and tenders, or invest in collaborative process improvements or systems integration.

1.10 **Transparency** is the willingness to share information. It depends on trust, because information can be misused: used to the advantage of one party at the other's expense (eg exploiting information on a supplier's problems to strengthen one's bargaining position); or released to unauthorised third parties (including a firm's competitors). Transparency supports a relationship by enabling a mutual understanding of both parties' needs, concerns and potential contributions: it is the basis of collaboration.

1.11 **Commitment** is the intention or desire of one or both parties to continue in a relationship, and to invest in maintaining it. If parties are committed to the relationship, they are more likely to be loyal and reliable, and to contribute to shared goals – over and above mere compliance with contract terms or basic expectations. Commitment is therefore important for adding value and minimising risk, especially in long-term supply chain relationships.

1.12 **Co-operation and collaboration** foster relationships. One of the key principles of relationship management is that commercial relationships can be co-operative rather than adversarial or competitive: buyers and suppliers, and even competitors, can work together to add value, to mutual benefit, in supply chains and networks of alliances.

1.13 **Mutuality**, exchange or reciprocity are all terms to express the idea that both parties gain some benefit from the relationship, and ideally share the benefits and risks of the relationship fairly between them. Mutuality is essential for any sustainable commercial relationship: if both parties don't get something out of it, the relationship will be exploitative (which may be seen as unethical) – and probably short-lived.

What kind of relationship?

1.14 It is important to realise that relationships are not a matter of 'either you have one or you don't'. Relationships can be viewed on a continuum or spectrum from *very low* levels of intensity, mutuality, co-operation and commitment (transactions) to *very high* levels of each (say, a partnership), with a wide range of options in between. We will explore this **relationship spectrum** in detail in Section 3 of this chapter.

1.15 No one type of relationship is 'best': different types of relationship – distant and transactional or close and collaborative – may be appropriate, depending on the situation and the parties involved. There is generally no point investing in close relationships for low-value or one-off purchases, for example: both supplier and customer will simply want to get the best deal from the transaction, without any 'strings attached'. However, ongoing, high-investment purchases may require a high degree of mutual understanding and trust.

1.16 This is why it is important to *prioritise* relationships, in order to decide what level of investment is required. We will look at several models for prioritising relationships, in Chapter 2 of this Course Book, but basically, an organisation may seek to develop supply relationships with:

- Suppliers who are most potentially beneficial or profitable to the organisation (and therefore offer a good return on relationship investment)
- Suppliers who present a potential risk to the organisation (which can be managed and minimised by closer relationship)
- Suppliers who offer realistic potential for deepening, ongoing development and added value.

1.17 Relationships only develop and deepen over *time*, as trust and linkages are established. Various writers see this happening in a series of distinct stages: from the birth of the relationship, developing to its maturity and, often, going on to decline and 'death' (termination of the relationship by one or both parties). This is sometimes called the **relationship lifecycle**, and we will discuss it in Section 5 of this chapter.

2   Internal and external relationships

Internal and external supply chains

2.1   In most cases, a supplier is an external organisation providing the buying organisation with goods or services for use in its business, in return for a consideration. In some cases, however, the 'supplier' of goods or services may be other members or units of the buying organisation itself.

2.2   'The supply chain encompasses all organisations and activities associated with the flow and transformation of goods from the raw materials stage, through to the end user, as well as the associated information flows' (Handfield & Nichols, *Supply Chain Redesign*).

2.3   The **inter-business supply chain** describes the traditional commercial supply model: a linked sequence of organisations from raw material producers to component manufacturers to assemblers to distributors – each contributing some kind of value as work in progress 'flows' towards the end customer or consumer.

2.4   Part or all of such a supply chain may be brought within the control of a single holding company. Large oil companies, for example, typically have control over all the main stages of exploration, production, refining and retailing. In most cases, however, supply chains are controlled through supply contracts and collaborative relationships between separate, autonomous entities. This is why managing contracts and supplier relationships is so important.

2.5   The **internal supply chain** describes a similar flow of information and other resources *within* – into and through – a given organisation: from inbound activities (purchasing and receiving inputs), to conversion activities (transforming inputs into outputs) to outbound activities (moving outputs onward to customers). For example, a road haulage company might have operational units for maintenance and servicing of vehicles, loading and driving. The procurement department is an internal supplier of tools, machine oil and overalls (among other things) to the mechanics, who are in turn suppliers of repair and maintenance services to the vehicle drivers – who are suppliers of the finished products to the company's external customers.

Procurement as an internal supplier

2.6   Seeing internal processes and relationships as a kind of supply chain therefore highlights the extent to which each function in an organisation acts as a link in the chain which delivers value to end customers. This is an important idea for the **internal customer concept**, which suggests that any unit of a firm whose task contributes to the task of other units can be regarded as a supplier of goods and services to those units. In order to fulfil its objectives, the supplying unit will need to anticipate and satisfy the requirements of these internal customers – just as a supplying firm will seek to do for its external customers.

2.7   This is a constructive way of looking at internal relationships, because it helps to integrate the objectives of different units throughout the value chain; it focuses on the process of adding value for the ultimate customer (rather than the separate goals and methods of each unit or function); and it makes each unit look carefully at what added value it is able to offer.

2.8   As a service function and internal consultancy, the procurement function has many different customers and clients in the organisation. They may include any of the following.

- Senior management, who expect their strategic objectives to be met through effective procurement and supply chain management
- Related functions in the internal supply chain, such as finance, engineering, manufacturing, warehousing and logistics, which depend on co-ordination with purchasing to secure the efficient flow of information and goods into, through and out of the organisation

- Managers in 'user' functions, on whose behalf purchasers procure goods and services, and who expect timely supply of the right quality and quantity of resources to meet their own objectives. Most obviously, this would include the production function in a manufacturing organisation, for whose processes purchasers procure raw materials, components and consumables. However, purchasing may also procure computer hardware for the finance department, advertising agency services for the marketing department, cleaning supplies for maintenance, office supplies for general use – and so on
- Staff in other functions who carry out some purchasing for their own units (sometimes called 'part–time purchasers'), and who may need advice and/or assistance from purchasing specialists: help with requisitioning, product specification, contracting or supplier management; advice on negotiation; and/or information on market prices or sources of supply, say.

Procurement as an internal consultancy

2.9 'Consulting' is a process in which one person or team (the consultant) helps another individual, group or organisation (the client) to mobilise internal and external resources so as to deal with problems. External consultants provide expertise and insight from outside the system they are attempting to help, with the benefit of an outsider's perspective: organisations often employ management, market research, logistics and other consultancy firms or agencies for this reason. *Internal* consultants operate as part of the system they are attempting to help or improve.

2.10 Internal consultancy is a complex role, requiring careful relationship management. The consultant will often have no direct authority over the client's decisions, and will have to use its expertise and influence to gain the client's agreement to implement recommendations and/or the support of executive management to enforce them. On the other hand, both consultant and client share the same external customer and overall goals (the increased effectiveness of their organisation), which should support collaboration.

2.11 Internal consultants are often called in to solve a particular problem or fulfil a need that cannot be efficiently or effectively satisfied with the internal resources and expertise of the client unit. The procurement function may adopt an internal consultancy role in the following circumstances.

- Procurement activity is undertaken by 'part-time' buyers or non-procurement staff in user or budget-holder departments. Since these staff may lack the specialist skills, disciplines and contacts for effective and cost-efficient procurements, the advice and guidance of procurement professionals may be required.
- Procurement is required for a multi-functional project (such as construction or IT development). The procurement function is ideally placed to research and recommend procurement solutions.
- Specific disciplines, skills or information are required by other functions, project teams or managers, which procurement is in a position to contribute. Procurement may be asked to provide advice or training for sales personnel in negotiation techniques, say; or may be asked to act as introducers and facilitators, putting the product development team in touch with potential supply partners (for early supplier involvement in designs and specifications); or may be asked to carry out a benchmarking exercise on competitors' logistics or quality management processes, to support competitive strategy development.
- Procurement lacks the formal organisational authority (mandate) to impose procurement disciplines, procedures or decisions on other departments – and must therefore exercise influence by promoting its value-adding expertise.

2.12 Internal consultancy may be structured as a discrete consultancy engagement or project: the procurement specialist works with the client to articulate specific desired outcomes from an intervention; gathers data on the problem or issue; feeds back findings to the client; and makes recommendations or works with the client to develop solutions (depending on the terms of the agreement between them). Such a consultancy project approach may be suitable for specific interventions such as the engagement or appraisal of an advertising agency on behalf of the marketing department; or a feasibility study for the introduction of a new computer system; the evaluation of make/do or buy decisions; or implementation of a sustainable procurement approach.

2.13   Internal consultancy – in the sense of offering other departments the benefit of procurement's specialist expertise – may also operate via a variety of operational mechanisms.

- Established procurement policies and procedures – acting as guidelines for buyers in other departments, to help them source and purchase inputs more cost-effectively and with less risk
- Preferred and approved supplier lists, framework agreements and call-off contracts – ensuring that buyers in other departments use suppliers pre-selected (and agreements negotiated) using purchasing expertise
- Purchasing research and information (eg supply market or category updates) – providing planners and buyers with relevant data to support their decisions, based on procurement's in-depth knowledge and contacts
- Standard terms and conditions in supply contracts – managing risk by providing sound contract terms and minimising the risk of legal problems
- Negotiation services and skills – conducting negotiations on behalf of other departments, or advising or training them in negotiation skills, as a way of maximising the organisation's share of value from transactions and relationships
- Management of supplier and supplier relationships – creating and developing sources of collaboration and information which may benefit other organisational activities

Characteristics of internal relationships

2.14   Internal relationships are different from external relationships in several key respects.

- Internal customers will often not have a legal 'contract for services', or even an explicit agreement on service requirements and standards, with internal service suppliers. Relationships are more often negotiated and based on over-arching corporate objectives and departmental performance measures. There is a risk that mutual expectations will not be clearly stated, creating potential for misunderstanding and conflict.
- There may not be a direct fee or charge levied for the internal provider's services, although the cost of the service will usually be accounted for in some way. This may raise questions about what level of service internal customers are entitled to demand ('you get what you pay for') – and what the service department gets in return for its services: where is the 'exchange' or reciprocity in the relationship, which is a feature of external transactions?
- Internal customers do not generally have the option to choose or switch suppliers – although it should be noted that purchasing (among other internal activities) can be outsourced to external service providers. This lack of competition may pose a challenge for maintaining service levels, but it also enables a high degree of integration and trust to be developed over time.
- Internal customers are generally personally known to internal suppliers, and there will be established channels for communication, information-sharing and collaboration. Even so, purchasing may have to put some effort into developing internal contacts and networks, and into marketing itself within the organisation.
- There may be conflicts and differences of interest between functions. Staff or service functions are often perceived as overly bureaucratic and 'interfering' in the more directly value-adding line functions such as production and sales, for example. Different functions will have their own priorities and objectives.
- In general, however – and unlike external buyer-supplier relations – the goals and objectives of internal customers and suppliers are (or should be) broadly shared or aligned, in the overall interest of the firm.
- Internal customer relations are increasingly developed using cross-functional teams, embedding representatives of diverse customer groups within the team. We will discuss this further, a bit later in this section.

Internal and external stakeholders

2.15   'Stakeholders are those individuals or groups who depend on the organisation to fulfil their own goals and on whom, in turn, the organisation depends.' (Johnson, Scholes & Whittington, *Exploring Corporate Strategy*)

'A stakeholder of a company is an individual or group that either is harmed by, or benefits from, the company or whose rights can be violated, or have to be respected, by the company.' (Jobber, *Principles and Practice of Marketing*)

2.16   From these definitions, you might note that the members (managers and employees) of an organisation are stakeholders in its activity and success. So are its supply chain partners (suppliers, intermediaries and customers) and others in direct business relationship with it (such as its owners or shareholders, the banks that lend it money and so on). An organisation therefore has both *internal* and *external* stakeholders.

2.17   The stakeholders of an organisation include internal, connected and external groups.

- **Internal stakeholders** are members of the organisation: the directors, managers and employees who operate within the organisation's boundaries. Key internal stakeholders in purchasing plans and activities include: senior management (who need purchasing to do its job in order for overall corporate strategies to be fulfilled); purchasing managers (who are responsible for purchasing performance); and the managers and staff of other functions or units of the organisation whose work and goals intersect with those of the procurement function.
- **Connected stakeholders** have direct legal, contractual or commercial dealings with the organisation. They include: shareholders (the owners of the firm) and other financiers, such as banks; customers and consumers; suppliers; and distributors.
- **External or secondary stakeholders** do not have direct contractual or commercial dealings with the organisation, but have an interest in, or are affected by, its activities. They include: the government and regulatory bodies (which seek to control business activity); professional bodies and trade unions (which represent the interests of their members within the organisation); various interest and pressure groups (which promote and protect the interests of their members, or a particular cause); and the local community (within which the organisation operates).

2.18   External stakeholders may be important stakeholders for a firm, and stakeholder relationship management may have an important role in relation to corporate social responsibility and reputation management. However, 'secondary' stakeholders do not have a direct commercial or contractual relationship with the firm, and so are beyond the immediate scope of this syllabus.

Procurement marketing

2.19   Procurement marketing is, simply, the way the procurement function 'markets' itself in the organisation. In the same way as the organisation (through its marketing function) promotes itself and its brands, products and services to potential customers in the external market, so the procurement function needs to promote itself and its services to its internal customers. This is particularly important if those internal customers have the option of obtaining services elsewhere (eg from a procurement consultancy or outsourced service provider, or by carrying out purchasing activity themselves).

Cross-functional relationships

2.20   In a 'functional' organisation structure, tasks are grouped together according to the common nature or focus of the task: production, sales and marketing, accounting and finance, purchasing and supply, and so on. This enables cost-effective use of specialist expertise and related resources (eg equipment, materials, management and training relevant to that particular specialism). Unfortunately, it can also create barriers between different functions: information and work flows are primarily 'vertical' within functions, which may be seen as separate 'silos' within the organisation.

2.21 Functional organisation can be a problem because business processes – such as the flow of products through the internal supply chain – are in fact 'horizontal': work and information must flow freely across functional boundaries, without the vertical barriers created by specialisation, departmental job demarcations and communication channels. Customer service, product development, cost reduction and quality management are all horizontal activities, requiring co-operation and information exchange across functional boundaries.

2.22 This is particularly important for procurement, which serves a diverse customer base, consisting of different value activities and functions. Lysons and Farrington note that, while in many organisations purchasing is a separate department responsible solely for the procurement of supplies, there is an increasing trend towards more integrated structures which take in the wider process of logistics or supply chain management: the whole sequence of activities from the acquisition of suppliers to the delivery of finished products to end-user customers. 'Such structures emphasise the importance of cross-functional decision-making', because business processes are *horizontal*, cutting across departments and disciplines: Figure 1.1.

Figure 1.1 *Business process flows across an organisation*

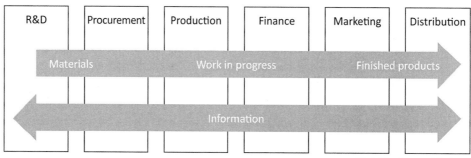

Adapted from Lysons and Farrington

2.23 For any given purchase or project, members of different functions will often have to work together, share information, communicate and co-ordinate their activities. Increasingly, this collaboration is structured using multi-disciplinary teams.

2.24 The same kind of imperatives extend cross-functional working to *external* supply chains and networks. Different members of the supply network fulfil their own specialist functions, as sourcers or manufacturers of supplies, components and assemblies, logistics providers, marketing and advertising consultancies, distributors and so on. Supply chain relationships are therefore also cross-functional or 'cross-disciplinary', which means that there is the same need for multi-directional communication, co-ordination of effort, and sensitivity to potential barriers and differences.

Cross-functional teams in procurement

2.25 Cross-functional teams comprise individuals from a range of disciplines. They may take different forms.

- *Multi-functional* or multi-disciplinary teams bring together individuals from different functional specialisms or departments, so that their competencies can be pooled or exchanged. This is often the case for product management and procurement teams, for example.
- *Multi-skilled* teams bring together a number of functionally versatile individuals, each of whom can perform *any* of the group's tasks: work can thus be shared or allocated flexibly, according to who is best placed to do a given job when required. This might be the case within a purchasing team, for example, where any member can undertake negotiations, draw up contracts, have knowledge of different categories, prepare investment appraisals and so on, as required.
- *Project* teams and task forces are short-term cross-functional teams formed for a particular purpose or

outcome (eg the introduction of a just in time approach, the integration of information systems, or the review of sourcing strategies) and disbanded once the task is complete. The members of such teams are usually seconded from various functional departments, for the duration of the team's existence, creating a matrix-type structure. However, longer-term projects (eg in the aerospace or construction industry) may require a full-time team, operating as a self-contained unit under a permanent project manager.

- *Virtual* teams are interconnected groups of people who function as a team – sharing information and tasks, making joint decisions and identifying with the team – but who are not physically present in the same location. Instead, they are linked by ICT tools such as the internet, e-mail, 'virtual meetings' via tele-/video-/web-conferencing, shared-access databases and data tracking systems and so on.

2.26   In addition, there may be an opportunity for procurement staff to work in cross-organisational teams: an extension of an internal cross-functional team to include representatives of suppliers or customers. Trent and Monczka argue that supplier participation, in particular, can result in better information exchange; supplier support for the team's objectives; and greater supplier contribution in critical areas (eg product innovation and development).

3   The relationship spectrum

3.1   Commercial relationships may vary widely in the extent of their intensity, mutuality, trust and commitment – in other words, their 'closeness'. Writers often refer to a relationship 'spectrum' extending from one-off arm's length transactions at one end to long-term collaborative partnerships at the other: Figure 1.2.

Figure 1.2 *The relationship spectrum*

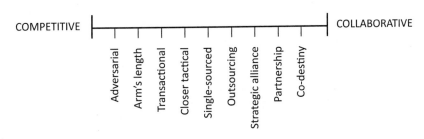

3.2   In Table 1.1 we highlight some of the main features of each relationship type.

3.3   There are various versions of the spectrum, although they often rely on concepts such as 'core competencies' and 'strategic alignment' which should be beyond the scope of this Unit (which focuses mainly on operational relationships).

3.4   **Cox's stepladder of contractual relationships** describes a spectrum including (in order of increasing closeness and mutual dependency):

- *Adversarial leverage*: multi-sourcing and hard-negotiated short-term contracts for routine purchases, where no unique competence is required of suppliers
- *Preferred suppliers*: a smaller list of potential suppliers on the basis of vendor rating and accreditation, for more important purchases where some special competence is required of suppliers
- *Single sourcing*: purchasing strategically important supplies from a single, high-quality supplier who can offer distinctive, important competencies
- *Network sourcing and partnerships*: partnerships between the main buyer and a 'first-tier' or immediate supplier, which takes responsibility for developing partnerships with second-tier suppliers, as a way of integrating and controlling the wider supply chain
- *Strategic supplier alliances or joint ventures*: the formation of a jointly-owned separate firm to produce the supplied product or service, where the buyer and supplier's competencies are complementary and of equal importance.

Table 1.1 *The relationship spectrum explained*

RELATIONSHIP TYPE	CHARACTERISTICS
Adversarial relationship	Buyer and supplier are opponents or competitors, each striving to obtain advantage (usually, on price) at the other's expense. There is little trust, communication or co-operation, and there may be open conflict or coercion in the pursuit of leverage. The potential for ongoing future transactions is not taken into account.
Arm's length relationship	A distant, impersonal relationship, where the buyer does not need close, frequent or collaborative access to the supplier. Purchases are generally infrequent and of low volume and value, so investment in closer relationship is not justified. Impersonal, efficient multi-sourcing methods (such as e-auctions or spot purchases) are used.
Transactional relationship	More regular dealings may be established with a supplier, but are still seen in terms of multi-source, one-off commercial transactions (generally aimed at securing competitive price and transaction efficiency) rather than relationship.
Closer tactical relationship	The buyer wants to secure quality and continuity of supply in addition to cost efficiency, and therefore seeks to foster a degree of mutual commitment (eg using fixed or call-off contracts) and collaboration (eg joint quality control) in an ongoing relationship with selected, reliable suppliers.
Single-sourced relationship	Supply continuity and quality are a key priority for the buyer, so it seeks to increase its control by securing the commitment and collaboration of a single, highly-trusted supplier: granting exclusivity in relation to a particular item or range of items. This implies a high level of trust, mutual commitment and collaboration. In practice, the risk of dependency on a single supplier may be too high, and the buyer may share the requirement between two suppliers (dual sourcing).
Outsourcing relationship	An organisation selects an external supplier to provide goods or services previously produced in-house, allowing it to (a) focus its resources on its own core competencies and (b) access external expertise and resources that will enable the requirement to be met more efficiently or competitively than was possible in-house. An even higher level of trust, commitment and collaboration is required to ensure that standards are maintained.
Strategic alliance	Two (or more) organisations identify selected areas in which they can collaborate to deliver a joint offering. For example, a software developer might form an alliance with a training firm, the trainer providing accredited courses in using the software.
Partnership relationship	Buyer and supplier agree to collaborate closely for the long term, sharing information and ideas for development. There is a very high level of trust and the aim is to find solutions that benefit both parties, with gains and risks shared between them.
Co-destiny relationship	An even closer relationship, in which buyer and supplier link their businesses together strategically for long-term mutual benefit.

3.5   Mark Moore (*Commercial Relationships*) offers a further version of the spectrum, which mixes the type and closeness of the relationship (as in our general model) with examples of purchasing approaches used (particularly at the transactional and arm's length end of the spectrum).

- *Spot buying*: making one-off purchases to meet requirements as they arise, taking advantage of best available terms at the time.
- *Regular trading*: giving repeat business to a group of preferred (known, trusted) suppliers.
- *Call-off contracts, framework agreements or blanket ordering*: establishing agreed terms of supply with suppliers for a defined period, against which individual orders can be made as required. (Effectively, an 'option to buy' from the supplier on agreed terms.)
- *Fixed contract*: establishing an agreed purchase volume and frequency, at agreed terms of supply, for a defined period.
- *Alliance*: agreement to work together with a supplier for mutual advantage in a particular area (eg a collaborative promotion, staff training or cost reduction)
- *Strategic alliance*: agreement to work together with a supplier for long-term mutual advantage in a particular area (eg systems integration or joint new product development)
- *Partnership*: agreement to work closely together in the long term, and on a range of issues, for collaborative problem-solving and development.

3.6 Lysons & Farrington argue (citing Tang) that the closeness of the buyer-supplier relationship – vendor, preferred supplier, exclusive supplier or partner – will influence (and be influenced by) a range of operational factors.

- The type and length of the supply contract
- The number of suppliers in the supply market (and in the buyer's supplier base)
- The product or service provided
- The amount and quality of information exchange
- The pricing scheme and delivery schedule
- The extent of senior management involvement
- The extent of supplier development and support offered by the buyer

From multiple to single sourcing

3.7 One approach to managing supply risk is to have *more* potential suppliers of a given item or category of purchases, pre-qualified and approved as being able to meet the buyer's requirements.

3.8 An advantage of multiple sourcing is that if there are supply shortages or disruptions (eg because of political unrest or bad weather in one supplier's area), or unforeseen peaks in demand (creating a need for extra supply), or a supplier failure, the organisation has established relationships with a wide range of approved alternative suppliers.

3.9 Another advantage of multi-sourcing is that as circumstances change – for both buyer and supplier – suppliers may become more or less compatible with the buying organisation, and more or less competitive in terms of their offering. Increasing the range of pre-qualified potential suppliers enables the buyer to be more *opportunistic*: taking advantage of the best available price, trading terms, quality, innovation and flexibility on offer at any given time. Such a policy is also likely to keep the supplier base competitive, as each supplier knows that it is competing for contracts with a number of other sources of supply.

3.10 However, there are disadvantages of multiple sourcing arrangements.

- They can lead to unnecessarily high procurement costs. A large supplier base usually means more small orders and higher transaction and administration costs: giving larger orders to fewer suppliers, on the other hand, would secure volume discounts and other savings (eg through systems integration with key suppliers).
- They can lead to waste, by retaining suppliers who cannot (or can no longer) meet the firm's requirements, or are otherwise not often used – and perhaps by increasing stock variety and proliferation, where different suppliers have slightly different products (so that ordering from multiple suppliers works against standardisation, variety reduction and inventory reduction).
- They fail to exploit the value-adding and competitive potential of concentrating on more collaborative relationships with fewer suppliers (eg continuous improvement over time, co-investment in innovation and quality, better communication and integration and so on).

3.11 More commonly, therefore, strong collaborative supplier relationships are used to 'narrow supply', enabling purchases to be concentrated on a smaller group of developed and trusted supply partners. Conversely, a reduced number of suppliers *enables* the buyer-side contract and supplier managers to focus on developing, maintaining and leveraging relationships with the selected suppliers.

3.12 At the very narrow end of the scale, a single supplier may be selected for the development of closer partnership relations or an 'exclusive supply' contract: an approach called **single sourcing**. Such an arrangement might be suitable for procurements for which the buyer hopes to gain supplier commitment and co-investment (eg for strategic or critical items) or preferential treatment (eg on price, for leverage items), by offering the supplier exclusivity.

3.13 Buyers now increasingly recognise that multiple sourcing is not the only way to minimise supply risk or secure competitive supply. Single sourcing may be considered appropriate in the following circumstances.

- The total requirement is too small to justify splitting orders among several suppliers, because the unit costs of handling and processing would rise as a result.
- One supplier is so far ahead of others in terms of reputation, quality, price etc that it would make no sense to use anyone else.
- Expensive set-up costs (eg tooling or systems integration) are required to enable supply: it may not make sense for the buyer to pay for such tooling several times over by using several different suppliers.
- The requirement is subject to supply risk, or in short supply: the buyer is likely to be treated more favourably by an exclusive supplier than by any one of several lower-volume and lower-value suppliers.

3.14 This is, of course, the most risky approach on the supplier base spectrum: if a single supplier fails, the buyer is left completely exposed. It might pre-qualify a 'back-up' supplier, as part of a contingency plan, in order to manage the risk of supply or supplier failure – but this may not provide sufficient incentive for the contingency supplier, or any guarantee that the contingency supplier will be ready or willing to supply when required.

3.15 For this reason, many organisations prefer the option of sharing supply between two suppliers: an approach called **dual sourcing**. This enables the buyer to maximise the advantages of narrow supply – while managing the risks of over-dependency on a single supplier.

Adversarial or competitive relationships

3.16 In adversarial or competitive relationships, each party seeks to obtain the best possible outcome for itself, at the expense of the other party if necessary. This can be seen as a potential 'win-lose' situation, where any gains for the buyer are at the expense of the supplier, and *vice versa*: for example, the buyer gets the best price by squeezing the supplier's profit margins, or the supplier enhances its profit margins by cutting corners on quality.

3.17 Such relationships are characterised by:

- Lack of trust and therefore little information sharing
- A one-off or short-term transaction focus
- The use of power and negotiation to seek the best possible deal (even at the expense of the other party and the potential for ongoing relationship)
- Rigorously enforced compliance with contract terms (in the absence of shared responsibility for quality or improvements)
- Little co-operation or recognition of mutual interests.

3.18 These relationships are 'transactional' rather than 'relational', in the sense discussed earlier. There is no consideration of the effect of an adversarial approach or win-lose result on the potential for future dealings – since in any case, the buyer uses multiple other suppliers to stimulate competition: if the buyer alienates one supplier with its hard bargaining, there is always another one available.

Co-operative or collaborative relationships

3.19 With a transactional approach, the benefits of doing business together arise purely from exchange: money in return for goods or services. In a *relational* approach, the benefits of doing business together arise from sharing, collaboration and synergy (2 + 2 = 5).

3.20 In collaborative relationships, the parties intentionally seek to develop long-term, mutually beneficial ongoing dealings. The strategic view is that both buyer and supplier share common interests, and both can benefit from seeking ways to add value in the supply chain: 'enlarging the pie' offers a win-win situation, where buyer, supplier and end-customer can all benefit.

3.21 The buyer therefore seeks to develop long-term, mutually-beneficial relationships with a smaller number of preferred suppliers. Relationship management is based on trust and mutual obligation, rather than mere compliance with contract terms. Both parties will participate in looking for improvements and innovations, secure in the knowledge that any benefits that are achieved will be shared. They will jointly set targets for improvements in cost and quality, and will meet regularly to discuss progress towards achieving these targets. Information will be shared more or less freely (in areas of shared activity) in both directions, to support joint problem-solving and development.

3.22 Note that a collaborative relationship is a proactive relationship with the aim of securing desired outcomes and improvements (in areas such as added value and competitive advantage, as discussed in Chapters 3 and 4). It should *not* be seen as a long-term 'cosy' customer-supplier relationship, pursued for its own sake, or for 'ease of dealing', where both parties grow complacent and used to the *status quo*.

3.23 The features of a constructive supply partnership, as distinct from a 'cosy customer-supplier relationship', can be summarised as follows.

- There is a joint and mutual search for greater efficiency and competitiveness.
- There is joint planning for the future by the customer and the supplier.
- They have agreed shared objectives.
- There is an understanding between the customer and the supplier that there should be a joint effort to eliminate waste from the supply chain in order to become more competitive.
- There is openness and transparency between the organisations.
- Each party understands the expectations of the other, and seeks to meet or exceed them.
- The relationship is one of equal partners, and the buyer does not adopt a 'master-servant' attitude.
- They recognise that the relationship might not last for ever, and have a prepared and agreed exit strategy, in the event that the relationship should come to an end.

Outsource relationships

3.24 The modern focus on 'core competencies' (Hamel & Prahalad) has led many companies to buy in products, components or assemblies previously produced in-house, and to *outsource* or *subcontract* a range of support functions (such as maintenance, catering, warehousing and transport, and staff recruitment and training) and even core functions such as sales and customer service (eg in call centres).

3.25 Lysons and Farrington (*Purchasing and Supply Chain Management*) explain the difference between outsourcing and subcontracting as a long-term strategic versus a short-term tactical approach: 'If you want a beautiful lawn in the neighbourhood and you hire someone to take responsibility for every aspect of lawn care, it's strategic outsourcing. But hiring someone to cut your lawn is subcontracting.'

3.26 Key contract and relationship management issues in outsourcing (and subcontracting) include the need for:

- The outsource decision to be based on clear objectives and measurable benefits, with a rigorous cost-benefit analysis
- Rigorous supplier selection, given the long-term partnership nature of the outsource relationship to which the buying organisation will be 'locked in'. In such circumstances, selection should not only involve cost comparisons buzt considerations such as quality, reliability, willingness to collaborate, and ethics and corporate social responsibility (since the performance of the supplier reflects on the reputation of the buying organisation).
- Rigorous supplier contracting, so that risks, costs and liabilities are equitably and clearly allocated, and expected service levels clearly defined

- Clear and agreed service levels, standards and key performance indicators, with appropriate incentives and penalties to motivate compliance and conformance
- Consistent and rigorous monitoring of service delivery and quality, against service level agreements and key performance indicators
- Ongoing contract and supplier management, to ensure contract compliance, the development of the relationship (with the aim of continuous collaborative cost and performance improvement), and the constructive handling of disputes. This is essential if the buying organisation is not to gradually surrender control of performance (and therefore reputation) to the supplier.
- Contract review, deriving lessons from the performance of the contract, in order to evaluate whether the contract should be renewed, amended (to incorporate improvements) or terminated in favour of another supplier (or bringing the service provision back in-house).

3.27 Some of the potential advantages and disadvantages of outsourcing are summarised in Table 1.2. (You should be able to convert this data into the corresponding arguments for and against *internal* service provision or in-sourcing.)

Table 1.2 *Advantages and disadvantages of outsourcing*

ADVANTAGES	DISADVANTAGES
Supports organisational rationalisation and downsizing: reduction in the costs of staffing, space and facilities	Potentially higher cost of services (including supplier's profit margin), contracting and management: compare with costs of in-house provision
Allows focused investment of managerial, staff and other resources on the organisation's core activities and competencies (those which are distinctive, value-adding and hard to imitate, and thus give competitive advantage)	Difficulty of ensuring service quality and consistency and corporate social responsibility (environmental and employment practices): difficulties and costs of monitoring (especially overseas)
Gives access to specialist expertise, technologies and resources of supplier: adding more value than the organisation could achieve itself, for non-core activities	Potential loss of in-house expertise, knowledge, contacts or technologies in the service area, which may be required in future (eg if the service is insourced again).
Access to economies of scale, since suppliers may serve many customers	Potential loss of control over areas of performance and risk (eg to reputation)
Adds competitive performance incentives, where internal service providers may be complacent	Added distance from the customer or end-user, by having an intermediary service provider: may weaken external or internal customer communication and relationships
	Risks of 'lock in' to an incompatible or under-performing relationship: cultural or ethical incompatibility; relationship management difficulties; supplier complacency etc.
	Risks of loss of control over confidential data and intellectual property

3.28 Outsourcing should only be applied to:

(a) Non-core competencies which, if outsourced:
- Will benefit from the expertise, cost efficiency and synergy of specialist supplier
- Will enable the firm to leverage its core competencies
- Will not disadvantage the firm with the loss of in-house capability or vulnerability to market risks
- Will enable the firm to exploit technology or other operational capabilities which it lacks (and would find too costly to develop) in-house

(b) Activities for which external suppliers have required competence or capability.

(c) Activities for which value for money is offered by outsourcing (due to the supplier's cost/profit structure, economies of scale, or potential for the buyer to divest itself of assets), in relation to the service levels that can be obtained.

Partnership relationships

3.29   Partnership relationships are at the highly co-operative and committed end of the relationship spectrum. They are more 'strategic' (concerned with the long-term objectives of the organisation) and of longer duration. There is more trust and sharing of information. The supplier is seen as an integral part of the organisation's competitive advantage and future plans.

3.30   Partnering is defined as: 'A commitment by both customers and suppliers, regardless of size, to a long-term relationship based on clear, mutually agreed objectives to strive for world class capability and effectiveness.' (*The Partnership Sourcing Initiative*)

3.31   The key characteristics of partnership sourcing are as follows.

* Top-level management commitment
* Involvement by all the relevant disciplines and functions
* Customer and supplier working together (eg there is likely to be early supplier involvement in new product design)
* A high level of trust, knowledge sharing and openness between customer and supplier, extending to the sharing of cost data by both parties (cost transparency)
* Clear joint objectives
* Commitment to a long-term relationship
* A proactive approach to improving and developing the partnership (rather than a reactive approach to dealing with problems after they have arisen.)
* A total quality management philosophy, focused on co-operative efforts to maximise quality and secure continuous improvement
* Flexibility, as a result of enhanced trust and communication
* A high degree of systems integration (eg using EDI).

3.32   Lysons and Farrington note that: 'Partnering aims to transform short-term adversarial customer-supplier relationships focused on the use of purchasing power to secure lower prices and improved delivery into long-term co-operation based on mutual trust in which quality, innovation and shared values complement price competitiveness'.

3.33   However, they also quote Ramsay on the downside view.

'As a sourcing strategy, partnerships may be generally applicable to only a small number of very large companies. For the rest, although it may be useful with a minority of purchases and a very small selection of suppliers, it is a high-risk strategy that one might argue ought to be approached with extreme caution. In Kraljic's terms, the act of moving the sourcing of a bought-out item to a single-sourced partnership increases both supply risk and profit impact: thus partnerships tend to push all affected purchases towards the strategic quadrant. Strategic purchases offer large rewards if managed successfully, but demand the allocation of large amounts of management attention and threaten heavy penalties if sourcing arrangements fail.'

4   Which type of relationship is best?

4.1   From our discussion above, the temptation may be to think that a collaborative relationship would be 'best' or 'ideal' – or at least 'more enlightened' – even if, in practice, adversarial relationships are common. This is not necessarily the case, however, and you should be prepared to take a contingency view of the most appropriate relationship type for a given purchasing situation: in essence, 'it all depends'.

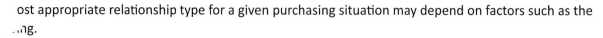

...ost appropriate relationship type for a given purchasing situation may depend on factors such as the ...ng.

- *The nature and importance of the items being purchased*: low-value, routine or one-off purchases are unlikely to justify heavy investment in long-term collaboration – whereas complex, customised, high-value purchases in unstable supply markets may well justify such investment, in order to secure control over the supply specification, quality and availability
- *The competence, capability, co-operation and performance of the supplier* (and reciprocal conduct of the buyer), and therefore the degree of trust developed between them: trust being a necessary foundation for closer relationships
- *Geographical distance*: close relationships may be more difficult to establish and maintain with overseas suppliers, especially if there is little communication infrastructure
- *The compatibility of the supply partners*: if their strategic aims, values and systems are incompatible, it may be too costly to attempt to bridge the distance or overcome the barriers (as long as more compatible alternatives are available)
- *The organisation's and procurement function's objectives and priorities*: best available price, security and quality of supply and so on
- *Supply market conditions*: if supply is subject to risk (eg because of weather or economic conditions), the buyer may wish to multi-source; if prices are fluctuating, it may wish to use opportunistic spot-buying – or to lock in advantageous prices through fixed contracts; if the market is fast-changing and innovative, it may avoid being locked into long-term supply agreements; if there are few quality, capable and high profile suppliers, it may wish to enter partnership with them – and so on
- *Legal and regulatory requirements*. Within the EU, for example, some types of relationships are regulated to protect competition (eg by forbidding cartels, collusion and mergers that would unfairly dominate a market and distort competition; or by ensuring compulsory competitive tendering in the public sector). As another example, in some developing economies, foreign suppliers are required to partner with local companies

When is a transactional approach appropriate?

4.3   A collaborative approach is not necessarily more suitable than a competitive approach to dealing with suppliers.

- A more adversarial approach may well secure the best commercial deal, and the biggest share of value from the relationship – where this is the priority.
- Developing collaborative relationships takes time and effort, and it is unrealistic to devote such resources to *all* relationships. They may not be possible for particular suppliers (eg because the supplier isn't interested) or suitable (eg because the supplier is incompatible), and they may not be cost-effective for routine items (eg office stationery), or items which are only purchased rarely, so that collaboration would not add value in any significant way.
- There are risks in long-term relationships, as identified by Jespersen and Skjøtt-Larsen, for example: the risk of supplier complacency or opportunistic behaviour, based on the security of the relationship; the risk of being locked into relationship with the 'wrong' partners; the difficulties of measuring the effectiveness of co-operation in meaningful ways; problems in obtaining an equitable sharing of the risks and rewards of co-operation (if the coalition is dominated by one more powerful party).

Drivers of collaborative relationships

4.4   However, a number of drivers have contributed to the trend towards more collaborative supply chain relationships.

- Perception of strategy has widened to embrace competitive advantage from supply chain management. Whole supply chains – not just individual firms – compete with each other in the global marketplace.
- Product lifecycles have shortened: that is, they come into and out of 'fashion' more quickly. This has

created the need for faster product development, more frequent product 'updating', and responsive product customisation (eg Dell's customer-specified computer packages) – all of which put pressure on supply chain communication and collaboration.

- Organisations are increasingly outsourcing non-core activities to external contractors, enabling them to concentrate on core activities where they have distinctive competencies and where most value can be added. This creates a need for close relationships, so that the firm can minimise risk by retaining some control over output quality and other potentially reputation-damaging issues (such as environmental and ethical performance).
- ICT developments have enabled and supported inter-organisational networking and relationships.
- In economies increasingly dominated by service-based and knowledge-based sectors, and consumer branding, there is pressure for companies to protect and leverage their intellectual property, knowledge, relationship networks and brand values: this depends on close, trusting co-operation within the supply network.
- In an increasingly challenging business environment, a focus on arms' length, opportunistic transactions fails to leverage the competitive and value-adding potential in supply chain relationships: eg opportunities to gather customer feedback; or to collaborate on product improvement or cost reduction; or to share knowledge and best practice with other companies to improve the performance of the industry as a whole.
- There are costs of adversarial relationships, which tend to encourage compliant (rather than committed) performance, disputes, win-lose negotiation and opportunistic behaviour, loss of preferential treatment that might arise from goodwill and trust, loss of potential synergy and improvements (eg from information-sharing) and so on.
- With competitive pressures towards 'lean' supply, closer relationships and integration help to reduce waste in supply chains. Partners can work together to identify wastes such as unnecessary or duplicated activity, bottlenecks, delays, errors and rejects, and excess inventory – and opportunities for improvements. Closer relationships often also result in integration of information systems, which streamlines transaction processes.
- 'Best practice' supply techniques, such as total quality management and just in time supply, reduce tolerance for delays and errors in the supply process. This causes increased dependence on the supply chain, which in turn requires strong supplier relationships, and the closer integration of people, plans and systems, both internally and externally (Lysons & Farrington).
- From the supplier's point of view, there has been a major shift towards relationship marketing (especially in business-to-business markets), mainly because it is more profitable to retain and develop existing customer relationships than to acquire new customers.

4.5 Partnership Sourcing Limited has identified a number of contexts in which partnership sourcing, in particular, may be most beneficial.

- Where the customer has a high spend with the supplier
- Where the customer faces high risk: continual supply of the product or service is vital to the buyer's operations, regardless of its market value
- Where the product supplied is technically complex, calling for advanced technical knowledge by the supplier (and making the cost of switching suppliers high)
- Where the product is vital and complex, requiring a lot of time, effort and resources ('high hassle') to manage
- Where the supply market for the product is fast-changing, so that an up-to-date knowledge of technological or legislative changes in the market is essential
- In a restricted supply market, where there are few competent and reliable supplier firms – and closer relationships could therefore improve the security of supply.

4.6 The advantages and disadvantages of collaborative or partnership relationships, from both the buyer's and the supplier's perspective, are summarised in Table 1.3.

Table 1.3 *Advantages and disadvantages of partnering*

ADVANTAGES FOR THE BUYER	DISADVANTAGES FOR THE BUYER
Greater stability of supply and supply prices	Risk of complacency re cost and quality
Sharing of risk and investment	Less flexibility to change suppliers at need
Better supplier motivation and responsiveness, arising from mutual commitment and reciprocity	Possible risk to confidentiality, intellectual property (eg if suppliers also supply competitors)
Cost savings from reduced supplier base, collaborative cost reduction	May be locked into relationship with an incompatible or inflexible supplier
Access to supplier's technology and expertise	Restricted in EU public sector procurement directives (eg re-tendering after 3–5 years)
Joint planning and information sharing, supporting capacity planning and efficiency	May be locked into relationship, despite supply market changes and opportunities
Ability to plan long-term improvements	Costs of relationship management
More attention to relationship management: eg access to an account manager	Mutual dependency may create loss of flexibility and control
ADVANTAGES FOR THE SUPPLIER	**DISADVANTAGES FOR THE SUPPLIER**
Greater stability and volume of business, enabling investment in business development	May be locked into relationship with an incompatible or inflexible customer
Working with customers, enabling improved service, learning and development	Gains and risks may not be fairly shared in the partnership (depending on power balance)
Joint planning and information sharing, supporting capacity planning and efficiency	Risk of customer exploiting transparency (eg on costings, to force prices down)
Sharing of risk and investment	Investment in relationship management
Cost savings from efficiency, collaborative cost reduction, payment on time	Dependency on customer may create loss of flexibility and control
Access to customer's technology and expertise	Restricted by EU public sector procurement directives
More attention to relationship management: eg access to a vendor manager	May be locked into relationship, despite market changes and opportunities

A portfolio of relationships

4.7 In the end, an organisation may need to develop a *portfolio* of relationships, appropriate to each supply situation.

- Using the Pareto principle or 80:20 rule, the organisation might focus relationship investment on the 20% of suppliers who provide 80% of total supply value – or the 20% of customers who provide 80% of total sales revenue. It might also prioritise suppliers and customers according to other measures of importance, risk or value – as we will see in Chapter 2 – and develop closer relationships with more important players.
- The organisation may use a blend of approaches. An 'adversarial-collaborative' approach, for example, might allow it to work co-operatively with a supplier on product development, cost reduction or continuous improvements – *and* to negotiate hard in order to secure the best possible share of the resulting value gains. In other words, collaboration 'enlarges the pie'.

4.8 A writer called Ralf (cited by Lamming and Cox) sums up the situation.

'The good old-fashioned Rottweiler approach to buying must co-exist with a more collaborative approach internally and externally... Adversarial relationships exist, and rightfully so. What is needed, however, is a balance between both approaches and a sophisticated understanding of which tactic to use to develop the strategic goals of the organisation. Deciding which relationship is necessary and when is crucial. If this is not done, then companies can be sucked into relationships they do not want, and that often generate higher costs, or time consuming activities and behaviour that are dysfunctional.'

4.9 So how do you 'decide which relationship is necessary and when'? We will look at tools to support this decision in Chapter 2, where we discuss the segmentation and prioritisation of relationships.

5 The relationship lifecycle

5.1 Like organisms, relationships can be seen as progressing through lifecycle stages of birth, growth, maturity, decline and death: Figure 1.3. (Similar models are used to describe the growth and decline of products and markets. You may have come across the idea of **product lifecycles**, for example: the period over which a product is launched, becomes increasingly popular and profitable, declines, and becomes unprofitable or obsolete – requiring updating or replacement.)

Figure 1.3 *The relationship lifecycle*

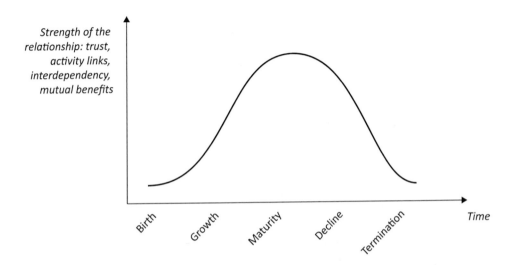

5.2 Each stage of the lifecycle raises challenges and opportunities for the participants. At its most basic, the lifecycle model highlights the need for suppliers and clients to manage:

- *Relationship 'birth'*: selecting suitable relationship partners; attracting them into the relationship; negotiating each party's terms and expectations in regard to the relationship; and setting up systems for ongoing interactions, joint activities and communication.
- *Relationship growth*: progressively upgrading the relationship through increasing contacts, co-operation, closeness, trust and (hopefully) benefits to both parties. This involves improving communication and integration; managing emerging issues and conflicts; resolving distance and barriers; managing the risks of closer involvement (discussed in Chapter 4); and continually checking that objectives are being met, and benefits accrued, to both parties' satisfaction.
- *Relationship decline*: progressively downgrading the relationship, or disengaging from it. Relationships run their course: they achieve their aims, or become stale and complacent, or cease to be profitable; they come up against limitations, or run into problems. The needs and circumstances of either or both parties may change. As a supply relationship declines, roles will have to be re-defined and resources diverted. Internal and external stakeholders will have to be informed and supported through the change.
- *Relationship termination*: ending the relationship. This needs to be done constructively, with a view to: keeping the door open to future relationship or further business; learning lessons for future relationship management; avoiding unnecessary conflict and reputational damage (eg law suits for breach of contract by a supplier or negative PR due to supplier redundancies); and being ethical and socially responsible in regard to stakeholders (eg consumers who may lose access to goods as a result of terminating a distribution contract).

Stages of relationship development

5.3 A more specific relationship lifecycle model (Ford *et al*, 2003) is often used to analyse the stages of relationship development between industrial or business buyers and their suppliers: Figure 1.4.

Figure 1.4 *Stages of relationship development*

Pre-relationship stage

Evaluation of new potential suppliers. There is initial inertia, due to familiarity with existing suppliers, the costs of finding and evaluating new suppliers, and the risks of change and 'distance' (unfamiliarity, incompatibility etc) with new suppliers. Basic questions are asked about potential costs and investment, benefits and compatibility issues. What do both parties want from the new relationship? How much investment will be required to make it work? What kinds of change and learning will be required?

Exploratory stage

Contact and discussion or negotiation about ways of testing each other out: eg trial orders, one-off service purchases (eg a short-term consultancy) or development of a specification for a capital purchase. Both parties invest time in learning about each other and reducing 'distance', but no commitments or routines have yet been established.

Developing stage

Business is growing in volume or changing in character in a positive way: purchases are being built up, or contracts are signed for a capital purchase. There are increasing personal contacts, familiarity, trust, information sharing and problem-solving. This is an intensive period of mutual learning and trust-building through investment in, and adaptations made for, the relationship.

Mature or stable stage

Deliveries have become routine, or several major capital purchases have been made: there is now high trust and proven commitment, leading towards interdependence. There is further investment in adaptation and integration and greater partnership, leading to established, ongoing patterns of trading. Routines and procedures are established, reducing risk and increasing efficiency.

5.4 Ford *et al* emphasise that 'it is not possible to put a time-scale on reaching [the mature] stage, as some relationships may never achieve it and others will quickly become quite stable, if only a little learning and investment are required'.

5.5 Ford et al also acknowledge that at any stage, the relationship may cease to develop further, or may be dropped by one or both parties, because of factors such as: changing supply requirements; wider experience; insufficient resources; or lack of commitment. This recognition is built into other variations on the model. For example, Dwyer, Schurr & Oh (*Developing buyer-seller relationships*) call their stages Awareness, Exploration, Expansion, Commitment and Dissolution. Tsokas & Saren's trust-based model likewise includes a final stage where the relationship faces either Renewal or Dissolution.

Using the lifecycle model

5.6 Lifecycle models draw attention to helpful questions such as these.

- Where in the lifecycle is the relationship with a given supplier or client?
- Where *should* it be, in light of the type of purchase – and how can this be managed?
- What risks and conflicts of interest are likely to arise at each stage of the cycle, and how can they be managed? For example, at the mature stage, might complacency set in? At the decline stage, might suppliers push their prices up to milk the last available profits from the relationship? How can purchasers prepare for constructive termination and smooth handover to another supplier? What contingency plans will need to be in place if relationship with a strategic or critical supplier is entering decline?
- What opportunities are presented at each stage? For example, at the exploratory stage, what innovative projects might be trialled? At the developing stage, what collaborative approaches to continuous improvement might be negotiated?

5.7 It is important to be aware, however, that such models represent an ideal linear progression. In practice, relationships ebb and flow. The degree of closeness and trust may rise and fall as each party's needs change, as opportunities present themselves, as expectations are met or disappointed, and as barriers get in the way. Moreover, as we have already suggested, not all supply chain relationships need to develop towards long-term collaboration: participants may be content to benefit from exchanges at a lower level of intensity, avoiding the risks of over-dependency and over-commitment.

5.8 We will look at some of the issues in managing each of the stages of the relationship in Chapter 10 on Supplier Relationship Management.

Chapter summary

- The concept of a buyer-supplier relationship implies longevity, plans for future interaction, meaningful links and ties, and commitment from both parties.
- Relationship drivers include quality of interaction, trust, transparency, commitment, co-operation and mutuality.
- Relations with external suppliers (and customers) form an external supply chain. A similar concept (the internal supply chain) describes flows of information and resources within an organisation.
- The procurement function has many different clients within the organisation and acts to some extent as an internal consultancy.
- Stakeholders in an organisation can be categorised as internal, connected and external.
- There is a spectrum of buyer-supplier relationships: adversarial; arm's length; transactional; closer tactical; single-sourced; outsourcing; strategic alliance; partnership; co-destiny.
- There is no single 'best' or 'ideal' relationship type. Instead, buyers must consider each supplier and/or each category of supply and determine which relationship is best in each case.
- Relationships go through a lifecycle comprising stages such as birth, growth, maturity, decline and termination.

Self-test questions

Numbers in brackets refer to the paragraphs where you can check your answers.

1 In what ways may buyers and suppliers demonstrate mutual commitment? (1.6)

2 Explain what is meant by the quality of interaction between buyer and supplier. (1.8)

3 In what circumstances is it worthwhile to invest in collaborative relationships? (1.15)

4 Define an external supply chain. (2.2)

5 What is meant by an internal supply chain? (2.5)

6 What is meant by the internal customer concept? (2.6)

7 In what circumstances may procurement adopt an internal consultancy role? (2.11)

8 List differences between internal and external relationships. (2.14)

9 Describe different types of cross-functional teams. (2.25)

10 List the different types of relationship along the relationship spectrum. (3.1, 3.2)

11 According to Lysons & Farrington, what factors influence the closeness of buyer-supplier relationships? (3.6)

12 What are the key disadvantages of multiple sourcing? (3.10)

13 In what circumstances may single sourcing be appropriate? (3.13)

14 What are the key characteristics of partnership sourcing? (3.31)

15 Why may it not always be appropriate to develop collaborative relationships? (4.3)

16 What factors have driven the modern trend towards collaborative relationships? (4.4)

17 List stages in the relationship lifecycle. (5.1)

18 What kinds of questions may be raised by use of the lifecycle model? (5.6)

CHAPTER 2

Planning the Relationship Portfolio

Assessment criteria and indicative content

 1.2 Apply portfolio analysis techniques to assess different commercial situations

- Probability and impact assessment of risks
- Matrices to identify supply, supplier and purchaser positioning
- Developing action plans

Section headings

1 Relationship management
2 Risk assessment
3 Supply and supplier positioning
4 Supplier preferencing

Introduction

In the previous chapter we highlighted the fact that an organisation was likely to have a portfolio of relationships – to match its portfolio of procurement items and categories. No one relationship type, on the spectrum from adversarial to partnership, is 'best'. It is necessary to take a contingency approach: essentially, 'it all depends'. In Chapter 1, we discussed some of the circumstances in which transactional or collaborative approaches might be most appropriate, together with their advantages and disadvantages.

We also noted that, even if a collaborative, long-term relationship is deemed desirable, it is not *possible* to develop such relationships with a large number of suppliers. Relationship development and management requires a considerable investment of time, effort and cost.

An organisation will therefore have to *profile*, *segment* and *prioritise* its portfolio of procurements and suppliers: leveraging its relationship investment by applying it where it will bring most benefit, in terms of added value, competitive advantage or reduced risk.

In this chapter we start by introducing the concept of 'relationship management': a process which includes the segmentation of the supply and supplier portfolio to support the prioritisation of key relationships, and the selection of appropriate relationship approaches.

We then go on to look at some of the available tools for portfolio profiling, analysis, segmentation and prioritisation. In each case, we consider what kinds of relationship 'action plans' may result from the analysis.

1   Relationship management

1.1   As a consumer, you may be familiar with the concept of 'relationship marketing': a long-term marketing strategy in which the emphasis is not just on *acquiring* customers, but on *retaining* them: building long-term, continually deepening, mutually beneficial relationships with them, in order to maximise their life-time value (in profitable ongoing business) to the marketing organisation. A sales transaction is not seen as the end of a process, but as the start of ongoing, mutually beneficial dealings with the customer, through loyalty programmes, Facebook or Twitter communities, special offers and so on.

1.2   In the same way, we can speak of 'relationship purchasing': an approach to procurement which looks beyond maximising the value of one-off transactions or exchanges with suppliers, to establishing strong, ongoing, mutually-committed supplier relationships, in order to secure added value, competitive advantage and reduced risk for both parties.

1.3   The difference between a 'transactional' approach and a 'relationship' approach to procurement is summarised in Table 2.1.

Table 2.1 *Transactional vs relationship approaches to supply chain dealings*

TRANSACTIONAL	RELATIONSHIP
Focus on sourcing lowest-price or best-value suppliers for one-off purchase transactions	Focus on retaining and developing value-adding, competitive-advantage-giving suppliers: repeat transactions and mutual development over time
Short timescale	Longer-term timescale
Arm's length, impersonal dealings	Aim for collaboration, trust and mutual commitment
Low level of contact and communication (mainly to process transactions)	High level of contact and communication (to share information, facilitate collaboration, deepen relationship and develop joint capability)
Primary concern with effective supplier outputs (compliance and conformance)	Primary concern with effective collaborative processes (leading to added value and competitive advantage outcomes)

1.4   **Relationship management** can therefore be defined as the process of analysing, planning and controlling an organisation's relationships, in order to be able to leverage the more important relationships to the long-term benefit of the organisation.

1.5   Relationship management involves a range of activities designed to:

- Gather information about the other parties in the firm's commercial relationships, in order to help predict and manage their behaviour
- Segment and prioritise the firm's portfolio of commercial relationships, based on their relative profitability or potential impact on the organisation (eg strategically important suppliers, or supplies vulnerable to supply risk)
- Develop approaches and action plans for managing key relationships (What kind of relationship will be developed? What will the key issues or potential problems be? What kinds of communication and control will be used?)
- Implement action plans for communication and collaboration, using appropriate mechanisms (eg extranets, contact structures, briefing and review meetings, and so on)
- Monitor and evaluate the effectiveness of relationships and communication, in terms of fulfilled objectives, partner satisfaction, relationship development and return on investment for the organisation.

1.6   You will be exploring the full range of these activities throughout this unit. In this chapter we look specifically at step two: the segmentation and prioritisation of the firm's portfolio of commercial relationships.

Portfolio analysis and segmentation

1.7   Portfolio analysis and segmentation involves categorising and dividing the firm's supplies and/or suppliers into different classes, according to relevant criteria such as volume and value of business, profitability, supply risk – or, broadly, 'importance' to the firm's strategic objectives. The segment into which a given supply or supplier falls indicates the purchasing resources, sourcing approach and relationship type that will be most important, as a basis for sourcing and relationship action plans.

1.8   Most purchasing operations these days face increasing operational pressures to sustain and extend cost savings – while also assuring the quality and continuity of supply. Portfolio segmentation allows the procurement function to:

- Focus and leverage available resources, while minimising identified supply and supplier risk factors
- Follow a standardised framework for decision-making and action planning in regard to supply and supplier portfolio management
- Justify supply and supplier portfolio management decisions on the basis of robust criteria and analysis.

1.9   We will look at a number of portfolio techniques mentioned in the syllabus. Note that the assessment criterion requires you to be able to *apply* or utilise these techniques (based on fairly basic data about a case study organisation and its procurement or supplier portfolio) – as well as to understand and explain their purpose and methodology.

2   Risk assessment

2.1   The syllabus deals with the assessment and classification of contractual and relationship risks (as part of the process of contract management) in a later section – and we will discuss this topic in Chapter 8.

2.2   However, 'risk' is also one of the key factors in prioritising supplies and suppliers for investment in relationship management. The higher the risk of disruption, failure or non-conformance of supply, the more the buying organisation will want to exercise control over suppliers and supply processes (such as demand management and quality control), in order to minimise the risk. And this desire for control will, in turn, influence the buying organisation's approach to contract and supplier relationship management.

2.3   The level of supply risk is used as a criterion for segmentation and prioritisation in many of the models discussed in this chapter. However, risk assessment may also be a prioritisation tool on its own.

Supply risk factors

2.4   We will look at the wide range of risks experienced by a buying organisation, and its supply chain network, in Chapter 8, but some of the key types of risk that should be analysed in assessing priorities for relationship management include the following.

- **Supply risk**: the broad category of risk associated with an organisation's supply chain being unable to supply, or being unable to supply on time, in full, or to required quality standards.
- **Supplier risk**: supply risks associated with the inadequacy or failure of the supplier. Examples include: the buyer's poor supplier appraisal, selection and management processes; lack of capability or capacity in the supplier; supplier failure (insolvency), cashflow problems or financial difficulties; supplier employee or industrial relations problems (eg strikes); supplier technology or IT systems breakdown; quality management issues; delivery delays
- **Environmental supply risks**: the risk of disruption to supply, or rising supply costs, arising from factors or changes in the supply market and external environment. Examples include: raw materials shortages; natural risks to supply (such as weather or disease); fluctuating commodity prices; market structures unfavourable to buyers (eg few, powerful suppliers); lead times for delivery and long, complex supply chains (leading to greater vulnerability); transport risks; exchange rate risks (among

other risks of international supply); political risks (such as disruption from war and conflict, or government policy such as export or import quotas); technology risks (obsolescence, incompatibility, security); and reputational risks (eg re ethical trading, labour standards, environmental protection and other corporate social responsibility issues).

- **Demand risks**, arising from factors such as: fluctuations in demand for the finished product (and related inputs); unexpectedly high demand (leading to poor service levels); unexpectedly low demand (leading to wastes); and the importance or 'criticality' of a given supply item or service to the buying organisation's business processes.

Probability and impact assessment of risk

2.5   Risk is commonly assessed as a function of:

- The *probability* (or likelihood) that an element of risk, or risk event, will occur, and
- The *consequences* or *impact* that will result if it does occur (both positive and negative – although negative or 'downside' impacts are most often the focus).

2.6   Risk levels can be calculated as a simple formula:

Risk = probability × consequence/impact

where:

- Probability is expressed as a percentage likelihood of a risk occurring
- Impact is expressed as a number from 1 to 10: 1 being a small adverse consequence, and 10 a disastrous (business-threatening) consequence.

2.7   So, for example, in appraising a proposed outsourcing of an information technology function, some key elements of risk may be identified as follows.

Element of risk	Probability	Consequence	Risk level
Systems failure	20%	10	2
Staff strike	30%	6	2
Teething problems	80%	5	4

2.8   The relative risks associated with different procurements, suppliers, or supply markets, can then be categorised as low, moderate or high – according to their total risk scores, or other decision rules (eg a consequence rating of 7 or more qualifies a risk as high risk, regardless of probability).

2.9   A simple risk or impact assessment can be performed by using a matrix on which procurements, suppliers or risk factors can be plotted according to probability and impact: Figure 2.1.

Figure 2.1 *Risk assessment grid*

		Impact/effect on organisation	
		Low	High
Likelihood of occurrence	Low	A	C
	High	B	D

2.10   Say we perform this analysis on a given supply market, focusing on categorising identified risks to supply. Taking the segments of the grid one by one:

- Segment A will contain risk events which are not likely to happen and would have little effect if they did: say, a power failure at all suppliers' factories at once, when they all have emergency back-up generators.
  Action plan: Given the low level of impact, the organisation can safely ignore such factors as low priority.
- Segment B will contain events which are relatively likely to occur, but will not have a major effect: say, an exchange rate fluctuation, if the organisation is not heavily exposed by international sourcing outside the EU.
  Action plan: The appropriate response is to monitor such factors, in case the situation changes and the impact may be greater than expected.
- Segment C will contain events which are not likely to happen, but will have a big impact if they do: say, the business failure of a supplier of critical requirements.
  Action plan: The appropriate response is to draw up a contingency plan to minimise the impact, in case the event occurs: perhaps having a back-up source of supply, and insurance.
- Segment D will contain events which are both likely to happen and serious in their impact: say, the emergence of a new technology that will alter the supply market.
  Action plan: The appropriate response is to respond to the perceived threat or opportunity, including it in strategic analysis and planning.

2.11 An alternative approach would be to use the same kind of probability and impact calculation to determine the level of risk for:

- Particular procurements or categories of procurement within the buying portfolio
- Particular suppliers (and their supply chains) or supply markets.

In such an analysis, procurements and suppliers in Segment A would require minimal managerial attention and controls. Segments B and C might require an action plan based on careful supplier selection, contract management, supplier performance or risk monitoring and contingency planning (eg back-up sources of supply). And Segment D would be the priority for the development of close supplier relationships, so that trust, collaboration, mutual commitment and control can be applied to minimise risk.

3 Supply and supplier positioning

3.1 A supply positioning model is a tool for determining what kind of supply relationships and sourcing approaches a buyer should seek to develop, in relation to the various items it procures for the organisation. The aim is to assess the importance or 'criticality' of the different items in the purchasing portfolio, and to prioritise contract and relationship management effort accordingly.

3.2 It is a costly and time-consuming exercise to carry out a supply positioning analysis – so such an exercise must itself be prioritised and justified according to potential benefits and value. Some of the target outcomes of supply positioning are summarised in Table 2.2.

Table 2.2 *Target outcomes of a supply positioning exercise*

OUTCOME	EXPLANATION
Better understanding of relative importance of items in the purchasing portfolio	The exercise forces buyers to think very carefully about important aspects of each item they buy, such as supply risk, and relative cost and value to the organisation.
Decision rules for sourcing and relationship approaches, as a basis for developing action plans	Segmentation on the basis of the nature and importance of the item provides a framework for determining the most appropriate sourcing approach and supply relationship.
Better understanding of stock requirements, supporting efficient and effective inventory management	Items of low cost are relatively inexpensive to hold in stock, and if they are items with high supply risk (ie strategic security items) this suggests a deliberate policy of stockholding (contrary to modern thinking in most cases, but indicated by the results of the analysis).

3.3   Let's look at some popular tools for positioning supplies – and suppliers.

Pareto (ABC) analysis

3.4   Italian economist Vilfredo Pareto (1848–1923) formulated the proposition that: 'In any series of elements to be controlled, a selected small factor in terms of number of elements (20%) almost always accounts for a large factor in terms of effort (80%).'

3.5   The Pareto principle (or '80/20 rule') is a useful technique for identifying the activities that will leverage buyers' time, effort and resources for the biggest benefits. It is a popular way of prioritising between tasks or areas of focus.

3.6   In the context of supply or supplier positioning, the Pareto principle can be interpreted as 80% of spend being directed towards just 20% of suppliers. This elementary form of segmentation can be used to separate the critical few suppliers (who supply important, high-value, high-usage items, which can only be sourced from a limited supply market) from the trivial many (who supply routine, low-value supplies which can easily be sourced anywhere). Most procurement and relationship management resources need to be focused on the critical or Category 'A' suppliers and the products procured from them.

Kraljic's procurement positioning or relationship matrix

3.7   The Pareto approach to segmentation is based on the value and volume of business we do with each supplier. However, this is not the only factor that a procurement or supply chain function should consider when segmenting suppliers.

3.8   Peter Kraljic (1973) developed a tool of analysis that seeks to map two such factors.

- The **importance** to the organisation of the item being purchased (related to factors such as the organisation's annual expenditure on the item, and its profit potential through enabling revenue earning or cost reductions)
- The **complexity** of the supply market (related to factors such as supply risk, the difficulty of sourcing the item, the vulnerability of the buyer to supply or supplier failure, and the relative power of buyer and supplier in the market)

3.9   The matrix therefore has four quadrants, as shown in Figure 2.2.

3.10   At a strategic level, the Kraljic matrix is used to examine an organisation's procurement/supply portfolio and its exposure to risk from supply disruption. For the purposes of this syllabus, it can be seen more simply as a tool for assessing what types of supplier relationships are most appropriate for different types of purchases.

- For **non-critical or routine items** (such as common stationery supplies), the focus will be on low-maintenance routines to reduce procurement costs.
  Action plan: arm's length, transactional approaches such as blanket ordering (empowering end users to make call-off orders against negotiated agreements) and e-procurement solutions (eg online ordering or the use of purchasing cards) will provide routine efficiency. The main focus of management will be monitoring expenditure against regular reports received from vendors, end-users or e-procurement systems.
- For **bottleneck items** (such as proprietary spare parts or specialised consultancy services, which could cause operational delays if unavailable), the buyer's priority will be ensuring control over the continuity and security of supply.
  Action plan: security may suggest approaches such as negotiating medium-term or long-term contracts with carefully pre-qualified and selected suppliers; developing alternative or 'back-up' sources of supply; including incentives and penalties in contracts; and performance monitoring and expediting, to ensure the reliability of delivery.

- For **leverage items** (such as local produce bought by a major supermarket), the buyer's priority will be to use its dominance to secure best prices and terms, on a purely transactional basis.
  Action plan: leveraging buyer power may mean multi-sourcing; taking opportunistic advantage of competitive pricing (eg through competitive bidding, tenders or e-auctions); standardising specifications to make supplier switching easier; and consolidating orders or engaging in buying consortia to enhance buyer power (where necessary) and secure economies of scale.
- For **strategic items** (such as key subassemblies bought by a car manufacturer, or processors bought by laptop manufacturers), there is likely to be mutual dependency and investment, and the focus will be on the total cost, security and competitiveness of supply.
  Action plan: develop long-term, mutually beneficial strategic relationships and relationship management disciplines (eg cross-functional teams; vendor and account management; executive sponsorship); collaborative planning; data sharing and systems integration; and so on. (We will discuss detailed action plans for developing supplier partnerships in later chapters of this Course Book.)

Figure 2.2 *The Kraljic procurement portfolio matrix*

Complexity of the supply market

	Low		High	
High	**Procurement focus** Leverage items	**Time horizon** Varied, typically 12-24 months	**Procurement focus** Strategic items	**Time horizon** Up to 10 years; governed by long-term strategic impact (risk and contract mix)
	Key performance criteria Cost/price and materials flow management	**Items purchased** Mix of commodities and specified materials	**Key performance criteria** Long-term availability	**Items purchased** Scarce and/or high-value materials
Importance of the item	**Typical sources** Multiple suppliers, chiefly local	**Supply** Abundant	**Typical sources** Established global suppliers	**Supply** Natural scarcity
	Procurement focus Non-critical items	**Time horizon** Limited: normally 12 months or less	**Procurement focus** Bottleneck items	**Time horizon** Variable, depending on availability vs short-term flexibility trade-offs
	Key performance criteria Functional efficiency	**Items purchased** Commodities, some specified materials	**Key performance criteria** Cost management and reliable short-term sourcing	**Items purchased** Mainly specified materials
Low	**Typical sources** Established local suppliers	**Supply** Abundant	**Typical sources** Global, predominantly new suppliers with new technology	**Supply** Production-based scarcity

3.11 Applying Kraljic's matrix to a particular context is a fairly straightforward process that offers a useful general framework for action planning. However, it does have some limitations.

- The analysis largely ignores the fact that not all supply risks arise within the buyer-supplier relationship, or can be mitigated by developing and managing such relationships. External environmental and competitive factors can impact greatly – as discussed in Chapter 3.
- The analysis applies to supplies (products or services) rather than to suppliers. A supplier of non-critical items may also supply strategic ones, for instance – and treating such a supplier as 'non-critical' (on the basis that some of its transactions appear in this category) would be a clear mistake.
- The perceptions of the buyer and its suppliers (eg in relation to the importance of the business, and the relative power and leverage of each party in the relationship) may differ. A given item may

be a 'leverage' item for a buyer (as a high-spend procurement within its portfolio) – but this may not represent high or significant spend for a large supplier with many other customers: a 'leverage' approach would therefore be ineffective. (The 'supplier preferencing' approach, discussed in the next section of this chapter, is one way of taking the supplier perspective into account.)

4   Supplier preferencing

4.1   Procurement positioning models (such as the Kraljic matrix) illustrate the buyer's perspective: how important is a given purchase or supplier in the buyer's portfolio; and how can procurement processes and relationships best be managed to maximise value for the buying organisation? However, in this module it is equally important to see the other side of supply chain relationships. A buyer may find it desirable to leverage (or coerce) a supplier, or to enter into a collaborative long-term relationship with a supplier – but what is the supplier's view? Is the buyer's business sufficiently important for it to make concessions? Will it want or accept the buyer as a long-term customer or partner?

4.2   The supplier preferencing model is another matrix, this time illustrating how attractive it is to a supplier to deal with a buyer, and the monetary value of the buyer's business to the supplier: Figure 2.3.

Figure 2.3 *The supplier preferencing model*

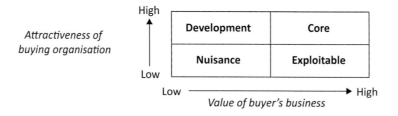

4.3   Looking at each quadrant in turn:

- Nuisance customers are neither attractive nor valuable to do business with. Suppliers practising customer relationship management will regularly review their customer base and downgrade or cease service to unprofitable customers – or raise their prices (in such a way as to turn them into exploitable customers).
- Exploitable customers offer large volumes of business, which compensates for lack of attractiveness. The supplier will fulfil the terms of the supply contract – but will not go out of its way to provide extras (and any extras demanded will be charged at additional cost).
- Development customers are attractive, despite currently low levels of business. The supplier may see potential to grow the account, and may court extra business by 'going the extra mile' in fulfilling contracts: if all goes well, the customer may be converted to 'core' status.
- Core customers are highly desirable and valuable for suppliers, who will want to establish long-term, mutually-profitable relationships with them if possible.

4.4   This is a useful model for operational supplier relationship management, because it suggests strongly that in order to get the best from suppliers, a buyer needs to maintain its attractive customer status. There are various factors that might make a supplier keen to do business with a buying organisation, and therefore (potentially) more co-operative, flexible and committed.

- Glamorous or high profile brand: suppliers will want to deal with the organisation in order to enhance their own reputation and attractiveness to customers
- Good reputation and standing in the market eg for environmental or ethical leadership (eg The Body Shop or Marks & Spencer)
- Fair, ethical and professional trading practices (eg paying suppliers promptly, not entering into unnecessary disputes, keeping suppliers well informed, not squeezing supplier profit margins excessively)

- Willingness to collaborate and co-invest in capability and performance improvements (eg through supplier training and other forms of supplier development, information-sharing for collaborative cost reduction and continuous improvement programmes etc)
- Willingness to share risks, costs and value gains equitably with supply partners (ie seeking reciprocity or win-win: not making excessive demands and hard bargaining techniques, without offering any benefits or concessions in return)
- Constructive interpersonal relationships with contacts at the buying firm (although these are vulnerable to change, if contacts leave the firm).

4.5   As a contrast to the benefits of maintaining positive relationships and status with suppliers, there is a potential downside to establishing a reputation as a 'negative' or 'unattractive' customer. Although suppliers have the business objective of providing their products or services to customers, and satisfying their needs and expectations where possible, this cannot be taken for granted. Part of the modern trend towards customer relationship marketing includes the prioritisation of customers; the leverage of relationships with the most attractive customers (loyal, influential, reliable, high-lifetime profitability) by offering them priority levels of service and satisfaction; and the 'downgrading' of effort on less attractive customers – the 'flip' side of supply positioning.

4.6   A buyer may become less attractive to suppliers if, for example:

- It often makes late or incomplete payments, or negotiates highly unfavourable terms
- It constantly queries, changes or disputes order details and terms
- It uses (and demands) excessive red tape or bureaucracy in its ordering procedures, causing delays in authorisations, payments and so on
- Its personnel are rude or otherwise disrespectful to sales and service staff
- Its personnel prove dishonest or unethical in dealings (eg soliciting bribes or collusion in fraud)
- It has a bad reputation (in regard to ethical dealings, labour standards, customer service or product safety, say) which would reflect badly on its supplier network
- It is excessively litigious (suing repeatedly for damages for minor infringements of terms and conditions).

4.7   Such a customer might suffer the penalties of such conduct, and poor relationship management, in the form of:

- Refusal of higher-quality suppliers to deal with it, or to bid for business, or to enter into long-term agreements
- Loss of supply, if suppliers find more attractive contracts (perhaps with the buyer's competitors)
- Lower priority for suppliers, leading to poorer delivery, information-sharing, service quality and so on
- Higher prices, or less favourable credit terms, to compensate suppliers for added costs of doing business. (This may also reflect a 'leverage' or opportunistic profit-maximising orientation on the part of suppliers, since there is little loyalty, goodwill or desire for long-term relationship.)
- More law suits, if suppliers reflect the customer's litigious approach.

Chapter summary

- Relationship management is the process of analysing, planning and controlling an organisation's relationships, in order to be able to leverage the more important relationships to the long-term benefit of the organisation.
- Portfolio analysis and segmentation involves categorising and dividing the firm's supplies and/or suppliers into different classes according to relevant criteria.
- Key types of risks for buyers are supply risk, supplier risk, environmental supply risk, and demand risk.
- Risk can be expressed as a combination of likelihood and potential impact.
- A supply positioning model is a tool for determining what kind of supply relationships and sourcing approaches a buyer should seek to develop.
- Supply positioning tools include Pareto analysis and Kraljic's matrix.
- The supplier preferencing model examines how attractive it is to a supplier to deal with a particular buyer, and how valuable in monetary terms that buyer's business is.
- It is important for buyers (in cases where the supply or supplier is sufficiently critical) to attain and maintain 'attractive customer' status so as to get the best from suppliers.

Self-test questions

Numbers in brackets refer to the paragraphs where you can check your answers.

1   List differences between transactional and relationship approaches to supply chain dealings. (1.3)

2   List activities involved in relationship management. (1.5)

3   What are the benefits to buyers of segmenting a supply portfolio? (1.8)

4   List different categories of risk that are of interest to buyers. (2.4)

5   How can risk be calculated as a combination of probability and impact? (2.6)

6   What is a supply positioning model? (3.1)

7   Explain the use of Pareto analysis by buyers. (3.4–3.6)

8   Explain action plans related to each quadrant of a risk assessment grid. (Figure 2.2)

9   Sketch Kraljic's matrix. (Figure 2.2)

10   What factors make a buyer an attractive customer in the eyes of a supplier? (4.4)

11   What are the potential consequences if a buyer does not achieve 'attractive customer' status? (4.7)

CHAPTER 3

The Competitive Environment

Assessment criteria and indicative content

 Classify the competitive forces that impact on relationships in supply chains

- Sources of competitive advantage
- Competitive forces: sources of competitive rivalry, bargaining power of buyers and suppliers, threat of new entrants and potential substitutes
- STEEPLE factors that impact on supply chains (social, technological, economic, environmental, political, legislative and ethical)

Section headings

1 The supply environment
2 STEEPLE analysis
3 Competitive forces
4 Sources of competitive advantage

Introduction

In this chapter we explore the competitive and other external forces that impact on supply chains. This discussion is relevant to the management of supplier relationships in several ways.

Firstly, as we will see, there has been a shift in perspective from competition between organisations (eg suppliers of the same or similar goods or services) to competition between *supply chains*: organisations' whole supply chains impact significantly on the quality, price and availability of their goods and services, or (as we will discuss in Chapter 4) the total 'value' that flows towards the end customer or consumer.

Secondly, therefore, one of the key objectives – or desired outcomes – of effective supplier relationship or supply chain management processes is the achievement of *competitive advantage* by the buying organisation (and its supply chain) over its competitors: supplying value to customers, and satisfying their needs and wants, more effectively and efficiently than competitors.

Thirdly, competitive forces in the supply market will affect the *competitiveness of supply*: the ability of the buyer to leverage suppliers' desire for competitive advantage over their competitors, in order to secure the best available deal – and committed and continuously improving performance over the life of a contract.

Since the syllabus also specifies a range of external environmental factors impacting on supply chains, and supply chain competitiveness, we will place our discussion in the context of the supply environment in general.

1   The supply environment

1.1   The supply environment of a given procurement function can be seen as a series of concentric circles: Figure 3.1.

- The internal environment of the organisation includes its various functions and personnel; its style or 'culture'; its objectives and plans; systems and technology; rules and procedures and so on.
- The immediate operating or micro environment of the organisation includes the customers, suppliers and competitors who directly impact on its operations.
- The general or macro environment incorporates wider factors in the market and society in which the organisation operates: industry structure, the national economy, law, politics, culture, technological development and natural resources.

Figure 3.1 *The procurement environment*

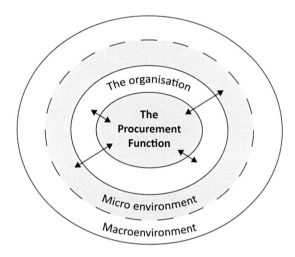

1.2   Supply chain management activity will be strongly *influenced* by factors in all three 'tiers' of the environment: from internal purchasing procedures, to supplier changes, to national contract law or international commodity prices. In turn, a procurement function has a measure of *influence* or control over:

- The *internal* environment (most obviously, by managing the flow of materials into and through the organisation, and the formulation of procurement policies and procedures) and
- The *micro* environment (most obviously, by seeking to manage supplier behaviour and relationships, and by contributing to the organisation's competitive advantage).

1.3   The *macro* environment, however, is *not* generally within a buying organisation's direct control: it will merely seek to anticipate, identify and manage emerging threats and opportunities, to its own advantage – and, ideally, more efficiently and effectively than its competitors. The procurement function is particularly important in this context, because buyers – by means of their contacts with the external supply market – span the boundary between the organisation and its environment. The marketing function performs a similar role by means of its contacts with external customers.

1.4   The 'open systems' model of organisations emphasises the importance of taking the environment into account. Firstly, because an organisation *depends* on its environment as the source of its inputs; the market for its outputs; and a key source of feedback information to measure and adjust its performance. And secondly, because an organisation also *impacts* on its environment, in the process of taking in inputs and creating outputs (both products, such as goods and services, and 'by products' such as waste, pollution, supplier development or local employment).

1.5   The external environment exerts an important influence on the organisation and its supply chain and supplier relationships, in three basic ways.

- It presents *threats* (such as restrictive legislation, competitor initiatives, technology obsolescence or supply shortages, say) and *opportunities* (such as consumer demand, technological improvements or innovative suppliers entering the supply market). These affect the organisation's ability to compete in its market and fulfil its objectives. Environmental threats and opportunities are key factors in the formation of business – and supply chain – strategies and plans.
- It is the source of *resources* needed by the organisation (labour, materials, supplies and services, energy, finance, information and so on). Environmental factors determine to what extent these resources are, or are not, available in the right quantity, at the right time and at the right price – and what sort of supply chain strategies, policies and practices will help to secure supply.
- It contains *stakeholders* who may seek, or have the right, to influence the activities of the organisation. These include suppliers and their supply chains – and also law makers, regulatory bodies, industry associations and other parties with an interest or 'stake' in supply chain ethics, management and performance.

Purchasing research

1.6 To achieve its strategic objectives for supplier relationship and supply chain management, it is clearly essential for the procurement function to understand its supply markets – and any threats, opportunities or stakeholder influence which might affect supply. Purchasing research may be defined as: 'the systematic study of all relevant factors which may affect the acquisition of goods and services, for the purpose of securing current and future requirements in such a way that the competitive position of the company is enhanced' (van Weele).

1.7 This is obviously a broad remit. It may include various forms of information gathering and analysis, including the following.

- **Environmental analysis**, including: environmental (STEEPLE) factor analysis and strengths, weaknesses, opportunities and threats (SWOT) analysis
- **Industry analysis**: focused on the structure of the buyer's industry and supply market(s), its key players, and the nature and intensity of competition in the industry
- **Competitor analysis**: focused on the resources, actions and plans, strengths and weaknesses of key competitors
- **Critical success factor analysis**: focusing on what objectives must be achieved in order to secure competitive advantage in a given industry or market
- **Supply, demand and capacity forecasting**: eg using statistical analysis or expert opinion gathering to estimate future sourcing requirements (and related requirements for supply chain capability
- **Vendor analysis**: evaluating the performance, and potential capacity and capabilities, of current vendors, and of other prospective suppliers in the supply market
- **Supply market analysis**: appraising general supply conditions in the market, in relation to factors such as: likely availability and the risk of shortages or disruptions; market prices, price fluctuations and trends; and environmental factors affecting supply or demand.

1.8 The research into supply markets conducted by procurement departments is generally of an ongoing nature – involving constant market scanning and analysis – although there is sometimes cause for a defined project of research to supplement this (eg in the case of new procurements or identified risk factors). Its objectives are as follows.

- To provide information on which the organisation can plan to adapt to changes in the supply environment (ideally, earlier and better than its competitors) – whether to take advantage of new opportunities or to take defensive action in the light of perceived threats
- To secure competitive advantage by means of early information on innovations in supply markets.

1.9 Basic supplier and supply market data – eg on supply factors and risks, supplier capabilities and performance, market prices, and supply market structure and competition – can be used to support supply chain management decisions at different levels.

- At a strategic level: eg in relation to make-do or buy, local or international sourcing, supply base rationalisation or partnering decisions
- At a tactical level: eg in relation to supplier appraisal criteria, sourcing policies and methods, price targets and risk management
- At an operational level: eg in relation to negotiating and communications procedures; the conduct of price negotiations, auctions and tenders; and supplier performance and relationship management

1.10 However, a procurement function may also need to respond to a wide range of factors in the external purchasing environment.

- Emerging economic opportunities and threats, such as: the opening up of new supply markets; falling or rising prices for critical supplies; or competitors tying up the best sources of supply (or developing other supply-chain based sources of competitive advantage)
- Changes in social values, preferences and expectations, which may give rise to demand for new or modified products (eg using recyclable materials) or business processes (eg e-commerce) or higher expectations on the part of suppliers and other stakeholders (eg for 'fair trade' dealings or sustainable sourcing)
- Technological developments: supporting new products, materials and supplier management approaches (such as e-procurement), while rendering others obsolete
- Constant amendments and additions to the law and regulation of business activities by the EU, national governments and other agencies. One major example is the 2015 revision of EU regulations on public sector procurement – but much of the law affecting purchasing is also constantly altered by decisions made in the courts.

1.11 Power, Gannon, McGinnis and Schweiger offer a checklist of environmental variables and their impacts on supply markets and supply chains: Table 3.1.

Table 3.1 *Environmental variables and their impacts*

VARIABLE	EXAMPLE	IMPACTS ON...
Societal changes	Changing customer preferences Population trends	Product demand or design Distribution; product demand and design
Political and legal changes	New legislation New enforcement priorities	Product costs Investments, products, demands
Economic changes	Interest rates Real personal income levels Exchange rates	Expansion, debt costs Demand Domestic and overseas demand and profit
Competitive changes	Adoption of new technologies New competitors Price changes New products	Cost position, product quality Prices, market share, margin Market share, contribution margin Demand, advertising expenditure
Supplier changes	Change in input costs Supply changes Changes in number of suppliers	Prices, demand, contribution margin Production processes, investment Costs, availability, risk
Market changes	New uses of products Product obsolescence New markets	Demand, capacity utilisation Prices, demand, capacity utilisation Distribution channels, demand, capacity utilisation

1.12 We will focus, however, on the model specified by the syllabus: STEEPLE analysis.

2 STEEPLE analysis

2.1 A popular tool for analysing external macro environment or supply market factors is described by the acronym PEST (and more comprehensive variants such as PESTLE). The most comprehensive version of this model – specified in your syllabus – is STEEPLE: Table 3.2. We have chosen some illustrative examples of STEEPLE factors which impact most clearly on supply chains and supplier relationships.

Table 3.2 *The STEEPLE framework*

FACTORS	EXAMPLES
Socio-cultural	Demographics (age, gender, population movements and so on) affecting demand for goods and services, and the availability of skills Consumerism and consumer power (affecting the value demanded by consumers from supply chains) Values (eg re ethical products and services, value for money) Attitudes to work and employee relations (impacting on supplier risk) International cultural differences (affecting international supplier relations)
Technological	Information and communications technology (ICT) developments broadly supportive of supply chain management and co-ordination, including: Supplier relationship management systems Communication tools such as web-conferencing and extranets E-procurement and e-contract-management systems Delivery/inventory tracking and data sharing systems (such as EPOS, RFID)
Economic	Indicators of the economic strength and stability of markets, including consumer spending and employment levels Rates of inflation, interest and taxation (impacting on disposable incomes, the costs of finance, and market price sensitivity) In *international* supply markets: exchange rates, comparative wages and taxes, freedom of labour and capital movements, trade agreements and so on.
Environmental (or 'ecological')	Consumer demand and public pressure for eco-friendly products and processes Law and regulation (and related compliance risks) on environmental issues such as pollution, carbon emissions and waste management Emerging or local priorities re green 'issues': eg water management, de-forestation, climate change and greenhouse-gas emissions The availability, scarcity and price of natural resources and commodities Risks from weather and other natural factors (eg earthquakes, diseases).
Political	Government policies (eg on tariff and non-tariff barriers to trade) Grants and subsidies available for supply market or supplier development Political risk in supply markets (eg political or civil unrest or war)
Legal	A wide range of law and regulation affecting: commercial contracts; employment rights and obligations in a transfer of undertakings (including outsourcing); workplace health and safety; environmental protection; consumer rights; data protection; and (in the public sector) procurement procedures.
Ethical	Consumer demand for ethically sourced and produced goods and services (eg fair pricing, supply chain labour standards, avoidance of animal testing, sustainable sourcing of non-renewable resources) Ethical codes and standards published by buyers or suppliers, professional bodies (such as CIPS), and pressure groups Ethical and reputational risk arising from exposure of, or association with, unethical practices in the supply chain.

2.2 It is well worth remembering these categories: if you are asked in the exam to comment on the external environment or supply market of an organisation, they provide a good 'checklist' around which to build a systematic and well-structured answer.

Socio-cultural factors

2.3 The socio-cultural environment embraces 'people' aspects of the society, product markets and supply markets within which the organisation operates, and from which it draws its suppliers, customers and workers.

2.4 Socio-cultural factors include: demographic characteristics (age, gender and geographical distribution, population density and movements, educational and occupational trends and so on); cultural norms, values and customs; emerging values (such as 'green' consumerism); attitudes to work, work-life balance and consumer spending; lifestyle and fashion trends; consumer buying preferences and so on. These factors reflect the needs and expectations of the organisation's target market, helping to forecast demand for products and services and to identify market segments which can be targeted for competitive advantage. However, they also reflect other stakeholder groups: shaping relationships with suppliers from different cultures, say; determining expectations of 'fair' and 'ethical' dealings and labour standards in supply chains; and affecting the availability of the skilled labour needed by the organisation.

2.5 Sources of socio-cultural data include: published demographic surveys and reports (eg the *Economic and Labour Market Review*); media and specialist analysis of trends; market research programmes (and/or access to published research reports); market-focused consultancies; customer feedback and preference-monitoring (eg via online data gathering); and general 'scanning' of the environment.

Technological factors

2.6 The technological environment embraces the technological sophistication of the organisation's national or international supply markets, and developments in the particular fields that are relevant to the organisation. Technology becomes more important every day, as innovations and developments:

- Increase the speed and power of information gathering, processing and communication (via information and communications technology or ICT) – supporting streamlined, automated procurement transactions and buyer-supplier data sharing
- Enable 24/7 global business activity (including supply chain communication), via the internet and telecommunications systems – particularly supportive of international supply chain management
- Enable new products (such as downloaded music), and business processes (such as e-commerce and computer-assisted design and manufacture) – to which supply chains must adapt
- Shorten the shelf-life of products (or 'product lifecycles'), owing to the increasing pace of changing demand, obsolescence and modification – creating pressure for product innovation, with fast, flexible supply chains to support it
- Increase competition, choice and supply chain diversity, by enabling small competitors to offer differentiated or customised, small-volume products and services to a global market
- Create 'virtual' teams and organisations, in which people share data and work together linked mainly by ICT – allowing firms to source and collaborate with supply chain partners regardless of location.

2.7 Information and communications technology can be used as a strategic tool for supply chain and supplier management in a number of ways.

- To improve supply chain productivity and performance, eg through the use of computer-aided design and manufacturing (CAD/CAM) or JIT systems; speeding up supplier communication using email or extranet; or reducing the need for expediting, using integrated information systems
- To facilitate supply chain innovation, learning and improvement, with access to global information eg on a pool of diverse, small, specialist and overseas suppliers and products; and on global best practice and competitor activity for benchmarking and imitation
- To support best practice in contract and supplier management through automated procedures and reporting by exception – minimising the risk of 'maverick' behaviour where contract management is devolved to user departments
- To develop loyal, mutually beneficial supplier relationships and collaboration, by:
  - Providing information on supplier capabilities, capacity, performance, contacts, contracts and agreements (eg on service levels or continuous improvement) to support relationship and performance management
  - Providing real-time information for transaction processing, delivery tracking and other value-adding services

- Streamlining procurement and delivery processes for higher levels of customer service and reduced costs
- Creating knowledge communities – sharing best-practice, supply market and competitor information via extranets, for example
- Facilitating the coordination of collaborative activities through improved communication.

2.8 Information on the technology environment is available from: technology surveys; specialist journals; media analysis; trade conferences and exhibitions; technology-based consultancies and providers (eg R&D companies, software and systems developers, robotics companies and so on).

Economic factors

2.9 The economic environment embraces the general level of activity and growth in the economic system, and the effect of economic cycles (boom, recession, recovery, growth). These are related to more detailed economic factors such as the government's fiscal (tax) and monetary (money supply) policy; foreign exchange rates; interest rates and the availability and cost of finance; inflation and prices; consumer spending; labour costs and unemployment levels; the mobility of capital and labour across international boundaries; international trade agreements and so on. Making informed judgements and assumptions about future economic events may therefore be crucially important for planning business strategy.

2.10 At the same time, organisations operate within an immediate industry and supply market ecosystem. *Industry analysis* explores such questions as these.

- What are the essential economic characteristics of the industry?
- What is the level of industrial concentration (what percentage of total capacity is controlled by the five or six largest companies) and competition?
- What is the apparent relationship or correlation between industry sales and demand, and economic indicators (eg gross national product or employment)?
- What are the possible consequences of economic factors and changes for supply chain decisions such as: demand forecasting and management; investment in supplier development; the financial stability of suppliers; and other supply risks?

2.11 Sources of economic data include: published government forecasts, reports and statistics; media analysis; industry projections and reports; and industry conferences and contacts.

Environmental factors

2.12 The natural environment embraces factors such as: legislation, international obligations (such as the Kyoto Protocol on climate change) and government targets in regard to environmental protection and sustainability; consumer and pressure-group demand for eco-friendly products and business processes; issues of pollution, waste management, disposal and recycling; the depletion of non-renewable natural resources; the protection of habitats and biodiversity from urbanisation and industry; the reduction of carbon emissions; the risk of natural forces (such as weather) affecting supply; and so on.

2.13 All these factors will impact on supply chains in areas such as materials specification; supplier selection and management (to ensure good environmental practice); the planning of logistics (eg transport) to minimise adverse impacts (such as pollution and fuel usage); the increasing use of reverse logistics (eg returns and recycling); and compliance and risk management. Specific industries and firms will also have particular concerns: you might like to think what 'green' issues might be a priority for a car manufacturer, an airline, a brand of canned tuna or a hospital, say; or what kinds of supply are most likely to be subject to weather risk.

2.14 As a side note, you should be aware of the potential for misunderstanding in exam questions, if you are asked about 'environmental factors': be clear whether such a question is asked in the context of environmental analysis (eg STEEPLE factors) – or whether it applies specifically to the *natural* environment or 'green' issues.

Political factors

2.15 The political environment embraces factors such as the economic and social goals of the government (and wider political blocs such as the EU); the role of government as an employer, consumer or supplier (in the public sector); the support given to industry (in the form of capital provision, regional grants, assistance to small firms, expert services etc); the strength or weakness of trade unions (and the stability of employee relations in firms); the influence of lobbying groups and public opinion on government policy and the practice of firms; and the stability of governing regimes and other forms of political risk (particularly in foreign markets).

2.16 Sources of such information include: published government policy; direct contact with government representatives and lobbyists; media analysis of the political scene; published, online or specially commissioned surveys and reports; and specialist consultancies dealing in political risk analysis.

Legal factors

2.17 The legal environment includes the operation of the justice system (the law and how it is enforced) and the organisation's contractual relationships with various parties (including suppliers). There is a wide range of national and trans-national (eg EU) law and regulation on areas such as: parties' rights under commercial contracts; the rights and obligations of employers and employees in the employment relationship; health and safety at work; consumer protection; environmental protection; data protection and so on. In addition to principles laid down by statute, there are principles developed by judges' decisions in the courts, which determine how the law is interpreted.

2.18 Strategic and operational compliance with relevant legal provisions is essential to demonstrate corporate social responsibility – protecting the organisation's brand and reputation (including its ability to retain quality supply chain partners) – and to avoid penalties and sanctions for *not* doing so.

2.19 Information on legal provisions and changes is well-publicised, and regularly scrutinised by specialist advisers. However, purchasing professionals will need to keep up to date with developments in their own areas of interest: *Supply Management*, for example, offers regular briefings and updates on relevant law and cases.

Ethical factors

2.20 The ethical environment embraces a range of issues to do with corporate social responsibility (CSR) and business ethics: what constitutes 'right conduct' for an organisation in its context. This overlaps with the legal and ecological environments, since compliance and environmental protection are generally regarded as ethical responsibilities. However, it also includes industry and professional Codes of Practice and stakeholder pressure in areas such as: fair trading and the ethical treatment of suppliers; the fair and humane treatment of employees (over and above legal minimum requirements); supporting local communities (with investment and employment); and selecting and managing suppliers so that they comply with good practice in these areas.

2.21 Industry associations and professional bodies such as CIPS publish Codes of Ethics to provide guidelines in these areas. Many organisations also develop their own objectives for corporate citizenship or corporate social responsibility, and codes of ethics or codes of practice to support them. Debate in the media, attitude and feedback surveys, and the activities of pressure groups are also good sources of information about the ethical concerns of the wider stakeholder environment. Fair and ethical trading and employment practices are also actively promoted by organisations such as the International Labour Organisation (ILO), the Ethical Trading Initiative (ETI) and the Fair Trade movement.

SWOT analysis

2.22 Strengths, weaknesses, opportunities and threats (SWOT) analysis is a strategic planning technique, used to assess the resources of an organisation, function or supply chain to cope with and/or capitalise on factors in its environment.

2.23 Strengths and weaknesses are *internal* aspects of the business or supply chain that enhance or limit its ability to compete, change and thrive. Internal appraisal may cover aspects such as the following.

- Physical and financial resources: plant and machinery, availability of raw materials, owned assets, revenue-earning potential, profitability
- The product and service portfolio, its competitive strength (eg brand positioning and market share) and sources of sustainable (eg hard to imitate) competitive advantage
- Human resources: management expertise, staff skills, labour flexibility
- The efficiency and effectiveness of processes, operations and systems (eg for quality control, inventory management, communication, information processing)
- Structure and relationships: adaptability, efficiency, co-ordination and communication, teamwork and collaboration, commitment and trust
- Distinctive competencies and resources: things the organisation or supply chain does differently and better than its competitors.

2.24 Opportunities and threats are factors in the *external* environment that may emerge to impact on the business or supply chain (as identified by STEEPLE analysis). What potential do they offer to enhance or erode its competitive advantage, profitability, reputation or other sources of value?

2.25 Internal and external factors can be mapped in a SWOT grid as follows: Figure 3.2.

Figure 3.2 *SWOT analysis*

INTERNAL	**Strengths** New technology Quality management systems Stable, high quality staff Market leading brands	**Weaknesses** Low new product development Poor financial controls Non-renewable resources
EXTERNAL	**Opportunities** E-commerce Consumer values re quality Tax breaks for regional development	**Threats** Environmental protection law Fashion trends Ageing demographic

2.26 SWOT is used to identify areas where strategic responses are required in order for the organisation or supply chain to maintain or enhance its position in relation to the environment.

- Plan to build on strengths and/or minimise weaknesses – in order to be able to capitalise on the identified opportunities (or create new ones) and to cope better with the identified threats.
- Plan to convert threats into opportunities – by developing the strengths (and contingency plans) to counter them more effectively than competitors, and by being prepared to learn from them.

3   Competitive forces

Porter's Five Forces Model

3.1   Some of the key texts on competition and competitive advantage were written in the 1980s by Professor Michael Porter. He suggested that 'competition in an industry is rooted in its underlying economics', and that 'competitive forces exist that go well beyond the established combatants in a particular industry'.

3.2   Porter developed a framework which argues that the extent of competition in an industry – and therefore its attractiveness or potential profitability to any given player within it – depends on the interaction of five forces in the organisation's industry environment: Figure 3.3.

Figure 3.3 *Porter's five forces model*

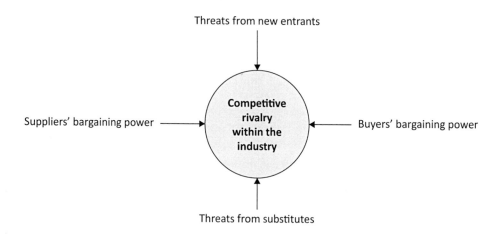

Potential new entrants

3.3   Potential new entrants to an industry may make it more competitive by: expanding supply (without necessarily increasing market demand); striving to penetrate the market and build market share, perhaps by innovating or competing aggressively; and increasing costs, as they bid for factors of production.

3.4   It is therefore in the interests of existing competitors to deter new entrants. The strength of the threat from new entrants will vary from industry to industry, according to the strength of 'barriers to entry' – and the response of existing competitors to any new entrant. (If existing players typically respond to new competitors by competing aggressively on price, a prospective entrant might think twice about whether entry will be profitable...)

3.5   *Barriers to entry* are factors which reduce the attractiveness or profitability of a market to potential new competitors from outside, and therefore reduce the likelihood that they will enter the market. In perfect competition, no such barriers exist – but in oligopoly and monopoly markets, firms will have an interest in erecting such barriers (if they do not already exist) in order to protect their power and profits.

3.6   The main barriers to entry include the following.

- Economies of scale and other cost advantages for established competitors (eg bulk purchasing and production economies, lower marketing costs, no learning curve, preferential access to necessary inputs), allowing them to squeeze out new entrants with a price war if necessary
- High capital investment requirements in order to enter the market
- Product differentiation and brand identity: hard-to-imitate offerings with costly-to-counter market profile and customer loyalty. Established competitors can afford to spend heavily on advertising, the

cost of which will be spread over a large number of units sold: newer, smaller entrants may struggle to advertise at levels required to create awareness and woo customers away from existing players.

- Switching costs (eg time, inconvenience, unfamiliarity with the new product, perhaps cost of getting out of existing contracts) and customer loyalty to existing brands, hindering new product trial and adoption by the market
- Existing players' control over supply and distribution channels (perhaps on a selective or exclusive basis which would hinder competitors)
- Existing players' control over a natural resource for which no close substitutes exist (eg ownership of or access to minerals or forests)
- Restricted labour or skill supply (eg the provision of accountancy and legal services being restricted to members of appropriate professional bodies)
- Government policy and legislative barriers: for example, laws protecting established players' intellectual property (eg design patents and copyrights) or physical property (such as mineral or fishing rights).

Potential substitute products

3.7   Substitute products are alternative products that serve the same purpose (eg postal services, courier services, fax machines and email in the field of communication), making it easy for buyers to switch to alternative suppliers, and therefore limiting the price that suppliers can charge for their products. At the same time, there may be the risk of substitute products in the buying organisation's own product market – weakening its power in relation to its own customers. There is a particular risk in that a company may not see a substitute coming, if it results from genuine innovation.

3.8   Where there are plenty of substitutes available, demand for a product is likely to be relatively price sensitive: buyers are more likely to switch in response to price rises (or price cuts by competitors). Improved price or value positioning in substitute products is therefore a significant threat to suppliers in a given supply market.

Buyer and supplier power

3.9   **Buyer power** may make an industry or supply market more competitive by enabling buyers (customers) to: force down prices; bargain for higher quality or improved services; or play competing providers against each other. Porter suggested that buyers are particularly powerful in the following situations.

- They are limited in number and/or large in size, relative to supplying firms.
- Their spend is a high proportion of suppliers' revenue (but not a high proportion of their own spend, since this will make them dependent on the supplier).
- Products and services are undifferentiated, or there are substitute products, making it easy to switch suppliers.
- There is potential for 'backward integration' (ie buyers can own or control their suppliers: a book publisher taking over a printing company, say).

3.10   **Supplier power** in a given industry or supply market is generally exercised to raise prices, squeezing buyers' profits (especially if they are unable to recover their cost increases by raising their own prices). Suppliers are particularly powerful in the following situations.

- They are limited in number and/or large in size, relative to buying firms.
- There are few substitute products and/or the supplier's product (and/or service) is highly differentiated.
- The volume purchased by the buyer or industry is not important to the supplier.
- The supplier's product is an important component in the buyer's business.
- The switching cost for buyers is high (eg because of investment in the relationship with a particular supplier, or contract penalties for switching).

- There is potential for 'forward integration' (ie suppliers can own or control their buyers: a clothing manufacturer opening retail stores, say).

3.11 A member of the supply chain can seek to increase its power in a relationship by manipulating some of these factors. A supplier may differentiate its product offering in an area of strategic importance to the buyer, for example, in order to increase the buyer's dependence on it, and the cost and difficulty of switching to another supplier later. A buyer may standardise its requirements, so that more suppliers can compete for the business, decreasing dependence on existing sources of supply. And so on.

Competitive rivalry

3.12 The intensity of competitive rivalry among current competitors may range from collusion between competitors (in order to maintain and share the profits available in the industry) to the other extreme of aggressive competitive strategies such as innovation, price wars and promotional battles, where one firm's gain is another firm's loss. Rivalry is likely to be more intense in the following situations.

- There are many equally-balanced competitors.
- There is a slow rate of industry growth. (If the 'pie' isn't getting larger, the only way firms can grow will be to compete for a bigger 'slice'.)
- There is a lack of product and service differentiation.
- There are high fixed costs of production, since firms need higher revenue to cover them and make a profit.
- There are high 'barriers to exit', so it is less costly to compete harder than to withdraw from the industry.

3.13 *Barriers to exit* are factors which make it difficult for an existing supplier to leave an industry, if it proves unattractive or unprofitable. Here are some barriers to exit.

- A lack of assets with significant break-up, re-sale or re-use value, so that the firm will not be able to realise any value from them (other than by continuing to use them)
- The cost of redundancy payments, if workers have to be laid off as a result of the closure or change of activity
- Effects on other divisions or activities maintained by the firm: loss of morale and/or strategic direction due to the divestment, loss of complementary products (which may have an impact on the sale of other items in the product range), loss of managerial talent (if not transferred to other divisions)
- Reputational damage, as a result of factory closures, product withdrawals and so on – which may impact on the firm's other product lines
- Corporate social responsibility and/or government pressure to maintain employment and the production of essential goods and services (even if they are unprofitable).

Using Porter's model

3.14 The Five Forces Model has long been the standard model for analysing forces in the competitive environment. It helpfully distinguishes key competitive variables in an industry, enabling systematic analysis of industry power structures and competitive pressures. It therefore enables managers to judge the likely profitability of different industries; identify competitive opportunities and threats; and seek to manipulate the various forces to increase profitability (add value) and improve their competitive position.

3.15 It is a simple framework, facilitating discussion and communication of findings, and it focuses on the forces most relevant to profitability – which is likely to be a key strategic objective for business organisations.

3.16 However, you should be aware that the model has limitations.

- It focuses on profitability, which may not be the primary or sole objective for all organisations. This is most obviously true for not-for-profit organisations, but other organisations may take a long-term view of profitability in order to prioritise market or product development, technology, innovation or ethical leadership and so on.

- It only offers a static 'snapshot' of the competitive environment at a particular point in time. In a highly dynamic environment, it may go out of date very quickly as the forces change (eg if legal or political barriers to entry come down or a substitute product arises from technological innovation), or as competitors make moves and counter-moves to overcome adverse forces.
- It considers only five forces in the immediate competitive environment. This can create an oversimplified picture, unless the connections between the competitive forces (which are not independent of each other) and the influence of key drivers in the macro-environment (STEEPLE factors) are also considered. The five forces on their own may not adequately capture the main competitive variables in a particular industry: eg core competencies, the pace of technology or intellectual property development, the length of product lifecycles (eg in industries subject to consumer fashions and fads) and so on.
- It is designed to be applied at the level of strategic business units (SBUs), and not at the level of the whole organisation or supply chain: organisations may be diverse in their operations and markets, and the impact of competitive forces may therefore vary.
- It typifies a 'positioning' approach to strategy development, which suggests that the source of an organisation's competitive advantage is mainly in how it achieves strategic 'fit' with its external environment. As we will see in the following section of this chapter, it has been argued that competitive advantage based on positioning is not sustainable in the long term, because of the speed and unpredictability of change in the environment and the ability of competitors to imitate strategies based on generic sources of advantage.

Monitoring competitors

3.17 Competitors are an important part of the external micro (market and industry) environment of supply chain management.

- An organisation's strategies and products will, to an extent, be influenced by the need to gain or maintain an advantage over competitors in the market. Managers will attempt to predict what competitors will do, in order proactively to counter threats (or exploit opportunities) arising from their plans. So, for example, purchasers may need to monitor competitors' materials costs and quality, in order for their own supply chains to stay competitive.
- Competitors may be used as benchmarks for key competencies that are valued by the market. The organisation may measure the customer service, quality management, procurement efficiency or ethical values of its supply chain, say, against the standards set by the supply chains of key competitors or market leaders. (We discuss benchmarking as an aspect of supplier performance management, in Chapter 11.)
- Competitors may seek competitive advantage by controlling the best quality supply and distribution channels, eg by forming preferential relationships with suppliers or distributors, or negotiating exclusive supply and distribution contracts. An organisation's supply chain managers are therefore in direct competition with competitors' supply chain managers, especially where supplies are limited or scarce – and this puts additional pressure on the quality of supply chain relationships.

3.18 Competitor analysis is therefore a key component of environmental analysis. It involves analysing competitors' goals, capabilities (strengths and weaknesses), strategies (on what basis is it aiming to compete: price, product differentiation, niche markets?) and likely response to environmental threats and opportunities. Purchasers may, for example, need to look at competitors' relationships with key suppliers; whether they have (or may be able to obtain) control over sources of key or scarce supplies; how well they are able to control or reduce purchasing, materials handling or supply chain costs (enabling greater profitability and/or price competition); and so on.

Competition and competitive supply

3.19   Public sector procurement, in particular, seeks to ensure that suppliers are selected not on the grounds of political expediency, socio-economic goals or favouritism, but by transparent procedures which (a) are open to audit (justifying the use of public funding) and (b) promote best value and ethical practice by giving all eligible suppliers an equal opportunity. There has been a particular emphasis on promoting – or enforcing – *competitive sourcing procedures*, as the best guarantee of quality and value for money.

3.20   It is important to note that the aim of competitive sourcing is not just **competition** for its own sake (as a mandated process), but its judicious use to achieve the value-adding outcome of **competitive supply**: that is, the extent to which a supply arrangement provides supply which matches or exceeds requirements at a cost which represents best value in relation to a given supply market.

3.21   **Competitiveness** is the strength and intensity of competition within a market, which results in genuine buyer choice, supplier commitment (to win the business) – and therefore potential for value-adding price, quality and innovation gains.

3.22   One key issue is whether competitive sourcing (such as the use of competitive tendering or e-auctions and short-term, frequently re-tendered contracts) actually results in supply solutions, bids and relationships that represent competitive supply.

- In some cases, there may be a need to generate greater competition in a supply market eg through: encouraging new entrants or substitute products and processes; expanding the supply market (from regional to EU/global, say); collaborative sourcing to increase buyer power; or making contracts more accessible and attractive to a wider range of potential suppliers (such as small and medium sized enterprises, third sector suppliers, or minority-owned suppliers).
- In some cases, competitive sourcing may actually work *against* competitive supply, by deterring potentially innovative suppliers (such as small suppliers, who cannot compete on economies of scale), or undermining the potential for sustainable competitive advantage that might arise from longer-term supplier development and supply chain partnerships (eg competing on innovative solutions, responsiveness or quality, rather than price).

Regulation of competition

3.23   While we are on the subject of competition in general, it is worth noting that governments can, through legislation and other means, significantly influence the nature of relationships between a firm and members of its micro and competitive environments.

- Controlling prices (eg in the case of privatised utilities) and competitive practices (eg outlawing the formation of cartels and competition-distorting monopolies and market dominance)
- Giving new producers access to markets with high barriers to entry (eg by offering development grants and subsidies)
- Regulating quality, testing and environmental standards (and in some industries, the adoption of new products, eg pharmaceuticals)
- Offering grants, tax incentives and other subsidies to encourage competition and innovation; and so on

4   Sources of competitive advantage

4.1   Essentially, a business can achieve competitive advantage by performing strategically important activities more cheaply or better than its competitors: offering customers a better bundle of desirable benefits than competitors, at the same cost – or offering a comparable bundle of desirable benefits, at lower cost.

4.2   Success in securing competitive advantage – or successful competition – is measured mainly by **market share**: that is, the proportion of sales volume or value in a given market that is gained by a given provider.

An organisation might also measure sales growth (in volume or value) – but this would not necessarily indicate *competitive* success: any increase in sales may be a result of the growth of the market, rather than securing customer preference over competitors.

4.3 Competitive advantage can be achieved anywhere along the internal business value chain – but also, importantly, along the overall value system that embraces suppliers, linkages and customers. (We will look further at the concept of 'added value' and the 'value chain' in Chapter 4.)

Generic sources of competitive advantage

4.4 Porter (*Competitive Advantage*) suggested that a firm may seek two basic kinds of competitive advantage, or 'edge' over its rivals in a market: low cost or differentiation. In other words, competitive advantage is obtained *either* by:

- Providing comparable value to the customer more efficiently than competitors (low cost), *or* by
- Performing activities at comparable cost but in unique or distinctive ways, creating more value for customers than competitors and commanding a premium price (differentiation).

4.5 At the same time, an organisation can choose to apply either of these strategies *either* to a broad market *or* to a narrow-focused or targeted market (or market segment). Porter identified the various permutations as three generic strategies:

- **Cost leadership**: seeking to become the lowest cost producer in the industry as a whole
- **Differentiation**: seeking to exploit a product or service perceived as 'different' or 'unique' in the industry as a whole
- **Focus**: targeting activities to a selected segment of the market, *either* by providing goods or services at a lower cost to that segment *or* by providing a differentiated product or service for the needs of that segment.

4.6 You may have noticed that there are in practice two focus strategies (cost focus and differentiation focus), and therefore, arguably, four generic strategies. Subsequent commentators on Porter's model have taken that line, depicting the possibilities in a simple matrix: Figure 3.4.

Figure 3.4 *Porter's generic strategies for competitive advantage*

		COMPETITIVE ADVANTAGE	
		Lower cost	Differentiation
COMPETITIVE SCOPE	Broad (industry wide)	Cost leadership	Differentiation
	Narrow (market segment)	Cost focus	Differentiation focus

4.7 **Cost leadership** is the key source of competitive advantage for organisations competing in a price-sensitive market. Such organisations need a thorough understanding of their supply chain costs and cost drivers – and of their customers' definition of quality. Their essential task is to supply the required quality at the lowest possible unit cost: specifically, at a low cost level relative to competitors.

4.8 This enables them, if necessary, to compete on price with every other producer in the industry, while earning the highest unit profit margins. It raises barriers to entry to new competitors, and makes the firm less vulnerable to other competitive forces such as the threat of substitutes, buyer power (since customers cannot drive prices lower than the next most efficient competitor) and supplier power (since the firm has some flexibility to deal with cost increases).

4.9 Pursuing an overall cost leadership strategy will require a firm to adopt tactics such as: large-scale production to secure economies of scale ('high-volume, low-cost'); enhancing productivity through technology; seeking continual improvement and waste reduction; and minimising supply and materials handling costs. From a supply chain perspective, the major implication of a cost leadership strategy is the emphasis on cost reduction, through measures such as stock minimisation, materials requirements and transport planning, variety reduction and quality control, transaction streamlining, price negotiation, aggregation of supply for economies of scale and so on. (We discuss cost reduction as a source of added value in Chapter 4.)

4.10 Differentiation is a key source of competitive advantage for an organisation faced by a strong low-cost competitor. The strategy is to gain advantage by differentiating the product from lower-priced ones on the basis of some non-price factor: in other words, setting it apart in customers' minds. (Note that while cost leadership is measured in real terms, differentiation depends on the subjective perceptions of the market.)

4.11 **Differentiation** may be achieved via: product specification or added features; technology and performance (like Dyson engineering); a reputation for quality (like Marks & Spencer) or corporate social responsibility (like The Body Shop); 'style' or esteem value (like Apple products); strong brand identity (like Cadbury's chocolate); supply chain agility and responsiveness for late customisation of products (like Dell computers); customer service (like Virgin Airlines); or a total supply experience (like Amazon.com). Ideally, a product may be differentiated along several dimensions.

4.12 From a supply chain perspective, a differentiation strategy permits, encourages – and arguably, requires – closer collaborative relationships with suppliers. Supply chain expertise and effectiveness can contribute to a wide range of differentiation variables. Process and product improvement will be key aims, along with quality control and exchange of information.

4.13 Differentiation creates customer and brand loyalty, which is a barrier to entry to new competitors and reduces the firm's vulnerability to other competitive pressures such as substitutes, buyer power (since it is less easy to switch) and supplier power (since high margins can offset cost increases). However, differentiation does have its downsides. The customer perception of 'exclusivity' is often incompatible with high market share. Sooner or later, customers become price sensitive, and may not be willing to pay prices significantly higher than the industrial average even for perceived quality. Competitor imitation may also lower the value of differentiation over time.

Two views of competitive strategy

4.14 As we have seen, a systematic process of strategy formulation includes an analysis of the internal and external environment of the organisation, to determine the (internal) strengths and weaknesses and (external) opportunities and threats they present to the competitive position of the organisation. However, there are two views as to which of these sets of variables has a greater or more lasting impact on competitive advantage.

- A **positioning-based approach** to strategy suggests that the source of an organisation's competitive advantage is mainly in how it achieves strategic 'fit' with its external environment, exploiting opportunities and minimising threats. In other words, you set your strategic objectives by identifying product and market opportunities within a given environment, and then develop and deploy the organisational resources required to get you to where you want to be. In this 'outside-in' approach, you start with environment conditions, and adapt the organisation to exploit them.
- The **resource-based approach** suggests that the source of an organisation's competitive advantage lies mainly in how it exploits its distinctive (unique and hard to imitate) internal resources and competencies, setting strategic objectives based on what they enable it to do. In this 'inside-out' approach, you start with the organisation's strengths, and seek an environment that will enable you to exploit them: the organisation will change environments to suit what it does best – rather than changing what it does best to fit the environment.

4.15 The concepts discussed in this chapter so far have mainly been based on a positioning approach: starting with detailed external environmental analysis (STEEPLE and competitive and industry analysis); and selecting generic 'best fit' strategies to reposition the organisation for competitive advantage in a given environment. Porter's 'generic competitive strategies' typify this approach.

4.16 A number of writers, however, have argued that competitive advantage based on positioning is not sustainable in the long term, for the following reasons

- The speed and unpredictability of change in the business environment undermines the assumptions behind positioning. Product and market changes constantly overtake long-range strategies. A more effective source of lasting competitive advantage is the ability to **adapt flexibly and swiftly to such changes** – enabled by effective supply chain communication, relationships and processes.
- Positioning is based on generic sources of advantage (such as differentiation and cost reduction) which can eventually be duplicated by competitors. A more effective source of lasting competitive advantage is some **resource or capability** that competitors do not possess – and cannot easily imitate. Such resources and capabilities may be accessed (and protected from competitors) by forming strong (and where possible, exclusive) relationships with expert supply chain partners.

Competitive resources and competencies

4.17 Competencies are 'the activities or processes through which the organisation deploys its resources effectively' (Johnson, Scholes and Whittington, *Exploring Corporate Strategy*).

- **Threshold** competencies are the basic capabilities necessary to support a particular strategy or to enable the organisation to compete in a given market. (The effective use of IT systems would now be considered a threshold competency in most markets.)
- **Core** competencies are distinctive value-creating skills, capabilities and resources which (Hamel and Prahalad) add value in the eyes of the customer; are scarce and difficult for competitors to imitate; and are flexible for future needs. They offer sustainable competitive advantage: for example by enabling differentiation or cost leadership, or putting up barriers to competitor entry into an industry.

4.18 Hamel and Prahalad argue that 'senior managers must conceive of their companies as a portfolio of core competencies, rather than just a portfolio of businesses and products' – and the same could be argued of supply chains.

4.19 The notion of core competencies is a key determinant of supply chain structure and relationships, because it expresses those business activities which an organisation itself can perform and leverage to competitive advantage – and those which can be more advantageously sourced externally, through the supply chain. This will have an effect on:

- The activities that are carried out and controlled within the firm and those which are bought in or outsourced (strategic sourcing and outsourcing decisions)
- The extent of control the organisation seeks to exercise over resources and activities in the extended enterprise – and therefore decisions about supply chain tiering, lead provider approaches, partnering and so on
- The composition of the supply network – since the non-replicability of competencies may be vulnerable in a loose, information-sharing network where some members are also interconnected with competitors.

4.20 The notion of core competencies is also a key factor in the choice of supply chain relationships, because it reflects the extent to which an organisation will rely on its suppliers for the provision, development and protection of distinctive, non-replicable, value-adding competencies.

4.21 Cox's **relational competence model** ('Relational competence and strategic procurement management', *European Journal of Purchasing and Supply*: 2(1)) suggests that the greater this reliance is, the greater the depth of the supply relationship will need to be.

- If a supplier can offer significant complementary competencies, which are not readily available in the supply market, then investment in collaboration (or even shared ownership) may be justified. The organisation is effectively 'locked in' to partnership by the need to secure access to significant competitive competencies, and the costs of finding them elsewhere.
- If the competencies offered by suppliers are at best residual (there are many suppliers with similar levels of capability and the costs of switching are low), long-term collaborative relationships are unnecessary: simple transactional relationships, based on competitive leverage, are adequate to secure the competencies on the most efficient and advantageous terms.

4.22   Ramsay ('Purchasing's Strategic Relevance', *European Journal of Purchasing and Supply*: 7(4)) also suggests a number of specific ways in which an organisation can use its supply chain to develop non-replicable competencies.

- Identify and develop unknown suppliers, which competitors are unlikely to be able to access.
- 'Enclose' a supplier (eg by acquisition, joint venture, exclusive supply agreement or confidentiality agreement), in order to secure sole access to its resources.
- Apply procurement strategies which are hard for competitors to imitate eg exploiting high bargaining power in an industry or relationship, or exploiting 'special relationships' with suppliers (based on personal relationship, knowledge-sharing, relationship-specific investment, adaptations and integration and so on).

Chapter summary

- The supply environment can be pictured as concentric circles representing the internal environment, the operating or micro environment, and the general or macro environment.
- Purchasing research may include environmental analysis, industry analysis, competitor analysis, critical success factor analysis, forecasting, vendor analysis, and supply market analysis.
- A popular tool for analysing factors in the macro environment is STEEPLE: socio-cultural; technological; economic; environmental or ecological; political; legal; and ethical factors.
- SWOT analysis is a strategic planning technique for analysing the (internal) strengths and weaknesses of an organisation and the (external) opportunities and threats that it faces.
- Michael Porter argues that the extent of competition in an industry depends on the interaction of five factors (Porter's five forces): threats from new entrants; threats from substitutes; threats from suppliers' bargaining power; threats from buyers' bargaining power; and competitive rivalry between firms already in the industry.
- Competitors are an important part of the external environment, which means that competitor analysis is a key component of environmental analysis.
- Porter also argues that a firm may seek competitive advantage either by low cost or by differentiation; and that these strategies can be applied either to a broad market or to a targeted market.
- A positioning-based approach to strategy suggests that an organisation is competitive if it achieves strategic 'fit' with its environment; a resource-based approach suggests that competitive advantage lies in exploitation of distinct resources and competencies.

3

Self-test questions

Numbers in brackets refer to the paragraphs where you can check your answers.

1   Distinguish between a firm's internal, micro and macro environments. (1.1)

2   In what ways does the external environment influence an organisation? (1.5)

3   What types of analysis might be performed as part of purchasing research? (1.7)

4   Suggest a number of environmental factors under each of the STEEPLE headings. (2.1)

5   List specific impacts of technological development. (2.6)

6   How might a SWOT analysis be used to help shape strategy? (2.26)

7   List Porter's five forces. (3.2)

8   List possible barriers to entry to an industry. (3.6)

9   In what circumstances are (a) buyers and (b) suppliers particularly powerful? (3.9, 3.10)

10   List limitations of Porter's Five Forces Model. (3.16)

11   How may governments influence the nature of relationships between a firm and its environment? (3.23)

12   Describe Porter's generic strategies for competitive advantage. (4.4–4.6)

13   List means by which a firm may achieve differentiation for its products or services. (4.11)

14   Distinguish between a positioning-based approach to strategy and a resource-based approach. (4.14)

CHAPTER 4

Value-Adding Supply Chain Relationships

Assessment criteria and indicative content

 Analyse the sources of added value that can be achieved through supply chain relationships

- The link between relationships as a process and the achievement of added value outcomes
- Sources of added value: pricing and cost management, improving quality, timescales, quantities and place considerations in procurements from external suppliers
- The link between organisations in supply networks

Section headings

1 What is added value?
2 Sources of added value
3 Value-adding relationship management
4 Developing opportunities in supply chain relationships

Introduction

In this chapter we complete our overview of supplier relationship management and its context, by exploring the business case for contract and relationship management. We noted, in Chapter 3, that relationship management, as a process, is not carried out for its own sake – not merely for process compliance or more 'pleasant' dealings with suppliers: the cost and effort involved is justified only by a measurable contribution to the strategic objectives of the organisation, such as competitive advantage and market share.

In this chapter we broaden our discussion of the target outcomes of effective relationship management, to consider the sources of 'added value' that can be achieved by organisations through supply chain networks.

We start by explaining the concept of added value, from different perspectives. We then go on to explore various sources of added value: first, using the framework of the 'five rights of purchasing' (which is used in the syllabus to express this topic); and then looking in more practical terms at how value can be added (a) through relationship management itself, and (b) through various approaches to developing opportunities in supply chain relationships. We will return to some of these themes in Chapters 10 and 11, on the management of supplier relationships and supplier performance.

1 What is added value?

Value and added value

1.1 The influential writer on competition Michael Porter *(Competitive Strategy, 1980)* argued that an organisation's competitive advantage ultimately comes from the 'value' it creates for its customers. Value can be seen simply as the 'worth' of the product or service, which may be measured in two ways: what it costs the organisation to produce or provide, and what customers are willing to pay for it. In other words:

- An organisation creates value – by performing its activities more effectively or efficiently than its competitors *and*
- Customers purchase value – by comparing an organisation's products and services with those of its competitors.

1.2 The term 'added value' thus essentially refers to the addition of greater value or worth to a product or service, as a result of all the processes that support its production and delivery to the customer: marketing, design, production, customer service, distribution, maintenance and so on.

The value chain or value stream

1.3 Porter's 'value chain' model depicts the various primary and secondary activities of an organisation through which value is created: Figure 4.1.

Figure 4.1 *Porter's value chain*

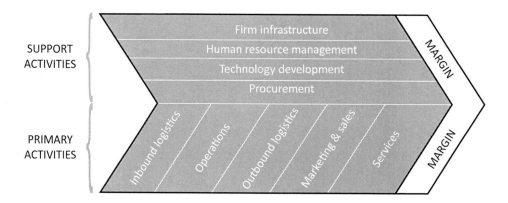

1.4 Every organisational activity can be seen as part of the value chain or value stream: the sequence of activities by which value is successively added to organisational resources as they 'flow' towards the customer.

- Primary activities are concerned with bringing resources into the organisation, transforming them by means of a 'production' process, moving finished products to customers, and marketing them.
- Secondary activities are concerned with supporting the primary business functions.

Note that value adding 'activities' are *not* the same as the *functions* of a business or business unit: they may be carried out across departments.

1.5 **Primary value activities** are grouped into five areas.

- *Inbound logistics* are the activities concerned with receiving, storing and disseminating inputs: materials handling, warehousing, inventory control etc.
- *Operations* are concerned with the transformation of inputs into finished goods or services. In manufacturing, these activities include assembly, testing, packing and equipment maintenance; in service industries, basic service provision.
- *Outbound logistics* are concerned with storing, distributing and delivering the finished goods to customers: warehousing, materials handling, transport planning, order processing and so on.
- *Marketing and sales* are responsible for communication with the customers to provide a means by which they can purchase the product (as well as an inducement to do so): market research, new product development, advertising and promotion, sales force management, channel management, pricing and so on.

- *Service* covers all of the activities which occur after the point of sale to enhance or maintain the value of the product for the customer: installation, repair, training, parts supply and maintenance.

1.6 **Secondary value activities** support all the primary activities, working across functional and activity boundaries.

- *Firm infrastructure* refers to systems and assets for planning, finance, quality control and management.
- *Human resources* are all the activities involved in recruiting, deploying, retaining and developing people in the organisation.
- *Technology development* activities relate to both equipment, systems and methods of work organisation: product design and improvement of production processes and resource utilisation.
- *Procurement* is – as you know – all the activities undertaken to acquire inputs for primary activities (or to support them in acquiring their own inputs).

1.7 At its simplest, this model suggests that procurement activities add value by supporting, or providing services, to the primary value-adding activities of the organisation.

- The procurement function may have direct responsibility for inbound and/or outbound logistics, or may manage the outsourcing of those functions (eg through third party storage and logistics providers).
- Procurement supports value addition through operational and service activities by fulfilling the 'five rights of purchasing': ensuring that the right goods, of the right quality, are delivered to the right place at the right time, and at the right price. (This is the main focus of the syllabus, in relation to sources of added value, and will be discussed in detail in Section 2 of this chapter.)
- It supports marketing and sales by providing product and delivery information, sourcing marketing services (eg advertising agency or printing services), or advising marketing staff on how to source requirements for themselves.

The value system or value network

1.8 The individual firm's value chain does not exist in isolation, and value-adding activities do not stop at the organisation's boundaries. As we argued in Chapter 3, a firm must also secure competitive advantage by managing the *linkages within its supply network:* the basis of techniques (discussed later in this chapter) such as lean and agile supply, total quality management and supply chain management.

1.9 This wider value chain, extended through the supply chain, is known as a **value system** or **value network**: Figure 4.2.

Figure 4.2 *The value system*

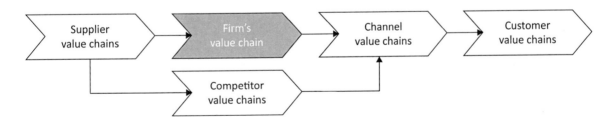

Supply chain linkages

1.10 A key point of the value chain and value network models, for the purpose of contract and supplier relationship management, is that activities within the value sytem are recognised as *interdependent:* each element can affect the costs, efficiency or effectiveness of another in the value chain, forming what Porter called 'linkages'. So, for example, improving the quality of materials purchased may reduce wasted effort on quality inspections or after-sales service. On-time delivery of finished goods to customers requires the integration of procurement, operations, outbound logistics and service activities.

1.11   Such 'linkages' require co-ordination in order to optimise the flow of value to the customer – which is why both internal and external supply chain relationships, and communication, are so important. Emphasis on optimising the flow of value to the customer through the management of linkages is foundational for the concept of 'supply chain management': we will discuss this in more detail in Section 4 of this chapter.

The concept of 'waste'

1.12   The value chain and value network models view business processes as a sequence of activities that successively add value to organisational resources, as they flow towards the customer. However, this raises the question of whether *all* activities of an organisation or supply chain, looked at in detail, actually add value – or whether some are effectively value neutral or negative: adding cost, without adding value in the eyes of the customer – or possibly even subtracting value in the eyes of the customer (eg through introducing poor quality or service into the value chain).

1.13   Activities and processes which add cost, without adding value, are identified as 'waste' activities: they contribute nothing to the flow of value to the customer – and should therefore be minimised or eliminated throughout the supply chain and value chain where possible.

The flow of value to the customer

1.14   It is also important to note that 'each activity within a value chain provides inputs which, after processing, constitute *added value to the output received by the ultimate customer* in the form of a product or service' (Lysons & Farrington).

1.15   Procurement can therefore be seen as an integral part of the flow of value *to the end customer* – not just as an internal administrative support function. In recent decades this has been increasingly recognised, giving procurement a more integrated and strategic role in organisational management, with input into strategic decisions such as: make/do or buy decisions; new product development; supply chain development; process re-engineering and so on.

The link between relationship 'processes' and added value 'outcomes'

1.16   The syllabus requires you to recognise the link between 'relationships as a process' and the achievement of 'added value outcomes'. In the most obvious interpretation of this syllabus caption, you should be prepared to demonstrate *how* relationship processes (such as the development of trust, or partnering, or performance management) contribute to the achievement of added-value outcomes (such as better cost management, reduced waste activities, enhanced profitability, improved quality or service, supply chain innovation or sustainable procurement). We will explore various aspects of this throughout this chapter.

1.17   However, it may also be helpful to distinguish clearly between 'outcome' and 'process'.

- **Outcomes** are what an organisation or procurement function is *aiming to achieve* – and/or what it *actually* achieves.
- **Processes** are the *means* or steps by which desired outcomes are pursued, or which an organisation follows in order to ensure good practice.

1.18   Processes must be justified by value-adding outcomes. However, organisations may become overly focused on narrow, short-term target outcomes such as cost reduction or maximised profits – at the expense of good practice and innovative, value-adding processes. So, for example, a short-term focus on lowest cost (outcome) may foster adversarial approaches to negotiation and supplier relationships and development (processes) – which may, in the long run, miss out on the value-adding potential for supply chain (process) improvement, sustainable procurement, collaborative whole-life cost reduction, agile or flexible supply, and so on.

1.19 Organisations may, on the other hand, become overly focused on 'correct' or 'accepted' processes and procedures – and lose sight of the need to add value. Excessive attention to 'doing things the right way' (as opposed to 'doing the right things') can create the kinds of cultural problems – and wastes – commonly associated with large bureaucratic organisations. In these, people don't seek to add value through initiative, discretion or innovation: they merely follow the procedure (which may, or may not, be a well-developed, up-to-date approach to a business or customer need).

1.20 A balance is needed between process compliance and outcome focus.

2 Sources of added value

Economic and customer value

2.1 According to Porter, the ultimate value a firm creates is measured by the amount customers are willing to pay for its products or services *over and above* the cost to the firm of carrying out all its value-creating activities (production, service, logistics and so on). A firm is profitable if the realised value to customers (what they are prepared to pay) exceeds the cost of value creation.

2.2 From an **accounting perspective**, therefore, added value is total revenue *minus* total cost of all activities undertaken to develop and market a product or service. This expresses the amount of economic value that has been added to the organisation's resources: how efficiently they are being used and how effectively they are being leveraged.

2.3 From this perspective, an organisation can add value by:

- Inducing customers to pay more (eg by providing additional features or services which attract a premium price) *and/or*
- Reducing costs or increasing the efficiency of processes.

2.4 From a **marketing perspective**, adding value means enhancing the offering to customers: 'augmenting' the core product or service with elements which customers value, and which differentiate the firm's offering or brand from competing offerings in customers' eyes (Kotler & Armstrong, 2003). Organisations can thus add value through enhancing product quality or design; value for money; delivery or availability; brand appeal; exclusivity; service levels; and so on. Porter and others have emphasised that value is effectively 'in the eye of the customer', and organisations must seek to understand exactly what aspects of their offering customers will place value on.

2.5 The main focus for procurement is value added either by **cutting costs** (without loss of quality or product features) *or* by **securing operational efficiency** (enabling superior quality or features at no additional cost). Ideally, it might aim to achieve both of these objectives: improved output at reduced cost.

2.6 We will now look in more detail at sources of added value, using the broad framework of the operational objectives of procurement: the 'five rights'. But let's start with the more general concept of eliminating wastes.

Eliminating wastes

2.7 As we suggested earlier, one of the key sources of added value is the reduction or elimination of waste activities and processes. One of the early manufacturing quality gurus, Taichi Ohno (at Toyota) introduced the concept of the 'seven wastes': areas that could be targeted in manufacturing operations in order to eliminate waste and improve the efficiency of the value stream (Table 4.1.) You should be able to see how the removal of non-value adding activities could equally well be applied to service provision.

Table 4.1 *Taichi Ohno's seven wastes*

WASTE ACTIVITY	COMMENTS
Over-production	Producing output (finished goods or work in progress) in excess of demand leads to stockholding costs, product deterioration, obsolescence and scrap. Good relationships in supply chains can help eliminate waste by accurate demand forecasting and responsive supply in response to demand, or JIT.
Transportation	Moving materials unnecessarily between different locations (eg to or within a production facility) adds cost, and risks damage and deterioration. Supply chain relationships can help eliminate waste through effective materials handling, and transport route and load planning.
Waiting	Delays or queues in processing mean that more time is taken than is really needed, without adding value. Supply chain relationships can help eliminate waste by facilitating effective scheduling to minimise waiting time – or by using waiting time for value-adding activity (such as training or maintenance).
Motion	Unnecessary motions (bending, reaching and so on) violate sound ergonomic principles: reducing productivity and causing fatigue (and possibly injury) to staff.
Over-processing	This can happen when procurements are over-specified (resulting in the production of unnecessary features) or when unnecessarily sophisticated equipment is used to produce relatively simple goods, adding to their cost. Supply chain relationships can help eliminate waste through techniques such as value analysis (and value engineering for new product design), to remove non-value adding features and processes.
Inventory	Unnecessary stockholding incurs cost without adding value, and can mask inefficiencies in production planning or processes. Supply chain relationships can help minimise inventory by accurate demand management and developing just in time (JIT) or responsive supply capabilities.
Defects/corrections	Rework and scrap add cost, without adding value. Supply chain relationships can help minimise waste through techniques such as quality assurance, continuous improvement agreements or a more radical supply-chain-wide approach such as total quality management (TQM).

Price and cost management

2.8　Reducing and eventually eliminating waste from the value chain is underpinned by a supply chain which eliminates activities that do not directly add value. This can be achieved through developing **lean supply**, which necessitates long-term relationships focused on the removal of waste from the value stream to the mutual benefit of both buyer and supplier (we shall come back to lean supply in Section 4 of this chapter). Lean supply chain management methods are specifically aimed at eliminating waste by leveraging the relationships that exist in the supply chain. Such methods include:

- Using electronic data interchange (EDI) to standardise and streamline business processes across participants in the supply chain (eg order processing, warehousing, logistics and inventory management)
- Focusing on supply chain participants' shared core competencies related to quality, delivery, financial information, operational excellence and performance measurement
- Using the knowledge that exists throughout the supply chain to continuously improve the value chain

2.9　The reduction and management of costs (including the procurement price of goods and services) will be a key objective to support the financial objectives of the firm (profitability, liquidity, return on capital invested and so on), even in the public sector (with goals such as value for money service provision and efficiency targets). It will also be the cornerstone of competitive advantage based on cost leadership.

2.10　*Emmett* argues, succinctly, that cost strategies are about 'knowing what the costs really are and then looking at how to reduce them'. You first have to apply effective cost analysis, with a particular focus on whole-life costing, total cost of ownership or total acquisition costs: purchase price *plus* delivery, support, consumables, staff training, inventory and handling costs, inspection, maintenance and repair, and so on, over the useful life of the asset. Then you are in a position to look at eliminating waste, negotiating on price and so on.

2.11　Price management involves managing input costs by ensuring that the organisation secures the optimum price for routine and leverage procurements (for which competitive purchase price – rather than whole-life value for money – is the priority).

- *Price analysis* is the process of seeking to determine whether the price offered is a fair and appropriate price for the goods. The 'right' price in this sense may be one which is advantageous or reasonable compared to: the prices offered by other suppliers (competitive tenders or quotations); the prices previously paid by the buyer for the same goods or services; the market or 'going' rate; and/or the price of any alternative or substitute goods.
- *Cost analysis* is often used to support price negotiations where the supplier justifies its price by the need to cover its costs (an approach called 'cost-based pricing'). Cost analysis looks specifically at how the quoted price relates to the supplier's costs of production. Suppliers may be asked to include cost breakdowns with their price quotations, to support this analysis. Not all suppliers will be willing to share their detailed cost information with buyers (an approach called *cost transparency*). However, if they can be persuaded to do so – often, as part of a trusting buyer-supplier relationship – there are several benefits. Cost analysis can keep prices realistic (ie no unreasonably large profit margins), in the absence of competition – for example, where there is a preferred supplier. It focuses attention on what costs ought to be involved in producing the goods or services, which acts as an incentive for cost control and reduction, and which may in turn lead to cost savings passed on to the buyer.
- *Price leverage* can be secured in the supply chain by means such as: aggregating demand or consortium buying; negotiating 'harder' on price; or using competitive leverage sourcing methods (such as e-auctions or competitive bidding). Such methods should only be used for appropriate procurements, where an adversarial or transactional approach is appropriate (and less value can be added through collaborative relationships).

2.12 Good supply chain relationships can contribute to cost reduction and management in a number of ways, at the strategic, tactical and operational levels. (If asked to recommend approaches for a case study organisation, in the exam, remember to select those which are appropriate to the organisational context, the level and time-scale of decision-making and so on…)

- Developing supplier relationships for cost and price advantages (whether by using competitive leverage to secure low prices *or* by developing collaboration to reduce sourcing and transaction costs, encourage mutual cost transparency and cost reduction and so on)
- Applying ICT and automation technologies to streamline processes across all participants in the supply chains (eg EDI and other e-procurement tools)
- Using key supply chain relationships to develop 'lean' supply and production: eliminating wastes from processes throughout the supply chain eg through better demand forecasting and materials planning; reduction of inventory through just in time techniques; efficient process layout and transport planning; minimal defects and wastage through quality management etc.
- Collaborating with supply chain partners on cost-reduction programmes, eg using 'target costing': estimating the selling price that the market will be willing to pay for the finished product, and working backwards through the supply chain to calculate the cost targets that must be achieved in order to support that price (providing reasonable profit margins for all parties).
- Improving specifications (based on constructive internal relationships with users and external relationships across the supply chain) and demand management through the supply chain, reducing waste by purchasing accurately to requirement.
- Using value analysis ('analysing the function of a material, part, component or system to identify areas of unnecessary cost': Zenz) and/or value engineering (the application of value analysis at the product development stage) to eliminate waste among supply chain participants. Value analysis asks whether the use of the item contributes value; whether its cost is proportionate to its usefulness; whether all its features are actually needed; and whether a lower-cost method could be used, while retaining the features and functions that add value.

- Managing supply chain relationships effectively, then selecting suppliers, supply chain quality assurance processes, and continuous improvement initiatives (eg improvement agreements, supplier development or quality circles) in order to minimise wastes such as inspection, defects and rework.
- Analysing and managing risk in the supply chain via supply market research and intelligence-gathering; appropriate supplier pre-qualification and financial appraisal; contract management; the formulation of contingency plans for identified supply risks; and so on.

Improving quality

2.13   Improved quality adds economic value by allowing the organisation to charge premium prices – and adds customer value by enhancing perceived product and service benefits. The supply chain has a crucial role in maintaining and assuring quality. Dobler *et al* (*Purchasing and Materials Management*) argue that: 'Quality must be built into a product. It is the buyer's responsibility to ensure that suppliers possess the ability, the motivation, and adequate information to produce materials and components of the specified quality, in a cost-effective manner. In fulfilling this responsibility, a buyer can exert positive control over the quality and attendant costs of incoming material.'

- At a strategic level, this may involve supplier relationship management, early supplier involvement, supplier selection and development policies, quality management and continuous improvement strategies and the establishment of systems for controlling supplier performance.
- At the operational level, it includes matters such as materials specification, service level agreements, contracting, supplier evaluation, quality control, benchmarking, contract management and so on.

2.14   Quality guru W Edwards Deming, in his analysis of Japanese companies, found that such companies were able to maintain high production standards primarily because of their ability to control the *quality of input materials* through close supplier relationships, characterised by co-operative quality assurance, the training of supplier personnel and the incentive of long-term relationships. He also argued that considerations such as quality and reliability should be at least as important as price when choosing suppliers.

2.15   The procurement or supply chain function can add value through quality improvement by managing supplier relationships with this end in mind.

- Developing a realistic mutual understanding of quality standards and procedures; providing incentives and rewards for high quality and continuous improvement; implementing lean supply and total quality management.
- Developing closer relationships with reliable quality performers; working with suppliers to resolve quality disputes, solve quality problems and/or make ongoing quality improvements: eg by providing consultancy, training, access to technology and so on (supplier development).

2.16   Quality management and improvement will be discussed in more detail in Chapter 11 on supplier performance management.

Timescales

2.17   Emmett *(Supply Chain in 90 Minutes)* offers some pithy advice for adding value: 'make it faster, move it faster, get paid faster'. Added value can be achieved by the use of efficient procurement and supply chain management techniques for the following purposes.

- Accurately negotiate, interpret and verify supplier lead times, in order to ensure timely replenishment or sourcing of inputs to maintain operations
- Shortening supplier lead times, where required: eg by negotiating incentive prices for 'priority' turnaround; working with suppliers to remove 'waste' time in the supply process; or negotiating contracts with supply partners to pre-manufacture and hold stocks of work in progress

- Reduce procurement cycle times, eg by streamlining and/or automating procurement processes, and effective contract and supplier relationship management
- Working with suppliers to ensure on-time delivery, eg by: selecting suppliers with good delivery capability; setting KPIs and contract terms for on-time delivery; issuing accurate and realistic delivery schedules to suppliers; giving regular suppliers advance notice (where possible) of ongoing or future demand; managing supply risks (eg transport delays) and expediting (or 'chasing') orders, if there are any concerns about progress.
- Reduce new product development (idea-to-market) cycle times, eg by the early involvement of suppliers in development processes.

Quantities

2.18 The key source of added value in relation to quantities is the **reduction of inventory** – minimising the costs and risks of holding stock – while still ensuring that there is *sufficient* stock to meet required service levels and maintain operations.

- Sufficient stock must be held (at each point in the supply chain) to meet anticipated demand. Stockouts may cause bottlenecks or shutdowns in production; costs of idle time; late delivery to customers; and related loss of credibility, goodwill and sales.
- 'Safety' or 'buffer' stocks allow the organisation to keep working if supply is disrupted by strikes, transport breakdowns, supply shortages, supplier failure, or long or uncertain supplier lead times: this is particularly important for items which are critical for operations.
- Buyers may be able to take advantage of bulk discounts, lower prices or reduced transaction costs by placing fewer, larger orders, for quantities in excess of what is immediately required. They may also be able to take advantage of advantageous spot prices by buying (or 'stockpiling') goods in advance of requirement.
- However, *excess* stock is a source of waste: tying up capital in 'idle' stock; wasting storage space; risking loss of value through stock deterioration, theft or damage; risking obsolescence or disuse; and incurring holding costs (warehousing, insurance and so on).

2.19 Efficient inventory management in the supply chain can be achieved by methods such as the following.

- Accurate demand forecasting through the supply chain, and transparency about demand data (eg to avoid the amplification of demand as each link in the supply chain builds in buffer or safety stocks)
- The use of appropriate stock replenishment systems for independent demand items (such as MRO supplies): monitoring levels of stock and planning to replenish them in time to meet forecast demand, based on usage rates and supplier lead times.
- The use of appropriate 'pull' inventory management techniques for dependent demand items, whereby buyers place orders with suppliers as and when items are required for production. Examples include just in time (JIT) supply and computerised systems such as materials requirements planning (MRP) or enterprise resources planning (ERP).
- Just in time (JIT) supply: a radical Japanese approach to inventory reduction which aims to ensure that goods only arrive at the factory 'just in time' to go into the production process. The philosophy of JIT is that 'inventory is evil': every effort is made to minimise stockholding, by securing demand-driven late delivery of required quantities of supplies. At the same time, given such 'tight' time and quantity parameters, the buyer cannot afford any defects in the supplies delivered: significant effort is also put into 'zero defects' quality management through the supply chain. Such a philosophy and practice requires strong integration and co-operation with suppliers. It is advantageous in reducing waste, minimising stock and lead times, and improving supply chain flexibility. But it comes at a risk: there are no time or stock buffers, if the supplier or system fails.
- Standardisation and variety reduction, to minimise the risk of stock 'proliferation': uncontrolled widening of range of stock items.

Place considerations

2.20 The key source of added value in relation to 'place' is the development of effective and efficient transport and logistics strategies throughout the supply chain, to secure timely, efficient and risk-managed supply. Value may be added throughout the supply chain by methods such as the following.

- The rationalisation and re-structuring of logistics and warehouse locations eg using regional distribution centres: to break bulk on large incoming deliveries for distribution to multiple sites or users ('hub and spoke') and/or to consolidate multiple in-coming deliveries for combined transport to sites or users ('merge in transit').
- The outsourcing of logistics (warehousing and/or transport) to third party providers, which may have better competitive and value-adding competencies and resources, to provide operations more efficiently than the organisation could do in-house
- Selecting the most efficient, effective and risk-managed mode of transport for a given procurement
- Planning transport loads and routes to minimise cost (eg driver and vehicle time, fuel usage, vehicle wear-and-tear) and environmental impacts (fuel usage, carbon emissions, traffic congestions, pollution) – in particular, minimising wasted vehicle space (eg incomplete loads and empty return trips).
- Ensuring that transport risks are effectively managed throughout the supply chain: eg by the use of transport packaging; insurances; delivery 'track and trace' systems; and haulier selection and management.

2.21 In summary, key sources of added value that an organisation can achieve through its supply chain relationships are:

- Price and cost analysis and management
- Shared information and use of technology to secure benefits such as reduced stock-holding, more effective and efficient logistics, and improved forecasting
- Better use of time by using JIT, cutting duplication, reducing the need to rework items and shortening the time-to-market
- Improving quality and reducing defects by working together to use standards and quality management systems
- Involving suppliers in developing features in the end product that customers value.

3 Value-adding relationship management

The benefits of positive relationship management

3.1 We have already noted that the development and management of supplier relationships is *not* 'an end in itself': it is a process (or 'means') to achieve certain desirable results or outcomes ('ends') – notably, added value and competitive advantage. You may be asked to justify the investment of effort in developing and maintaining a given supplier relationship – or supplier relationships in general – on the basis of a sound 'business case': demonstrating the link between relationship development and measurable added-value outcomes (such as those discussed above).

3.2 High-quality, motivated and committed suppliers have the potential to contribute significantly to a business in areas such as the following.

- **New product development and process innovation**: contributing ideas based on their expertise in the materials, components and technologies involved (ie 'early supplier involvement')
- **Availability and delivery**: offering swift, flexible delivery of inputs, so that the organisation can hold less inventory (and benefit from lower inventory costs) while still being able to fulfil orders. (This is the principle behind 'just in time' supply or JIT.)
- **Quality**: ensuring the quality of the materials and components delivered; collaborating with purchasing and operations to improve quality management processes; and committing to continuous

improvement programmes

- **Value for money**: keeping materials, supply and inventory costs low, or collaborating with the organisation on cost reduction programmes
- **Service, advice and information**: eg in the case of advertising agencies, management consultancies, third party logistics providers and so on.

3.3　In more general terms, however, positive supplier relationship management can itself offer a range of benefits for an organisation.

- **Stronger relationships**, through intentional efforts to develop trust, information sharing and co-operation; proactive conflict and issues management; and ongoing monitoring, evaluation and improvement of the relationship as it develops.
- **Sound risk management**. More is known about supply chain partners, so the organisation can predict and manage their behaviour. High-risk suppliers can be brought under closer control, through relationship management. Contract and relationship monitoring helps to minimise the risk of breakdown. This is particularly important where a firm's activities have been outsourced to external partners.
- **Better return on relationship investment**, by prioritising the few key relationships which can be most effectively leveraged (achieving larger returns and impacts for smaller investment and effort), and maintaining arm's length transactional efficiency in less value-adding relationships.
- **Improved business efficiency**, through the streamlining and integrating of supply chain information and communication systems; collaborative reduction of waste in the supply chain; better information sharing (enabling forward planning); the establishment of routines (rather than having to plan and communicate each transaction afresh); and so on.
- **Greater profitability** through reduced sourcing and input costs. It is more expensive to continually identify, evaluate and get used to new suppliers than it is to retain and leverage those you already have. Long-term suppliers may add increasing value (eg through cost reduction and improvement programmes) while the costs of dealing with them decrease (eg through systems integration and higher-volume orders).
- **Potential for value-adding synergy** (2 + 2 = 5). Goodwill and trust built up in well managed relationships can lead to collaboration, ideas sharing and loyalty – over and above compliance with a contract, specification or service level agreement. Suppliers may stay loyal in the face of problems (eg contractual disputes or reduced demand) and may give preferential treatment when needed (eg first call on scarce supplies, fast-tracked orders, willingness to be flexible). Opportunities may arise for collaborative promotions (eg between a supplier and retail buyers) and other strategic alliances.
- **Improved corporate social responsibility and reputation management**. In order to establish credentials for green and ethical sourcing and supply, organisations must (a) carefully select which supply chain partners they will do business with – and be identified with – and (b) monitor and manage the environmental and ethical performance of their supply chains. Positive relationship management should support both areas.
- **Competitive advantage.** If an organisation reaps any or all of the above benefits more effectively, consistently and efficiently than its competitors, it will have an advantage in securing and retaining customers (as discussed in Chapter 3). Positive relationship management may be a key factor differentiating a firm from its competitors in the perceptions of the market. Moreover, *all* relationships – not just customer relationships – can support the strength of a brand in the marketplace: relationships with suppliers support product quality and customisation, for example; relationships with intermediaries support preferential product display and promotion; and relationships with employees empower and motivate them to deliver competitive levels of service to customers.

Potential costs of poor relationship management

3.4　So what are the consequences of *not* managing relationships effectively? Remember, we are not talking here about the advantages and disadvantages of *close* relationships – or any particular type of relationship: we are talking about the advisability of a systematic and structured approach to managing relationships of all types. You should be able to think of the opposite effects to those listed above.

- Weaker relationships, or failure to develop and leverage potentially profitable and value-adding relationships
- Poorly controlled risks (eg risk of reputational damage from poorly managed supplier performance; supply risk of unforeseen supplier failure, or failure of contract performance)
- Waste of resources on too many relationships or non-profitable relationships
- Inefficient systems and processes, through lack of integration, co-ordination and communication
- Loss of opportunity to reduce sourcing and transaction costs
- Loss of opportunities arising from goodwill and synergy.

3.5   In addition, there may be significant costs arising more directly from poor relationship management.

- Costs of supplier disputes (costs of mediation or law suits, damages and so on): poor relationships create a more adversarial climate for dispute resolution
- Loss of employee morale due to constant disputes and complaints
- Loss of 'priority' status with suppliers, leading to poorer delivery performance, service quality, information sharing and so on
- Loss of 'attractive customer' status with suppliers, leading to loss of preferential treatment and flexibility when needed
- Refusal of higher-quality suppliers to deal with the buyer, or to bid for business, or to enter into long-term agreements
- Higher demands from suppliers (eg in relation to prices or payment terms) to compensate them for the added costs of doing business. (This may also reflect an opportunistic 'win-lose' approach, since there is little loyalty, goodwill or desire for long-term relationship to make a 'win-win' attractive.)
- Loss of supplier loyalty, which – in the face of further problems – may lead to relationship breakdown and lost business: suppliers may find more attractive contracts (perhaps even with the organisation's competitors).

4   Developing opportunities in supply chain relationships

Why develop opportunities in relationships?

4.1   If you see an opportunity, arising from positive supplier relationships, to improve *performance*, or to add value, or to enhance competitive advantage, why should you do something about it? Some key answers may be as follows.

- The organisation has invested time, energy and finance in developing relationships, and the only way a business case can be made for this investment is if the organisation reaps benefits and rewards from the relationships. This is sometimes known and measured as **return on relationship investment (RORI)**.
- The organisation should continually be looking to add value, protect its competitive position, improve its performance or reduce its costs, in order to survive and grow. Relationships represent organisational resources and competencies, which should be utilised in pursuit of such objectives
- This is a key way in which purchasing can add value in the organisation: it may be important in enhancing the function's credibility, status, influence and strategic role.
- Developing opportunities will ideally benefit both the organisation *and* the supplier, and this mutual benefit can further develop and deepen the relationship between them. One example is supplier development: the buying organisation helps the supplier to provide better service – benefiting and satisfying both parties.
- Relationships may be leveraged for a range of specific benefits: reduced supply costs, better specifications, better information for new product development, faster time-to-market of new products, better quality, faster and more flexible delivery, support for innovation or continuous improvement – and so on.
- Insisting on returns on relationship investment, and developing opportunities for performance

improvement within relationships, helps to keep suppliers 'on their toes'. It models a commitment to continuous improvement, and maintains a high level of expectations, without which long-term suppliers may become complacent and relationships may become 'cosy'.

4.2 Looked at the other way, what are the risks if an organisation *doesn't* develop opportunities within relationships? Again, some key answers are as follows.

- The organisation may invest in relationships indiscriminately (without prioritising or assessing their potential for added value), wasting resources on relationships which do not bring a return.
- The procurement function will not be able to make a compelling business case for its supplier management activity, and may lose credibility, status and stakeholder 'buy in' to its policies, procedures and advice.
- Strong relationships may become cosy and complacent over time, if they appear to be valued for their own sake – rather than as a source of added value and competitive advantage. Supply costs may rise (or may not be reduced), supplier performance may become inconsistent (or fail to improve continuously) and so on.
- External threats may be ignored or not countered (eg if the buying organisation is not able to use its strong supply base to cope with supply shortages, price fluctuations or unexpected peaks or troughs of demand).
- External opportunities may be ignored or not exploited (eg if the buying organisation is not able to use its supply chain to innovate, apply new technologies or respond quickly to emerging customer demand).
- The organisation's competitors may be reaping the benefits of supplier leverage (cost reduction, flexibility, innovation, continuous improvement etc) more effectively than it is, gaining competitive advantage. (Remember: supply chains compete, not just organisations.)

4.3 Let's now look at some selected methods of developing the opportunities inherent in strong supplier relationships. How can they be used to improve performance, added value, competitiveness and risk management?

Early supplier involvement

4.4 Early supplier involvement (ESI) is defined as: 'A practice that brings together one or more selected suppliers with a buyer's product design team early in the product development process. The objective is to utilise the supplier's expertise and experience in developing a product specification that is designed for effective and efficient product roll-out.' (Institute of Supply Management, USA)

4.5 The main purpose of ESI is to enable a supplier to make proactive suggestions relating to improving product or service design – which may also reduce costs. This contrasts with a more traditional approach to developing design, in which the supplier provides reactive feedback on designs which have already been developed. In an extreme case, a buying organisation may install a member of its own engineering staff in the supplier's plant (or *vice versa)* to secure these benefits, but collaboration may be achieved by a series of consultation meetings, or cross-organisational task force or project teamworking.

4.6 There are numerous ways in which suppliers can contribute to the product development process.

- Constructive criticism of designs: suggesting alternative materials, technologies or manufacturing and assembly methods (at a time when engineering changes are still feasible); suggesting potential for standardisation or customisation; or highlighting process issues (such as economic order sizes, lead times and safe inventory quantities)
- Technical information about performance and tolerances of materials or components, or any packaging and transportation issues that might arise
- Supply market information: the availability of materials and components (including supply risks, production capacity and market demand), their present and forecast costs, any intellectual property issues that may arise (eg design patents, copyrights and licences on designs or processes) and so on.

4.7 The advantages and disadvantages of ESI (according to Lysons & Farrington, Dobler & Burt and others), are summarised in Table 4.2.

Table 4.2 *Advantages and disadvantages of ESI*

ADVANTAGES OF ESI	DISADVANTAGES/PROBLEMS OF ESI
Quicker development lead time to bring a concept to the market	Longer development lead time, if the process is conflicted or inefficient
Improved product specifications and improved manufacturability of products	Heavy investment in inter-company communication
Enhanced quality and lower development costs	May get 'trapped' with incompatible supplier because of co-investment in R & D
Access to new technologies ahead of competitors	Potential for conflict from different goals and agendas
Shared expertise for problem-solving	Risk if supplier or technology is unfamiliar
Exchange of knowledge and information, building trust and alliance: making the supplier feel part of the organisation 'team'	Risk of leakage of information and intellectual property (especially if ESI suppliers become, or serve, competitors)
Improved understanding of supplier capabilities, with potential for future development and partnership	Risk if products or services are designed around the supplier (dependency)

Ethical, environmental or sustainable supply

4.8 Organisations can leverage their relationships with suppliers to improve ethical and environmental standards in the supply chain, where this is an important aspect of their own corporate mission and image. They may use their bargaining power to negotiate ethical and environmental (or 'sustainability') standards, or to impose policies and procedures (such as performance monitoring and standards accreditation) – or they may involve suppliers in collaborative initiatives to improve the performance of both organisations in these areas.

4.9 Here are some key sustainability issues that buyers may address with suppliers.

- The development of reverse logistics capability, so that materials and components can be returned for re-cycling or safe disposal, as part of 'green' commitments to reduce waste and landfill
- The monitoring and improvement of employment terms and conditions for suppliers' workers, particularly in developing countries where employment and human rights may not be covered by local legislation to a standard considered ethical by buyers (and consumers) in more developed economies
- The monitoring and improvement of standards for waste, emissions, pollution, environmental impacts (eg deforestation) and so on
- The potential to source materials that are more environmentally friendly (eg recyclable or biodegradable) and ethically produced (eg without animal testing)
- The opening up of opportunities for small and diverse suppliers as sub-contractors (where they may not have the capability or capacity to take on lead provider status).

4.10 Note that this represents an opportunity for the buying organisation, because ethical, environmental and sustainability performance – embracing the whole supply chain – is increasingly important to governments, consumers and the general public. The buyer's reputation can be damaged by bad publicity in these areas. On the other hand, there is growing demand and support for green, ethical and sustainable products and brands.

Total quality management and continuous improvement

4.11 Total quality management (TQM) is an orientation to quality in which quality values and aspirations are applied to the management of *all* resources and relationships within the firm and throughout the supply chain, in order to seek continuous improvement and excellence in all aspects of performance.

4.12 We will discuss TQM and continuous improvement agreements in detail in Chapter 11 on supplier performance management, but for our purposes here it is worth noting that such a radical quality management strategy depends on and leverages strong supplier relationships to maximise quality assurance and continuous improvement.

Outsourcing

4.13 Close, trusting relationships and information sharing may enable the organisation to outsource some of its internal activities to specialist external providers. Outsourcing allows the organisation:

- To focus its managerial, staff and other resources on its core and distinctive competencies
- To leverage the specialist expertise, technologies, resources and economies of scale of suppliers, with potential to add more value at less cost than the organisation could achieve itself, for *non*-core activities.

4.14 The benefits, however, can only be secured by excellent supplier relationship management, because of the risks of: selecting the wrong supplier; failing to control service standards; and potential reputational damage if service or ethical issues arise. High-profile case studies (such as British Airways' problems arising from poor employee relations at Gate Gourmet, to whom it had outsourced all its catering services) show that careful management is required to control the relationship, output and service quality, ethical and employment standards – and their consequences for the outsourcing organisation and its brand.

Developing supply chain management

4.15 Supply chain management (SCM) is a holistic, integrative and strategic approach to supply chain relationships. It may be defined as: 'the management of relations and integrated business processes across the supply chain that produces products, services and information that add value for the end customer… Use of the SCM concept entails that the links in the supply chain plan and co-ordinate their processes and relationships by weighing the overall efficiency and competitive power of the supply chain' (Jespersen & Skjøtt-Larsen, *Supply Chain Management in Theory and Practice*, 2005).

4.16 In other words, where supplier management, or supplier relationship management, looks mainly at the relationship between the buying firm and its own immediate suppliers, supply chain management looks at all the interactions and linkages between all the organisations that make up the supply chain.

4.17 SCM consists primarily of building collaborative relationships across the supply chain, so that the whole chain works together to add value for the end customer in a profitable way. Christopher *(Logistics and Supply Chain Management,* 2005) argues that, these days:

'The real competitive struggle is not between individual companies, but between their supply chains or networks… What makes a supply chain or network unique is the way the relationships and interfaces in the chain or network are managed. In this sense, a major source of differentiation comes from the quality of relationships that one business enjoys, compared to its competitors.'

4.18 The potential benefits of an integrated SCM approach include the following.

- Reduced costs, by eliminating waste activities and implementing cost reduction programmes throughout the supply chain. ('Often there are many activities that do not create value involved in trade between two companies. Jointly locating and eliminating these activities, as well as developing co-operative goals and guidelines for the future, can focus resources on real improvements and development possibilities' *Jespersen & Skjøtt-Larsen)*
- Improved responsiveness to customers' requirements (by focusing the whole business process on customer satisfaction) – hopefully resulting in greater customer loyalty and sales revenue
- Access to complementary resources and capabilities (eg joint investment in research and

development, technology sharing, ideas sharing and so on)

- Enhanced product and service quality (eg through collaborative quality management, continuous improvement programmes and improved supplier motivation)
- Improving supply chain communication, which in turn offers benefits for more efficient planning and co-ordination, reduced inventory, and potential for innovation and flexibility.
- Sharing demand forecasting and planning information enables suppliers to produce only what is required, when it is required – an approach which you may recognise as just in time supply.
- Faster lead times for product development and delivery also mean that new and modified products can be offered in response to changing customer demand – an approach which you may recognise as 'agile' supply.
- Better communication allows greater transparency. Information on costings, performance, and the status of individual orders and stock movements is available quickly or in real time: building trust, and enabling all parties to plan ahead and to manage contingencies as they emerge.

4.19 However, it is important (in exams, as in real life) to be realistic about the benefits claimed for SCM – and to analyse whether it is relevant, possible or beneficial for a particular organisation. It is not for everyone. For one thing, it requires considerable investment, internal support and supplier/client willingness – any or all of which may be absent. It also involves focusing on closer relationships with a smaller number of suppliers and clients, and this may be risky (if the relationships don't work out, for example, or if the firm becomes dependent on a supplier which later has problems, or a customer which later 'gets a better offer').

4.20 Remember: whether or not a firm adopts a supply chain management (SCM) orientation, supplier and supplier relationship management will still be important.

Lean supply

4.21 Lean thinking has its origins in Japanese production operations, but it can be applied to any organisational type (including service providers) and can be applied across all areas of the business. It is a three-pronged approach that incorporates a belief in quality, waste elimination and employee involvement supported by a structured management system.

4.22 'Lean production is "lean" because it uses less of every thing compared with mass production: half the human effort in the factory, half the factory space, half the investment in tools, half the engineering hours to develop a new product in half the time. Also, it requires far less than half of the needed inventory on site. The expected results are fewer defects, while producing a greater and ever growing variety of products' (Krafcik).

4.23 According to the CIPS paper *Lean and Agile Purchasing and Supply Management*, there are five key principles to lean thinking.

- Specify what creates value as seen from the customer's perspective: this implies a need for close relations with the customer to ensure that its perception of value is embodied in what the supplier is offering
- Identify all steps across the value stream: the aim is to eliminate non-value-adding activities and processes, leaving just a stream of value-adding activities
- Make actions that create value 'flow': link value-adding activities effectively to deliver total value to the end customer
- Only make what is pulled by customer demand, just in time (as opposed to production for stock, in advance of customer requirements)
- Strive for perfection by continually removing successive layers of waste: activities that add cost (or consume resources) but are not operationally necessary and do not add value.

4.24 Other cultural characteristics of lean organisations have been identified, including: positive, clear communications; 'no blame' culture (to encourage initiative); a high degree of staff involvement; the use of process maps to attract challenge and ideas (in order to remove non-value added steps); an orientation to fixing root causes, not symptoms; and a philosophy of continuous improvement.

4.25 Lamming defines lean supply as: 'the elimination of duplication of effort and capability in the supply chain, combined with a philosophy of continuously increasing the expectations of performance and self-imposed pressure to excel.' He goes on to argue that: 'This is achieved by recognition of mutual dependence and common interest between customer and supplier – beyond the principle of operational collaboration'. Lean supply requires close supply partnerships, based on single or dual sourcing and information transparency.

4.26 Here are some benefits claimed for lean supply.

- The progressive removal of wastes, reducing costs and improving quality
- Closer collaborative relationships within the supply chain, creating opportunities for shared competitive advantage and synergies
- Cross-functional teamworking, involvement and flexibility within the firm (with flow-on benefits for organisational learning and continuous improvement)
- Reduced inventories (also improving cashflow)
- Shorter cycle and delivery times, enabling better service to consumers
- More efficient process flows, allowing better resource utilisation
- Fewer defects, creating customer loyalty and lower failure costs.

4.27 Lean supply chains do, however, have their limitations – and are not suitable for all organisations in all circumstances.

- The reduction of wastes can reduce capability to respond flexibly to contingencies, eg by removing buffer stocks that would minimise vulnerability to emergency orders or supplier failure.
- Highly integrated, downsized supply chains can increase supply risk. They can also prevent the organisation from exploiting opportunities presented by global supply and e-business through short-term virtual (ICT-integrated) relationships.
- There may be a narrow focus on reducing cost (or on shop-floor technologies and techniques) rather than enhancing quality, service and creativity, for long-term customer value.
- Less powerful members of the supply chain may incur heavy costs becoming lean, and may make themselves vulnerable through open book costing, without sharing equitably in the value gains.
- Lean supply primarily suits high-volume industries with long lead times and relatively predictable demand: it is less effective in low-volume, dynamic industries.

Agile supply

4.28 The concept of agility is an acknowledgement that we operate in an ever-changing world with constantly changing demands. Agility implies proficiency at dealing adequately with change or unexpected events – both opportunities and threats. The CIPS paper on lean and agile supply describes agile supply as 'using market knowledge and a responsive supply network to exploit profitable opportunities in the marketplace'. An agile organisation, for example, is better able to exploit opportunities for product modification at any time that the market appears ready for it.

4.29 Rushton, Oxley and Croucher give two simple dictionary definitions to explain the difference between 'lean' and 'agile'.

- **Lean:** having no surplus flesh or bulk
- **Agile:** quick in movement, nimble.

Cox (cited in the CIPS paper) argues that lean philosophy is most powerful when the winning criteria are cost and quality, whereas agility is paramount where service and customer value enhancement are key.

4.30   Whereas lean thinking attempts to remove stock from the supply chain, as being a source of waste, agile thinking is more ready to accept stock, provided the reasons for holding it are sound. One example is a supplier who is asked by its customers to hold stock to enable response on very short lead times: this is an example where stock is not a source of cost, but of value enhancement for the customer.

4.31   Stock is also accepted by agile companies which practise late customisation: typically, the stocks held will mostly be in the form of work in progress, waiting to be converted into finished goods in response to customer orders. This concept will be familiar to anyone who has ordered a computer from the Dell website: Dell allows the online customer to specify exactly what components are required in the computer system and then manufactures it exactly to the customer specification. This can be done very rapidly, because all of the component parts are finished to a high degree and ready for incorporation in the finished product.

4.32   Christopher supports the view that agility resides in the supply chain: 'the key to agile response is the presence of agile partners upstream and downstream of the focal firm'. Achieving agility requires:

- Streamlining the physical flow of parts from suppliers (eg through process alignment and shared systems, or partnering with suppliers to reduce inbound lead times)
- Streamlining and synchronising the flow of information (eg through electronic data interchange, integrated information systems and ICT support for virtual collaboration between physically dispersed teams and the rapid formation of supply chain partnerships).
- Adaptability in responding to changing needs of the market (eg through concurrent planning and process redesign; rapid development and trialling of new processes; the use of e-commerce to improve direct contact with customers; and postponing the final configuration, assembly and distribution of products).
- Measuring the performance of the supply chain using suitable agility metrics.

Chapter summary

- Michael Porter argues that an organisation's competitive advantage comes from the value it creates for its customers. His value chain model depicts the primary and secondary activities through which an organisation creates value.
- Value-adding activities do not stop at an organisation's boundaries. They extend throughout its supply chain.
- There is a link between outcomes (what a firm is aiming to achieve) and processes (the means or steps by which outcomes are pursued).
- Procurement's role in adding value is a combination of reducing costs (without loss of quality) and securing operational efficiency.
- Taichi Ohno identified seven common sources of waste: over-production; transportation; waiting; motion; over-processing; inventory; and defects/corrections.
- Price management involves price analysis, cost analysis, and price leverage.
- Buyers can add value through quality improvement (eg by appropriate supplier selection).
- It is worthwhile to develop high quality, motivated and committed suppliers because they can contribute to adding value.
- Positive supplier relationship management offers many benefits to an organisation; conversely, there are significant downsides to poor relationship management.
- The rewards arising from good relationship management are sometimes quantified as 'return on relationship investment'.
- The objective of early supplier involvement is to utilise the supplier's experience and expertise in the early stages of product development.
- Modern thinking emphasises the value of an integrated approach to supply chain management. Such an approach is essential if an organisation is pursuing a strategy of lean or agile supply.

4

Self-test questions

Numbers in brackets refer to the paragraphs where you can check your answers.

1   List the primary and secondary activities in Porter's value chain model. (1.3, Figure 4.1)

2   According to the value chain model, how can procurement add value? (1.7)

3   Explain the link between relationship processes and added value outcomes. (1.16, 1.17)

4   Distinguish between the accounting perspective and the marketing perspective in relation to added value. (2.2–2.4)

5   What are the seven wastes identified by Taiichi Ohno? (2.7, Table 4.1)

6   Distinguish between price analysis and cost analysis. (2.11)

7   List means by which procurement can add value through quality improvement. (2.15)

8   List means by which inventory can be efficiently managed. (2.19)

9   Describe the potential contribution of high-quality and motivated suppliers. (3.2)

10   List the benefits of positive supplier relationship management. (3.3)

11   List potential costs that may arise from poor supplier relationship management. (3.4, 3.5)

12   What are the risks if an organisation does not develop opportunities within its relationships with suppliers? (4.2)

13   In what ways can suppliers contribute to the product development process? (4.6)

14   What are the potential benefits of an integrated SCM approach? (4.18)

15   List five key principles of lean thinking. (4.23)

16   Describe the different attitudes to inventory in (a) lean supply and (b) agile supply. (4.30, 4.31)

CHAPTER 5

Foundations of Contract Performance

Assessment criteria and indicative content

2.1 Evaluate the elements of a legally binding agreement

- Contract terms that regulate commercial agreements and relationships
- Oral statements and representations
- Model form contracts
- The use of standard contracts versus negotiated/bespoke contracts
- Applicable law and defined terms

2.2 Compare implied and express terms that affect performance issues

- Definition of express terms
- Implied terms through legislation, case law and custom
- Implications of international law

Section headings

1. Elements of a binding commercial agreement
2. Contract terms
3. Express and implied terms
4. Express terms relating to performance of contract
5. The implications of international law

Introduction

We now move on from our overview of commercial relationships to explore one of the key operational processes by which such relationships are shaped and controlled: the development and management of commercial contracts. The syllabus addresses this process from two perspectives: a 'legal' perspective (dealing with the legal principles and issues which underpin the performance – or non-performance – of contracts: Chapters 5–7) and a 'managerial' perspective (dealing with practical approaches to ensuring contract performance, known collectively as 'contract management': Chapters 8–9).

In this chapter we begin with the legal underpinnings of contract performance: the formation of legally binding commercial agreements, and the various terms that can be inserted or implied into contracts to express the rights, obligations and expectations of the contracting parties. Note that the emphasis here is on the *interpretation* of contracts for the purposes of monitoring and managing performance: detailed issues in the *development* of contracts are the focus of the *Negotiating and Contracting in Procurement and Supply* module.

In Chapter 6, we will go on to look at the legal aspects surrounding *non-performance* of contracts – and follow up with the related area of dispute resolution in Chapter 7.

In this chapter, the law of England and Wales is used as exemplar of the relevant legal rules.

1   Elements of a binding commercial agreement

Understanding legal aspects

1.1   There are a numberxxxxxxxxxxxxxxxxxxxxxxxxxxxxx of very good reasons why purchasers should try to have at least a working knowledge of commercial law.

- The organisation's response to the law is not 'optional' or left to managerial discretion: compliance is required and enforced by various sanctions and penalties.
- The requirements are constantly changing, as courts and tribunals define them through their decisions, and as legislators and regulatory bodies issue new provisions and amendments.
- Purchasing involves a number of activities which are the specific focus of law and regulation – notably, the development and performance of contracts with suppliers. It is essential for purchasers with responsibility for contract management to be able to interpret both their own organisation's obligations under contract (eg in relation to payment of suppliers) *and* the obligations of suppliers (eg in relation to delivery and quality) in order to monitor and enforce compliance with agreed terms.
- The common law principle that 'ignorance of the law is no excuse' means that the courts won't accept a 'we didn't know' defence from an organisation caught in non-compliance.
- As Lysons & Farrington note: 'a little knowledge is a dangerous thing'. If you know how complex the law is, you are more likely to seek professional advice from legal experts when you need to, in order to avoid the risk of making a costly mistake.

The nature and role of a contract

1.2   Contracts are a central feature of everyday life. The purchase of a study book, the boarding of a bus, the ordering of a meal in a restaurant: all constitute contracts. A contract is simply an agreement between two (or more) parties which is intended to be enforceable by the law. Note that the 'legally binding' aspect makes a contract different from a social agreement, such as arranging to borrow a friend's car for the day. In the latter case, if one party does not carry out his part, he will not be taken to court by the other to enforce the agreement. If the agreement is between two commercial enterprises, however, it is presumed that there is an intention to 'enter into legal relations': that is, to use the law to enforce the agreement if necessary.

1.3   The role of a contract is to set out the roles, rights and obligations of both parties in a transaction or relationship. For the purposes of the management of contract performance, a contract is basically a statement of:

- Exactly what two or more parties have agreed to do or exchange (specifications, prices, delivery and payment dates and so on)
- Conditions and contingencies which may alter the arrangement (eg circumstances under which it would not be reasonable to enforce certain terms, or agreement that if party A does x, then party B may do y)
- The rights of each party if the other fails to do what it has agreed to do ('remedies' for 'breach of contract')
- How responsibility or 'liability' will be apportioned in the event of problems (eg who pays for damage or loss of goods)
- How any disputes will be resolved (eg by arbitration).

Elements of a legally binding agreement

1.4   There are certain basic requirements for a valid contract to be formed. This is not just relevant to contracting with suppliers, or the development of contracts: it will be important in post-contract management to know whether or not you have a valid contract with a supplier, and whether you (and they) are therefore legally bound to comply with the terms set out in it.

1.5   In order for a contract to exist and to be legally binding, in the UK five essential elements must be present: agreement (offer and acceptance); consideration; intention to create legal relations; contractual capacity; and correct form.

1.6   One party (the 'offeror') must make a definite promise to be legally bound on specific terms: this is the offer. It may be an offer to sell ('This car is for sale for $5,000') or an offer to buy ('I will pay $5,000 for that car'). The offer can be made expressly (eg in spoken words or in writing) or by implication, where a person's behaviour implies the offer. It is important to note that not all 'statements' amount to an offer: an 'invitation to treat', such as a request for quotation sent to a potential supplier, is not an offer, but an invitation to the supplier to make an offer to sell (the quotation). Similarly, the display of goods in a sale catalogue is not an offer, but an invitation to make an offer to buy (expressed in a purchase order).

1.7   The other party (the 'offeree') must accept the offer, clearly, unconditionally and freely (ie not subject to duress or undue influence): this is the acceptance.

- Acceptance is an *unconditional* assent ('yes') to *all the terms* of an offer. If an offeree attempts to change the terms of the offer, use its own standard terms of business or stipulate conditions, this is taken as a *rejection* of the offer and the presentation of a *counter-offer* – which must then be accepted by the other party. (This gives rise to the 'battle of the forms' in the use of buyer and supplier standard terms, for example.)
- Any form of acceptance is valid, whether oral, written, or inferred from the conduct of the parties (eg the retailer takes your money, or you take the offered goods) – unless the offeror stipulates otherwise (eg by stating that acceptance must be in writing or within a certain time).

1.8   In most cases, a contract is only binding if the promises of the parties are supported by some form of consideration. The case of *Dunlop v Selfridge* (1875) offers a good definition of consideration as: 'an act or forbearance (or the promise of it) on the part of one party to a contract, as the price of the promise made to him by the other party to the contract.' In other words, a contract must be an exchange: one person does something (or gives up something, or promises to do something) because the other does, as part of a transaction.

- Consideration may include the barter or exchange of goods or services – but in most commercial purchasing contracts, consideration will be some form of payment for goods or services received.
- There may be some tricky issues around part-payments and variation of terms eg if the buyer is unable to pay the supplier in full – or offers to pay a supplier earlier than originally agreed, in return for a discounted rate. This will require legal advice, but essentially, any variation of terms is a new element in the contract, and there must be separate consideration for it. If a supplier agrees to accept a lesser amount than originally agreed, for example, it should receive consideration in the form of earlier payment, or payment of a smaller sum accompanied by some goods in exchange.

1.9   Intention to create legal relations means that both parties must intend that the agreement between them is legally binding. In other words, each party acknowledges that if a dispute arises (eg if the buyer refuses to pay the agreed price for goods), the matter can be taken to a court of law to decide the matter.

- In commercial contexts, there is a strong presumption that the parties intend agreements to be legally binding. However, this can be challenged if the opposite intention is clearly expressed in the agreement itself: eg in the form of a clause stating that 'any agreement entered into shall not give rise to any legal relationship but is binding in honour only'.

- Another special case is a situation where the parties are not yet ready to sign a formal contract, but intend to do so once final terms are agreed. They may therefore draft a 'letter of intent' offering assurance that the contract will go ahead – on the basis of which one party may commence work on its side of the bargain. This is very risky: until terms have been formally agreed, no binding contract exists, and the overcommitted party won't be able to claim damages for any wasted work.

1.10 Contractual capacity means that each of the parties must be legally able to enter into a contract. In simple terms, the parties should usually be 18 years of age or over, and of sound mind, and any individual entering into a contract on behalf of a business should have legal authority to do so: as the owner, partner or director – or as an agent with formally delegated powers to act on the company's behalf.

1.11 In relation to correct form, some types of specialty contract, such as a conveyance of land and an assignment of a lease (over three years in duration) must be made in the form of a deed: a written, signed and witnessed document. Other types of contract, such as share transfers, bills of exchange (such as cheques) and hire purchase agreements must be in writing. In general, however, oral agreements are binding – as long as the other elements are present. (In practice, it is preferable to put commercial agreements in writing to avoid later disputes about exactly what was agreed.)

1.12 There are detailed common law rules (and associated case law, based on decisions made in specific court cases) on the interpretation of each of these elements. These are beyond the scope of this syllabus, with its focus on contract performance: they are covered more appropriately in the *Negotiating and Contracting in Procurement and Supply* module.

Invalid contracts

1.13 A contract may be vitiated (flawed) by a number of factors, such as mistake, misrepresentation, duress or undue influence (meaning that there has not been a genuine offer and acceptance), or illegality (meaning that the parties cannot fulfil the terms of the contract, because doing so would be illegal). In such cases, the contract is either void (it has no legal effect on either party) or voidable (either party can make it void). Any goods which have been exchanged must be handed back.

1.14 Misrepresentation may be defined as a false statement of material fact made by one of the contracting parties, before or at the time of entering into the contract, which was intended to (and did) induce the other party to make the contract. (Advertising claims are usually regarded as 'mere puff', rather than representation, true or otherwise.) Contracts based on misrepresentation are voidable: they can be cancelled by the aggrieved party, who is released from his obligations. Additional damages may be payable, if the misrepresentation is fraudulent or negligent, rather than an innocent mistake.

1.15 Mistake describes a situation in which one or more of the parties end up bound by a contact to which they did not intend to commit themselves (although this is difficult to prove, given the common law principle: caveat emptor, or 'let the buyer beware') or which turns out not to be valid. As an example, a buyer and seller may contract in good faith for the sale of goods which – unbeknown to them – have been destroyed or do not exist: the contract is void. Another example may be where a seller offers a house for sale, and the buyer thinks he is offering a horse: the parties are at cross purposes, so there was no genuine agreement – and therefore no contract.

1.16 Duress and undue influence apply if pressure is placed on one party to agree to a contract, which does not therefore reflect the true intentions or wishes of both parties. Since one party has not freely consented to the agreement made, the contract is voidable, at the option of the coerced or influenced party. Note that 'duress' doesn't just mean threats or intimidation: it may also mean 'economic duress' eg undue commercial pressure by a major customer or employer (heavier than legitimate 'hard bargaining').

1.17 Legality may be another issue which renders a contract void. The courts will not uphold a contract (however valid in its formation), if its purpose, intent or effect is contrary to statute or common law: it is unenforceable. Obviously, you cannot sue a party with whom you have contracted to commit a crime, to make them carry out their part of the agreement, or to gain damages for their failure to do so. This may seem obvious in the case of fraudulent activity, say, but may be less so in more complex legal areas such as competition law (eg in the case of price fixing agreements) or equal opportunities law (eg contracting with a recruitment consultant to apply discriminatory selection policies).

1.18 'Rescission' (rescinding) of the contract is an equitable remedy (a remedy at the discretion of the court, based on the principle of fairness) in cases where the contract is voidable for the above reasons. Rescission can mean a formal order of the court, or the act of one party to the contract in cancelling or 'avoiding' the contract. This simply sets aside the contract as though it had never existed, returning both parties to their exact pre-contract position.

2 Contract terms

What are contract terms?

2.1 Contract terms are statements by the parties to the contract as to what they understand their rights and obligations to be under the contract. They define the content of the 'offer' (or counter-offer) which becomes binding once accepted by the other party.

2.2 Contract terms define both parties' rights and obligations, and it is important that there should be genuine and specific agreement on what these are, from the outset. After the contract has been made, it is too late for either party to alter its terms unilaterally: such a variation is effective only if it is made by mutual agreement (ie by another contract).

2.3 There are a number of important distinctions in regard to types of contract terms.

- **Express terms** (which are explicitly inserted into a contract by either or both of the parties) and **implied terms** (which are automatically assumed to be part of a contract, by virtue of relevant statute, custom or business and other factors). This distinction is discussed in Section 3 of this chapter.
- **Conditions** (vital terms of the contract, the breach of which entitles the wronged party to cancel or 'repudiate' the contract) and **warranties** (non-vital terms of the contract, the breach of which only entitles the wronged party to damages, with the mutual obligations of the contract otherwise remaining in place). This distinction is discussed in Chapter 6, since it is mainly relevant to the issue of non-performance and remedies for breach of contract.

Oral statements and representations

2.4 A statement, written or oral, made during negotiations leading to a contract, may be:

- A *term* of the subsequent contract; or merely
- A representation designed to 'induce' (or encourage the other party to enter into) the contract (for example, a claim about short lead times or price discounts).

2.5 It is important to ascertain whether a statement has become a term of the contract, or remains a mere representation, because the remedies available to a wronged party (in the event of a dispute) will differ depending on whether there has been a breach of a contractual term – or merely a misrepresentation.

- If a representation is subsequently included in the contract as one if its terms, and if it is then later found to be untrue, the party misled has remedies for breach of contract, as well as for misrepresentation.
- If the representation does not become a term of the contract, the party misled will have remedies only for misrepresentation.

2.6   Whether a statement becomes a term of the contract or not depends – like so much in contract law – on the intention of the parties. The test of the parties' intentions will depend on what was said and the circumstances in which the statement was made. The court deciding the issue will give weight to the following factors.

- **When the statement was made.** The greater the interval of time between making the statement and making the contract, the more likely it is that it will be a mere representation.
- **Whether the statement was put into writing after it was made**. If it was, it is more likely to be a term of the contract.
- **The importance of the statement to the recipient.** For example, if a statement about the quality of goods is the whole basis upon which the contract is made, as far as the buyer is concerned, then it will be a term.

     (In the case *Bannerman v White, 1861,* a buyer of hops asked the seller whether sulphur had been used in their treatment and added that if it had, he would not buy. The seller assured him that sulphur had not been used – but it turned out later that it had. The court decided that as the use of sulphur was a vital part of the contract, around which the whole deal revolved, it was a term.)

- **Whether the person making the statement has suggested that the other party checks its validity** (eg having goods checked out by a valuer or quality assessor), in which case it will probably not be a term. If the statement is particularly forceful and emphatic, however, the other party need *not* check its accuracy for it to be construed as a term.

     (In the case *Schawel v Reade, 1913,* a prospective buyer was inspecting a horse which he wanted for stud purposes. The vendor of a horse stated "You need not look for anything, the horse is perfectly sound. If there was anything the matter with the horse, I should tell you." The buyer ceased his examination of the horse – which later proved unsuitable for stud purposes. The court held that the seller's statement was a contractual term, as he had effectively taken responsibility for the soundness of the horse.)

- **Whether the person making the statement has special knowledge or skill in relation to the subject matter of the statement.** If he has, the statement is more likely to be regarded as a term, because the other party is more likely to rely on his expertise *(Dick Bentley Productions Ltd v Harold Smith (Motors) Ltd, 1965)*. Where a lay person, who does not normally deal in the kind of goods being considered, makes an assertion to an expert, the statement is unlikely to be a term, since the expert is in a better position to weigh up the credibility of the statement *(Oscar Chess Ltd v Williams, 1957)*.

Purchasers' and suppliers' terms

2.7   Most commercial concerns do not go to the trouble of drawing up a special contract every time they purchase or sell goods or services. Instead, they rely on standard terms. Each firm will draw up its own 'standard terms of business', and will seek to ensure that these terms are accepted by other firms with whom they deal.

2.8   It may be useful to consider some of the areas where the buyer and seller have opposite interests and may therefore use conflicting clauses.

- Is it a fixed price contract or has a price escalation clause been inserted?
- If the supplier delivers late, will the buyer be entitled to end the agreement?
- Who pays the costs of carriage?
- Who bears the risk of accidental loss or damage in transit?
- When is ownership of the goods passed to the buyer?
- If the supplier delivers goods which do not match the specification, or which are not of satisfactory quality, will the buyer be able to reject them and claim damages, or has the supplier tried to exclude or limit his liability for such a breach of contract?

2.9   Legal problems may arise if one firm's terms of purchase differ from another firm's terms of sale – because of the principle of offer and acceptance discussed earlier. If in its acceptance, the offeree seeks to vary the terms in any way (eg by stipulating that the transaction will be covered by its own standard terms of business), this is interpreted as a counter-offer. This creates what is known as the battle of the forms.

2.10   Think of the typical procurement cycle.

- The buyer may send a written enquiry to a potential supplier on a pre-printed form stating that any purchase made pursuant to the enquiry will be governed by the buyer's standard terms (printed on the reverse of the form).
- The supplier will reply quoting details of price and availability, stating that any sale will be governed by the supplier's own standard terms (printed on the reverse of the form): an invitation to treat.
- The buyer may place an order (make an offer) on a standard form repeating its own terms.
- The supplier may reply with an acknowledgement of order, repeating its terms: a counter-offer.

2.11   In such a case, the principle (known as the 'last document rule') is that the last set of terms and conditions sent constitutes the final counter-offer: the party who 'fires the last shot' wins. Usually it is the seller who is best placed to do this, by delivering the goods with a delivery note repeating its standard terms. If the buyer's goods inwards department has signed the delivery note, or simply accepted and used the goods, the courts are likely to judge that the final counter-offer was accepted and the contract was formed on the seller's terms.

2.12   It may well turn out that, because of careful counter-offers, both sides could be shown not to have accepted the other's terms. In such a case, where goods may have been transferred and used, but not paid for, the law uses the idea of 'quasi-contract': under the principles of equity, the buyer must pay what the goods are worth.

2.13   In order to prevent the battle of the forms, procurement staff may:

- Send acknowledgement copies of all purchase orders, which the supplier should sign and return, indicating agreement with the buyer's terms. If the seller acknowledges using its own documentation (and accompanying terms and conditions), the buyer should write back stating that delivery will be to the buyer's conditions.
- Negotiate contracts with suppliers, agreeing specific terms and conditions – which may include some of the buyer's standard terms and some of the seller's: this is likely to be a time-consuming process, only practicable for a large volume or value of business.
- Check any revised terms or conditions (counter-offers) which may be attached to supplier documentation: acknowledgement of orders, delivery notes, invoices etc.
- Stamp delivery notes 'goods received on buyer's terms and conditions' on receipt of goods.

Standard contracts

2.14   As you may already have gathered, it would be extremely time-consuming and expensive to negotiate and formulate contract terms and clauses afresh for every new contract with a supplier. In many situations, it would also be a case of 'reinventing the wheel', since the terms would be substantially similar for most business dealings of a similar type. Buyers and sellers may therefore agree to use a standard contract: a contract 'template' based on generally accepted practice in an industry or supply market, or based on past negotiated agreements between the two parties concerned.

2.15   Where an organisation has recurring dealings with a supplier, or recurring requirements for a product or service, it may develop its own standard contract for use in particular types of dealings. For example, a publisher might have a standard contract for authors, another for printers, another covering sale to book distributors and another for sale to bookshops. Each standard contract would incorporate standard terms and conditions which have proved acceptable and workable in each type of contractual relationship in the past. A supplier or buyer could accept the contract as it stands, or negotiate to vary specific terms.

2.16   Lysons & Farrington suggest a general contract structure, incorporating standard terms, as shown in Table 5.1.

Table 5.1 *General contract structure*

The agreement	Names and signatures of the parties to the contract (usually with a statement that the parties have read and understood all terms and conditions)
Definitions	Definition of names and terms, to avoid repetition of long sentences in the body of the contract.
General terms	<ul><li>*General agreements* clause</li><li>*Changes, alterations and variations* clause: eg that no variations to the contract can be made without written agreement</li><li>*Notice* clause: how and by what method any notice relating to the contract is to be sent</li></ul>
Commercial provisions	Rights and obligations of the supplier and of the purchaser. Standard terms of purchase, for example, might include:<ul><li>*Passing of title/ownership*: at what point the goods become the property of the buyer (eg after inspection and formal acceptance)</li><li>*Time of performance*: eg a clause stating that 'time shall be of the essence', so that late delivery constitutes a breach of condition</li><li>*Inspection/testing*: the allowance of reasonable time to inspect incoming goods.</li><li>*Delivery/packing*: stipulating that this should be in accordance with instructions contained in the purchase order</li><li>*Assignment*: eg that no part of the order shall be subcontracted to a third party without the buyer's written agreement</li><li>*Liability for damage or loss* in transit (and associated insurance costs)</li><li>*Rejection*: eg a clause stating the right of the buyer to reject goods for various reasons (eg unsatisfactory quality, late delivery)</li><li>*Payment* terms</li></ul>
Secondary commercial provisions	<ul><li>*Confidentiality and intellectual property protection* (where relevant)</li><li>*Indemnity*: eg the supplier guarantees to make good any losses suffered by the buyer as a result of product defects (eg in the form of consumer compensation claims or product recalls)</li><li>*Guarantee* clause: eg the supplier guarantees to make good any defects in the items supplied, provided that notice is received within a reasonable time.</li><li>*Termination*: eg when and how the contract will be discharged.</li><li>*Arbitration*: eg that contract disputes will go to arbitration prior to legal action being taken in the courts</li></ul>
Standard clauses	These may include:<ul><li>*Waiver*: failure to enforce a 'right' at a given time will not prevent the exercise of that right later</li><li>*Force majeure*: exclusion of liability if a 'major force' outside the control of the parties (eg an act of God, war, flood etc) prevents or delays the performance of the contract</li><li>*Law and jurisdiction*: which nation's laws govern the contract.</li></ul>

Model form contracts

2.17   Model form contracts are published by third party experts (such as trade associations and professional bodies), incorporating standard practice in contracting for specific purposes within specific industries, and ensuring a fair balance of contractual rights and responsibilities for buyer and seller. They are often used in particular industries to establish conditions of contract between buyer and seller which become an acceptable and familiar commercial and legal basis upon which business is usually conducted. Model form contracts can usually be adapted to suit particular circumstances and relationships.

2.18   The most common model form contracts are used in the construction and engineering industries, but other industries – such as logistics and facilities management – are also beginning to develop them. Here are some examples.

- CIPS has published a range of model form contracts and contract clauses, which members are licensed to use in support of their employment.
- The Institute of Civil Engineers (ICE), the Association of Consulting Engineers and the Federation of Civil Engineering Contractors issue standard forms for civil engineering. The ICE has also produced a new model for contract, standardising terms used across the construction industry: the New Engineering Contract (NEC) is intended for use for civil, engineering, building and electrical or mechanical works.

- The Joint Contracts Tribunal (JCT) publishes a Standard Form of Building Contract (including a model form for framework or call-off contracts).
- The Freight Transport Association has developed a model form of conditions of carriage, for carriage of goods by road in the UK.
- The Chartered Institute of Building has developed a model form contract for the commissioning of facilities management services.

Standard and model form contracts vs negotiated or bespoke contracts

2.19 A buyer may rely on its own standard terms and conditions for simple, low-value, low-risk and regular purchases, such as stock and MRO items. However, it must still be remembered that the buyer and the seller may have different standard terms and conditions, which are intended to protect their different interests in the transaction – leading to the 'battle of the forms'. It is therefore common for organisations to publish their standard terms wherever possible: on purchase order forms, order acknowledgements, invoices, receipts and so on.

2.20 The standard terms and conditions of buyers and sellers are likely to diverge in a wide range of areas.

- Payment terms (since sellers will want quick payment and buyers will want long credit terms, to support their respective cashflow positions)
- Transfer of title (when goods purchased become the property of the buyer, and title transfers from the seller, which affects who bears the risks in the mean time)
- Time of the essence (whether the delivery date is a condition, protecting the buyer, or a warranty, protecting the seller in the event of schedule slippage)

2.21 For more complex and/or larger, more strategically critical, high-risk or non-routine purchases, standard terms are very unlikely to include the level of detail, and specific provisions, that need to be addressed in the contract. In such cases, it would be worth the time and expense of negotiation and drafting of contact-specific terms and conditions. Model terms and conditions have been specifically written for particular types of complex contracts, and are used as industry standards: these are discussed a bit later in this chapter.

2.22 The advantages and disadvantages of using standard and model form contracts are summarised in Table 5.2.

Table 5.2 *Advantages and disadvantages of model form contracts*

ADVANTAGES	DISADVANTAGES
Helps reduce time and costs of contract development (including legal service costs)	Terms may not be as advantageous to a powerful buyer as if contract was negotiated
Avoids 'reinventing the wheel' – but can be adapted to suit particular circumstances	Terms may not include special clauses or requirements to cover the buyer's position
Industry model forms are widely accepted, reducing negotiation time and costs	Legal advice is still required if significant amendments or variations are to be made
Designed to be fair to both parties	Costs of training buyers to use model forms

3 Express and implied terms

3.1 Terms can be expressly or explicitly inserted into a contract by either or both of the parties (*express* terms) or can be implied or assumed to be included in the contract (*implied* terms) because they are a recognised part of common or statute law.

Express terms

3.2 Express terms are clearly stated and recognised in the contract between the parties, whether they are written or oral (or a bit of both). They are often said to constitute the 'small print' of the contract (because of the literally small size of the type in which they are commonly set out).

3.3 The most common examples of express terms would be where the parties specify price, delivery dates, how carriage and insurance costs will be shared, and so on. Another example is an exclusion or exemption clause, which states that one party will not be liable (or will have only limited liability) for some specific breach of contract, or a *force majeure* clause which specifies special circumstances in which a party will not be liable for failure to fulfil its contract obligations. (We will discuss a number of common express terms a bit later in the chapter.)

Implied terms

3.4 Implied terms are terms which are not expressly included in the contract by either of the parties, but which are nevertheless assumed to exist (eg by virtue of common law, statute or custom), and therefore form part of the contract. In other words, in contract management, the printed terms and conditions of a contract cannot be viewed in isolation: buyers and suppliers must bear in mind that they may have responsibilities or rights not specifically dealt with in the terms of the contract.

3.5 Terms may be implied into a contract by virtue of:

- The **nature of the contract** (eg an employment contract implies certain duties of an employer and employee, such as a fair day's work for a fair day's pay)
- The **need for business efficacy** (to make the contract workable), based on the presumed intentions of the parties. In the *Moorcock case* (1889), there was an agreement by a wharf owner to permit a ship owner to unload his ship at the wharf. The ship was damaged when, at low tide, it was grounded on a hard ridge at the bottom of the river. The court held that it was an implied term of the agreement that the river bottom would be reasonably safe – otherwise the parties would not have made the agreement.
- **Statute law** (legislation or Acts of Parliament), such as the Sale of Goods Act 1979
- **Custom of the trade**, such that both parties could reasonably be supposed to have had the customary term as their unstated intention. For example, in the case *Foley v Classique Coaches* (1934), in a contract to supply the petrol requirements of a bus company, no price was expressed or provided for. However, for some time before the dispute, petrol had been supplied at the supplier's standard price, to all of its customers. The court held that practice indicated what was to be implied, indicating a term which the parties intended to adopt but did not express.

3.6 As a general rule, implied terms take second place to the express provisions of the contract: express terms are taken to be the most accurate reflection of the intentions of the parties to a contract, which is what contract law seeks to discover and enforce. Express terms may therefore override implied terms – except in certain circumstances, where an express term is taken to be 'unfair'. We will discuss this as part of the Unfair Contract Terms Act, a bit later.

Terms implied by the Sale of Goods Act 1979

3.7 For buyers, the most important examples of implied terms are the group of terms automatically inserted into contracts by the Sale of Goods Act 1979. Although certain amendments have subsequently been made, the 1979 Act remains the leading statute.

3.8 The SGA draws together the legal principles relating to **contracts for the sale of goods**: that is, contracts in which a seller *transfers property* (ownership or title) in goods to a buyer in exchange for a *money consideration* (price). It covers both 'sales' (in which the buyer becomes the owner of the goods at the time when the contract is made) and 'agreements to sell' (when the buyer becomes the owner only at some future date, or on fulfilment of agreed conditions such as a certain number of instalment payments).

3.9 Sections 12–15 of the Act set out terms which are implied into all contracts of sale of goods, principally to protect the buyer: Table 5.3.

3.10 You should be able to come up with – and recognise in case study scenarios – examples for each scenario envisaged by the implied terms covered in Table 5.3. For example:

- A supermarket might purchase products described as 'biodegradable plastic bags' from a supplier, but subsequently find out that the bags are not biodegradable (s13).
- Raw materials may be of satisfactory quality in themselves, but contaminated with another agent which prevents them from being used (s14).
- Foodstuffs may arrive from an overseas supplier in a deteriorated (unusable or unsaleable) state, despite the fact that the seller should have been able to anticipate their 'going off' over the normal period of the journey, in normal conditions (s14).
- An office manager might buy wallpaper based on samples, only to find that the batch of paper delivered is of a slightly different colour – and the supplier hadn't warned that this could happen (s15).

3.11 Other sections of the Sale of Goods Act deal with detailed issues in relation to:

- When ownership passes from a seller to a buyer (Sections 16–20)
- The seller's duty to deliver, and the buyer's duty to accept and pay for, goods in various circumstances (Sections 27–31)
- Remedies for breach of contract by the buyer, eg if the seller isn't paid (Sections 41–50)
- Remedies for breach of contract by the seller, eg if goods aren't delivered as contracted (Sections 51–54).

We will discuss some of these aspects in Chapter 6, in relation to non-conformance.

Terms implied by the Supply of Goods and Services Act 1982

3.12 Similar provisions, in the context of the supply of goods and services, are contained in the Supply of Goods and Services Act 1982. This Act covers situations excluded from the definition of 'contracts for the sale of goods' (and therefore not covered by SGA 1979) in various ways.

- Contracts for the transfer of goods, including: contracts of exchange or barter (where the consideration for the transfer of goods is not monetary, but in the form of other goods or services) and contracts for work and materials (where the substance of the contract is the buying of a skill rather than the buying of a product)
- Contracts for the hire or hire-purchase of goods (since this does not involve a 'sale' or transfer of ownership)
- Contracts for the supply of services, in which the supplier agrees to carry out a service. (This does not cover contracts of employment.)

Table 5.3 *Terms implied by the Sale of Goods Act*

SECTION	IMPLIED TERM	EXPLANATION
12	*Title (ownership)*	The seller is deemed to undertake: • As a condition, that he *has a right to sell the goods*. This is important for a buyer if the seller turns out not to be the true owner of the goods (eg if they are stolen, or have already been sold to someone else) or if the seller does not have the right to sell the goods (eg if this would infringe a patent). • As a warranty, that the goods are free from any charge or encumbrance (such as an outstanding legal dispute) not disclosed to the buyer before the contract is made
13	*Sale by description*	In a sale by description, the offer includes some description (eg specification and quantity of goods, brand or model), on which the buyer relies when accepting. In such a case, the seller is deemed to undertake that the goods will correspond with the description. This may apply even if the buyer sees the goods, if the non-conformance with description is not obvious.
14	*Satisfactory quality and fitness for purpose*	Where the seller supplies goods in the course of a business, he is deemed to undertake that: • *The goods will be of satisfactory quality:* – Working and in good condition (so far as may be reasonably expected, in the light of any description applied to them, the price and other relevant circumstances) – Free from 'minor defects' (except defects drawn to the buyer's attention before the contract was made, or which a pre-contract inspection by the buyer revealed or ought to have revealed) • *The goods will be fit for:* – The purpose for which such goods are commonly used; or – Any specific unusual purpose, or any unusual circumstances in which the goods will be used, where (a) these have been notified to the seller, and (b) the buyer relies on the seller's judgment as to fitness for purpose. (The buyer is not protected if he has not told the seller of the special circumstances, or if he does not rely, or could not be expected to rely, on the skill or judgement of the seller in regard to the goods' fitness for a specific purpose.) – At the time of sale and for a reasonable time after sale. (For example, goods are not fit for purpose if they require repair or other treatment such as washing: *Grant v Australian Knitting Mills,* 1936.) Thus, a buyer cannot expect very cheap, second-hand or 'rush-order' goods to be of the same quality as expensive, new or normally-produced goods. However, goods used in the 'normal' way, which do not work properly, or fail after an unreasonably short time, or which are unsafe, are *not* of satisfactory quality. Nor are goods which are originally sound but damaged in transit (being badly packed by the seller, despite knowledge of the kind of journey they would have to make).
15	*Sale by sample*	Sale by sample occurs when the contract expressly gives the buyer an opportunity to examine a small part of goods to be bought, as typical of the whole (bulk). (It is not a sale by sample merely if part of the goods was shown to the buyer during negotiations or specification: both parties must agree by express contract term that the sale is by sample.) In such cases, the seller is deemed to undertake that: • The bulk will correspond with the sample in quality • The buyer will have a reasonable opportunity to compare the bulk with the sample • The goods will be free from defects rendering them unsatisfactory, which would not be apparent from 'reasonable' examination of the sample (which does not have to be a thorough examination: *Godley v Perry*, 1960). If a sale is both by description and by sample, it must satisfy the requirements appropriate for each. In *Nichol v Godts* (1854), a contract to sell 'foreign refined rape oil, warranted only equal to sample' was breached when the seller delivered oil corresponding to the sample, but not answering to the description 'foreign refined rape oil'.

3.13 Contracts for hire, hire purchase, exchanges and work and materials are covered by Part 1 of the Act. This implies terms about title, transfer or hire by description, satisfactory quality and fitness for purpose, and transfer or hire by sample – corresponding to the same terms in the Sale of Goods Act.

3.14 Contracts for the supply of services are covered by Part 2 of the Act, which implies a slightly different set of terms into contracts as shown in Table 5.4.

Table 5.4 *Terms implied by the Supply of Goods and Services Act, in relation to services*

SECTION	IMPLIED TERM	EXPLANATION
13	*Care and skill*	The supplier will carry out the service with reasonable care and skill. In the case *Greaves & Co v Baynham Meikle & Partners* (1975) the judge clarified: 'The law does not usually imply a warranty that the professional … will achieve the desired result, but only a term that he will use reasonable care and skill. The surgeon does not warrant that he will cure the patient. But when a dentist agrees to make a set of false teeth for a patient, there is an implied warranty that they will fit his gums.'
14	*Time of performance*	Where the time for the service to be carried out is not fixed by contract, but is left to be fixed (in a way agreed by the parties, or by the course of dealings), the supplier will carry it out within a 'reasonable' time.
15	*Consideration*	Where consideration for the services is not fixed by contract, but is left to be determined (in a way agreed by the parties, or by the course of dealings), the buyer will pay a 'reasonable' charge.
16	*Limitation of liability*	Exclusion or limitation of liability for breach of any of these implied terms is subject to the Unfair Contract Terms Act (see below).

The Unfair Contract Terms Act 1977

3.15 As a general rule, as we have said, implied terms take second place to the express provisions of the contract. The express terms of a contract may therefore attempt to exclude or limit terms implied by statute. A supplier might state, for example, that he accepts no responsibility for goods not conforming to description or sample.

3.16 However, this might unfairly limit the rights of buyers, and is therefore subject to certain restrictions. Some statutory implied terms are regarded as so important that they cannot be excluded even by express provision, or can only be excluded to a limited extent.

3.17 The Unfair Contract Terms Act 1977, together with the Consumer rights Act 2015, restrict the exclusion or limitation of liability for:

- **Negligence:** that is, the breach of a contract obligation (express or implied) to take reasonable care or the breach of the common law duty to take reasonable care.
- **Breach of implied terms**. Liability for breach cannot be excluded at all in consumer contracts (to protect consumer interests), and only in other contracts if the exclusion is 'reasonable' and fair, taking into account other factors: whether the buyer was forced by circumstances or inducements to agree to the term, whether the buyer understood (or ought to have understood) the implications of the term and so on.

3.18 We will look at the limitation of liability further in Chapter 6, in connection with breach of contract.

Caveat emptor

3.19 The common law principle *caveat emptor* (Latin for 'let the buyer beware') stated that a buyer could not claim damages for defects which made goods or services unfit for ordinary purposes, unless the seller had actively concealed these defects. In other words, the buyer had no warranty as to quality: it simply had to take responsibility for inspecting and choosing wisely before entering into contracts.

3.20 Now, under the legislation discussed above, 'satisfactory quality and fitness for purpose' are implied by statute. The buyer is much better protected – although it still has responsibility to make reasonable inspections and choices.

Why re-iterate implied terms?

3.21 There are two basic ways of drafting the terms and conditions of a contract.

- You can specify *only* those points where you are *changing* the ground rules as set out in the Sale of Goods Act 1979 or other statutes: that is, expressly excluding, limiting or varying implied terms.
- You can *specify all relevant obligations, rights and remedies* in the contract – even though they are already set out in the Sale of Goods Act 1979 or other statutes (and therefore implied into the contract). Thus, conditions of purchase frequently deal with issues such as compliance with the specification, satisfactory quality, rights of rejection, damages and remedies for non-delivery.

3.22 The second option is the most common approach – despite the extra work involved – since it clearly states the intention of both parties and avoids the potential for misunderstanding. Small organisations may not be aware of their rights and responsibilities under statute and common law, and an express (explicit) reference to their most important duties will put them on the alert. In the event of a dispute, it is often easier for a party to succeed if it can point to an express term of the contract, rather than having to rely on an implied term.

4 Express terms relating to performance of contract

4.1 Let's look at some of the basic contract terms you might need to interpret, in order to manage buyer-side and supplier-side performance of a contract.

Time of performance

4.2 Express stipulations as to time of performance (such as dates of shipment, transfer or delivery) are normally treated as *conditions* in commercial contracts and other contracts where time lapse could materially affect the value of the goods: *Bunge Corporation v Tradax* (1981) and *Hartley v Hymans* (1920).

4.3 Such time stipulations are generally treated as part of the essential description of the goods, and are governed by implied terms in relation to sale by description (s 13 of the SGA 1979). However, it is common to note expressly that 'time is of the essence of the contract', so that the buyer can insist upon the delivery date specified in the contract. In such cases, if there is a delay in performance, the injured party may treat it as breach of condition and pay nothing (and also refuse to accept late performance if offered).

4.4 Such a stipulation may be waived by the buyer, to give the supplier extra time or time flexibility – but the buyer can at any time, by giving reasonable notice, make time 'of the essence' again. In the case of *Charles Rickards v Oppenheim* (1950), for example, the contract was for delivery of a custom-built Rolls Royce car within seven months: the buyer agreed to wait three extra months. He then gave four weeks' notice to complete, at the end of which he cancelled the order. The court held that, at the expiry of his notice, the buyer was within his rights to cancel the order, as by serving notice he had made time of the essence. He could not have cancelled on expiry of the original delivery period, however, as he had waived his right to do so.

4.5 When a contract does not specify any time for the performance of obligations, they must be performed within a 'reasonable' time.

Price

4.6 Contract clauses may be used to stop the supplier from increasing the price through the life of the contract, or adding 'extras' (eg consumables) not included in the original quotation or tender. Here are some examples.

- A fixed price clause for the duration of the contract
- A contract price adjustment clause, detailing how new prices or price changes will be determined and jointly agreed
- Dispute resolution clauses, detailing how disputes on price will be resolved.

Passing of title/property

4.7 The passing of property means the transfer of ownership of goods. Note that this is not the same as transfer of 'possession' (ie who physically *has* the goods). In a cash sale, for example, possession may not be obtainable until the price has been paid. In the case of goods delivered on a sale-or-return basis, however, the potential buyer is given possession – but the *ownership* does not pass until some further action has been performed in relation to the goods.

4.8 The moment when the property in the goods passes from the seller to the buyer under a contract of sale may be important in many circumstances, including:

- If the goods are accidentally damaged or destroyed: the allocation of risk (ie who suffers the loss) may depend on who owns the goods at the time
- If the goods are damaged or destroyed through the negligence or other fault of a third party: an owner has stronger rights to claim for loss than a 'possessor'
- If a buyer fails to pay in full for the goods, or becomes insolvent: an unpaid seller can sue the buyer for the price of the goods, if title in the goods has passed to the buyer
- A sale of goods: only a person who owns goods is entitled to sell them (s 12 SGA 1979).

4.9 As a general principle, property in goods passes from the seller to the buyer at whatever time the parties *intend* it to pass. If the parties do not indicate their intentions, section 18 of the SGA 1979 lays down various rules for when property passes.

- In an unconditional contract for the sale of specific goods in a deliverable state, property passes at the time of the contract.
  In *Tarling v Baxter* (1827), a farmer sold a haystack which remained on his farm, ready to be collected by the buyer in the spring. Before collection, the stack was destroyed, through no fault of the farmer. The court held that ownership had passed to the buyer, who had to bear the loss.
- In a contract for the sale of specific goods where the seller has to do something to put the goods into a deliverable state, the property does not pass until this has been done and the buyer has notice of it.
  In *Underwood v Burgh Castle Brick and Cement Syndicate* (1922), the contract was for the sale of an engine embedded in a concrete floor, to be dug up by the seller – but the seller, in removing the engine, damaged it. The court held that at the time the damage occurred, the goods had not yet passed to the buyer: the seller had to bear the loss.
- In a contract for the sale of specific goods in a deliverable state, where the seller has to weigh, test or measure the goods in order to ascertain the price, the property does not pass until this has been done and the buyer has notice of it.
  In *Turley v Bates* (1863), the contract was for sale of a heap of clay at a certain price per ton, which the buyer was to weigh as he loaded. The court held that the goods were at the buyer's risk until they had been weighed.
- Where goods are delivered 'on approval', or on a 'sale or return' basis, the property passes to the buyer when he signifies his approval or acceptance to the seller – *or* if he retains the goods without rejecting them within a fixed or 'reasonable' time.
  In *Elphick v Barnes* (1880) the seller handed a horse to a buyer on approval for eight days – but the

horse died on the third day. The court held that ownership had not yet passed to the buyer, and the seller had to bear the loss.

- If the contract is for the sale of 'unascertained' goods (goods not specifically identified at the time of the contract) or 'future' goods (goods to be manufactured after the contract) sold by description, the property passes when goods of that description and in a deliverable state are unconditionally 'appropriated to the transaction' (identified as the goods contracted for, or delivered to the buyer) by the buyer, with the seller's assent.

  In *Carlos Federspiel v Charles Twigg* (1957), a contract was made for the sale of bicycles and tricycles. The buyer had paid the price and the seller had crated up and labelled the goods for shipping: the goods were in his yard when the seller went into liquidation. The court held that there was no 'unconditional appropriation' of the goods on both sides: setting aside goods was not sufficient to attach these particular goods irrevocably to the contract, since the seller could have changed his mind and delivered the goods elsewhere.

4.10 In order to avoid such complexities, a contract may stipulate an appropriate point at which the buyer assumes title.

- A buyer may wish to stipulate that ownership passes when the goods have been delivered and formally accepted, following inspection, testing or other procedures.
- A supplier may wish to stipulate that ownership passes only when goods have been paid for in full, so that it can repossess the goods if the buyer does not pay for them (or becomes insolvent).

  This is called a **retention of title clause**, or a **Romalpa clause**, after the case of *Aluminium Industrie Vaassen v Romalpa Aluminium Limited* (1976). The claimants supplied aluminium foil to the defendants, who subsequently went into liquidation. The contract stipulated that the title to the goods did not pass to the defendants until they had paid in full. The defendants had failed to pay for a quantity of goods (some of which they had resold) and the claimants sued to recover them. The court held that, in accordance with the conditions of the contact, the claimants were entitled to the goods belonging to them: at least, those which were still in the possession of the buyer and in their original (unmanufactured) state.
- A buyer may secure ownership of the goods upon inspection and payment, but may ask the supplier to retain *possession* of some or all of the goods, in order to reduce its own stockholding.
- There may be a sale 'on approval' for a defined period: ownership passes when the buyer signifies acceptance of the goods, or retains the goods without rejecting them within a stated time.

Passing of risk

4.11 Risk generally (or *prima facie* – 'unless proved otherwise') passes with property or title in the goods, but this may not always be the case. The passing of risk determines who is responsible for insuring the goods, and who bears the cost of any loss or damage to the goods.

4.12 This is particularly important in international contracts, where delivery is likely to comprise several stages, and goods are in the hands of various parties along the way. Who is responsible for insurance and loss at each step along the way? The standard terms for international commercial contracts – Incoterms 2010 – provide expressly for risk to pass at a number of different stages in the journey from the supplier to the buyer. We will discuss this in more detail in Section 5 of this Chapter, on the implications of international law.

Payment

4.13 Under the Sale of Goods Act, any time stated for payment is not 'of the essence' (ie a vital condition of contract), unless the contract states otherwise. In the absence of an express term, the seller is therefore not entitled to refuse to supply goods on the grounds of late payment.

4.14 However, under the Late Payment of Commercial Debts (Interest) Act 1998, statutory interest of 8% above base rate is automatically payable by the buyer if payment is late. In addition, there are many commercial considerations in regard to payment terms. The length of credit periods, for example, is important: in securing cashflow; as a bargaining tool (offering extended credit in return for other benefits); and as a source of short-term finance (eg by delaying payments).

4.15   Express payment terms generally therefore specify:

- When goods will be paid for (eg at the end of the month following the month in which the goods are received, or in which the invoice for the goods is received, whichever is the later)
- What interest, if any, the buyer will be liable for in the event of late payment (eg a rate which compensates the seller for losses directly caused by the late payment, so long as this does not exceed the rate of statutory interest)
- Whether time for payment shall be of the essence of the agreement. (From a buyer's point of view, ideally *not*…)

Liquidated damages and penalty clauses

4.16   A liquidated damages clause is used to guarantee the buyer damages against losses arising from a supplier's late or unsatisfactory completion of a contract – and to motivate the supplier to perform the contract. Such clauses are often used in large contracts (eg for construction works or capital equipment). We will look at these in detail in Chapter 6, since they relate specifically to non-performance of contract (by reason of breach).

Force majeure clauses

4.17   The purpose of *force majeure* (major force) clauses is to release the parties from liability in circumstances where their failure to perform a contract results from circumstances which were unforeseeable, for which they are not responsible, and which they could not have avoided or overcome. Examples of such circumstances include 'act of God'; flood, earthquake, fire, storm and other natural physical disasters; war, revolution, riot or civil disorder; general industrial disputes (not limited to the employees of the supplier or its subcontractors); and so on. Such circumstances do not automatically frustrate or end a contract, but may cause late delivery or non-delivery for which liability needs to be waived.

4.18   Again, we will look at such clauses in Chapter 6, since they relate specifically to non-performance of contract (by reason of frustration).

Other 'special' terms

4.19   As we saw in Table 5.1 above, there may be a range of other terms protecting the interests of either or both parties.

- **Confidentiality:** protecting either party, in cases where they need to give the other party access to information about their operations, in the course of the contract. A confidentiality clause should define 'confidential information' (eg information that would appear to a reasonable person to be confidential or is specifically stated to be confidential) and should provide that the other party will take all proper steps to keep such information confidential. In certain cases requiring stricter confidentiality, one party may require the other to sign a separate 'non-disclosure agreement', to be appended to the main contract.
- **Intellectual property rights:** enforcing legal protection for designs, patents and copyrights owned by either party.
- **Indemnities:** requiring an undertaking from the other party against loss arising from events including loss and damage to its property, or injury to its staff, caused by the negligence of the other party's personnel. A buyer will usually wish to confirm that the supplier has the ability to pay compensation in the event of law suits arising from these issues, and will usually make it a requirement of the contract

that the supplier has the necessary insurances to cover them. Examples include public liability insurance, professional indemnity insurance and product liability insurance.

- **Dispute resolution:** stipulating that a specified process will be used to handle contract disputes before recourse to legal action in the courts. It is increasingly common for clauses to stipulate that any dispute must be referred to mediation or arbitration, for example. (This will be discussed in detail in Chapter 7.)

Contract duration and renewal

4.20 A contract would normally expressly state a **duration** period, especially in the public sector (where maximum contract durations are set by the EU Procurement Directives, in order to promote competition and value). For long-term service contracts, a termination date encourages review, re-negotiation or re-tendering of the contract – which may be important if the contract proves unsatisfactory for either party, or if ongoing improvements in terms are desirable. If a contract is drawn up *without* a specified term, both parties are at greater risk of early termination by the other.

4.21 If the parties wish to keep open the possibility of continuing under the same contract, after the end of the original term of contract, they might include an **extension or renewal clause**, giving them this option. This would be particularly valuable in contracts for long-term service requirements, where contract performance is satisfactory to both parties (and/or where continuous improvement measures have been built into the original contract), because it saves the time and expense of re-letting the contract. A renewal clause may also act as an incentive to the supplier to maintain high levels of performance, if renewal is not automatic but made a 'reward' for good performance.

4.22 Provisions for renewal of contract may include:

- The initial duration of the contract
- The availability of an extension period, if any
- Criteria for qualifying for extension
- Procedures for terminating the contract
- Procedures for handing over to a new provider, where relevant.

5 The implications of international law

5.1 The fact that supply relationships increasingly take place in an international context gives rise to particular legal difficulties, in relation to issues such as: which country's law will govern the contract; and in whose courts will any dispute be heard. This is a vast area of study in its own right – and we can only give a brief overview here. In any case, our focus is still on interpreting contracts, for the purposes of appreciating potential issues in the management of contract performance. Other aspects of international contracts and transactions (such as international transport modes, import documentation and procedures, the use of Incoterms and the use of international payment methods such as letters of credit) are covered in other Level 4 modules such as *Sourcing in Procurement and Supply* and *Negotiating and Contracting in Procurement and Supply*.

Harmonisation of law

5.2 In managing international contracts, it is very important to understand certain key issues of contract law, the legal requirements of other countries, and protection for breaches of contract. Terms and conditions linked to international trade have not always been interpreted in the same manner by different national legal systems, and this raises an important issue for a buyer sourcing from overseas. Many attempts have been made over the years to standardise the terms on which export and import transactions are made.

5.3 Some of the common issues arising are as follows.

- When does an offer or acceptance become effective in an international trade transaction?

- When do title, property and risk in the goods sold pass from the overseas seller to the UK buyer?
- What are the rights of a party when goods do not conform to the contract?

5.4 The United Nations Commission on International Trade Law (UNCITRAL), based in Vienna, has as one of its key objectives 'to further the progressive harmonisation and unification of the law of international trade'. Under the Vienna Convention, it has formulated two basic instruments (or 'Uniform Laws'), although these have not yet been ratified by all the world's trading nations.

5.5 The **Uniform Law on Sales** defines a sale of goods as international when the parties reside or operate in different nation states and the goods are to be transported from one nation state to another, or where both offer and acceptance are made in one nation state and delivery is made in another. Under UK law (the Uniform Law on International Sales Act 1967), a UK buyer is not compelled to adopt the Convention when buying from overseas, but if it does so, then buyer and seller accept certain obligations under the Uniform Law on Sales.

- The seller has three fundamental duties: to deliver the goods; to deliver the relevant documentation; and to transfer the property in the goods
- The buyer has two duties: to pay the price expressed in the contract of sale, and to take delivery of goods according to the terms of the contract of sale.

5.6 The complementary **Uniform Law on Formation** tries to resolve the considerable differences between English and European law in particular, on the basic tenets of contract law: offer and acceptance. For example, under English law an offer can, in theory, always be revoked until it is accepted, while in most European countries, an offer is binding as soon as it is made. Under the Uniform Law an offer can, in principle, be revoked *unless* the offer states a fixed time for acceptance or otherwise expresses that it is firm or irrevocable, or if revocation is not made in good faith or in conformity with fair trading.

Applicable law and jurisdiction

5.7 It is essential to know the applicable law governing an international contract of sale, and which country's courts have jurisdiction (or power) in any subsequent dispute. The EC's Rome Convention on the Law Applicable to Contractual Obligations 1980 (The Rome Convention) was designed to replace common law rules to determine the law that applies to a contract, in any situation involving a choice between the laws of different countries. It was enacted into UK law by the Contracts (Applicable Law) Act 1990.

5.8 The Rome convention allows the parties to the contract to agree on which law will be applicable. They may do this by an express clause in the contract – and this is certainly the safest option – even if it is difficult to negotiate. Any stipulation as to applicable law must always be undertaken via negotiation, and with the express agreement of both parties.

5.9 If the applicable law is not expressed in the contract, and questions or disputes arise, it may be inferred from the nature of the contract and the prevailing circumstances. The general rule is that the choice of law should be the law with which the contract is most closely associated: generally, the law of the country in which the contractual work is to be performed.

5.10 The Rome Convention applies to any kind of contract, including contracts for the sale of goods, and employment contracts. However, it does not apply to arbitration agreements and agreements on the choice of court (among other exemptions).

Bills of lading and shipping conventions

5.11 The documentation used in international trade is beyond the scope of this syllabus. However, it is worth noting briefly the nature of a particularly crucial document: the bill of lading.

5.12   The bill of lading is a vital document in international trade where sea carriage is the mode of transportation. It is customarily regarded as a receipt issued by the ship owner to the shipper (usually the exporting company or seller), covering:

- The quantity of the goods received
- The condition of the goods when received
- Marks which clearly identify the goods.

5.13   A bill of lading generally contains the terms of carriage – but it is only evidence of a contract of carriage if the holder of the bill is the shipper. It is only after a bill of lading is issued and made out to a third party, ie a consignee or endorsee, that it becomes the contract of carriage.

5.14   When the goods are on board the ship, the bill of lading is signed and dated by the ship's master or his nominated agent, and marked either 'freight paid' or 'freight payable at destination'. If all is well with the consignment, the bill of lading will be signed without endorsement (a clean bill of lading). If there is something wrong with the consignment, the bill of lading will be signed but endorsed with the appropriate comment, making it an 'unclean' or 'claused' bill of lading. This may be important for the determination of liability for problems with the consignment on receipt by the buyer.

5.15   Most bills of lading issued are subject to international conventions such as the Hague Rules (1924), the Hague-Visby Rules (1968) and more recently the Hamburg Rules (1992). These conventions specified minimum responsibilities and liabilities on carriers, which cannot be lessened with express terms in the contract of carriage. The UK has implemented the main proposals in the Carriage of Goods by Sea Act 1971.

5.16   Bills of lading not within the ambit of these rules are governed by common law, which implies a number of general obligations on the part of both the ship owner and the shipper.

- The ship owner will provide a seaworthy vessel (ie one that is fit for its purpose).
- The shipper will proceed with due despatch.
- The shipper will proceed taking the direct route to the agreed destination.
- The ship owner will use due care in navigating the ship and carrying the goods.

The use of Incoterms

5.17   The communication difficulties involved in international trade have long been recognised as a problem. The translation and interpretation of contractual terms is of key importance to both buyers and suppliers, since both parties' understanding of contract requirements must be absolutely free from ambiguity in order for a contract to be fulfilled successfully – and without dispute.

5.18   With this in mind, the concept of Incoterms (International Commercial Terms) was introduced by the International Chamber of Commerce (ICC) in 1936. It was felt that if the parties concerned in an international transaction adopted standard terms, many problem areas could be averted, as all parties would be clear on their areas of risk and responsibility at all stages of transaction – and there would be no ambiguity of law or jurisdiction in the event of a dispute.

5.19   Incoterms is a set of contractual conditions or terms that can be adopted into international contracts, which are designed to be understood and interpreted on a worldwide basis. It sets out agreed explanations of many of the terms used in international trade to define the obligations of seller and buyer. The document is regularly updated in line with developments in commercial practice: the most recent edition being *Incoterms 2010* (effective from 1 January 2011).

5.20   There is no legal requirement to use Incoterms when drawing up an international commerical contract: buyers and suppliers may contract with each other on whatever terms they think most suitable. However, if they specifically refer to an Incoterm (or 'adopt' an Incoterm into the contract), both parties agree to be bound by the detailed specifications laid out in *Incoterms 2010*: in the event of a dispute, the courts will 'imply' the standards of Incoterms in law.

5.21 The use of Incoterms in a contract can save pages of detailed negotiation as, when adopting Incoterms into the contract, the detailed specifications relating to the relevant Incoterm will apply, defining areas of risk and responsibility. Areas detailed within Incoterms specify the obligations of buyer and seller at each stage of delivery, and can therefore be used as a framework for checking and managing performance of the contract at this crucial stage.

5.22 Parties may negotiate to determine which type of Incoterm agreement is most suitable. Table 5.5 contains a brief overview of all eleven of the 2010 Incoterms.

International arbitration

5.23 The International Chamber of Commerce (ICC) is committed to best practice in international trade so is well placed to offer advice when it comes to settling contractual disputes with an international dimension.

5.24 Arbitration is the most commonly used form of dispute resolution for international disputes. The ICC cite three main reasons for this.

- The final and binding character of arbitral awards. Under a number of international conventions, awards made in one country are generally legally enforceable in other countries.
- Wide international acceptance. More than 140 countries have signed up to the 1958 United Nations Convention on the Recognition and Enforcement of Foreign Arbitral Awards (the New York Convention).
- The neutrality and fairness of the forum. Neither of the disputing parties need be unduly advantaged or disadvantaged in regard to: the location of proceedings; the language used; the procedures or law applied; the nationality of arbitrators; or legal representation.

Table 5.5 *Incoterms*

EXW *(ex works) ...* *named place*	This is the easiest form of export that can be used by the seller: the buyer collects the goods, and the EXW price is for the goods alone, free of any delivery charges, insurances etc. The obligations of the seller are to place the goods under the contract at the factory gate or other named area in the factory vicinity that will enable the buyer to uplift the goods. The buyer must then make all arrangements to uplift the goods from the premises and ship them to the destination at its own risk and expense.
FOB *(free on board) ... named* *port of shipment*	Suitable for conventional cargo (eg break-bulk) shipments sent by sea or inland waterway: for other transport modes, the term FCA is more appropriate. The seller has responsibility for delivering to the port and vessel nominated by the buyer, and responsibility/risk remain with the seller until the goods have passed the ship's rail at the port of shipment.
FCA *(free carrier)* *... named place*	Unlike FOB, this term is applicable to all modes of transport to a specific carrier or specific destination: it is particularly relevant for multi-modal, containerised transport. The seller retains responsibility and risk until it has handed the goods over, cleared for export, into the charge of the carrier named by the buyer at the named place. The place stipulated by the buyer could be an inland clearance depot, rail or airport terminal, shipping berth, or freight agent's warehouse.
FAS *(free alongside ship) ...* *named port of shipment*	Similar to FCA, but used only for sea or inland waterway traffic. The goods must be delivered to the berth or quay alongside a shipping vessel nominated by the buyer or his agent: the buyer takes on responsibility for getting the goods from the quayside to the vessel, plus all costs and risks after that point.
CFR *(cost and freight) ... named* *port of destination*	The seller bears the responsibility and cost of delivery from its premises to the port of *destination*, using sea and inland waterway freight. The seller is required to provide all export documents (certificate of origin, export licence, pre-shipment inspection certificates etc) if required. However, *risk* is transferred to the buyer when the goods pass over the ship's rail at the port of *shipment*: the cost of marine insurance is borne by the buyer.
CIF *(cost, insurance and* *freight) ... named port of* *destination*	Similar to CFR, but the seller is also responsible for marine insurance (for the benefit of the buyer) to protect the goods against loss or damage during carriage to the named place of destination. If the buyer requires a higher level of insurance than the supplier would arrange as standard (often a minimum level), this should be clarified when drawing up the sales contract.
CPT *(carriage paid to) ... named* *place of destination*	Designed for use with containerised and multi-modal transport. Responsibility and costs of transit are borne by the seller, up to the point at which the goods are delivered to the place of destination designated in the sales contract. However, responsibility for insurance is borne by the buyer.
CIP *(carriage and insurance* *paid to) ...* *named place of destination*	Similar to CPT, except that the seller also arranges all insurances for transit.
DAT *(delivered at terminal) ...* *named terminal at* *destination port/place*	The seller pays all costs of carriage to the named destination terminal, including taxes and delivery charges, but *not* including costs related to import clearance. The seller also assumes all risks up to the point at which the goods are unloaded at the terminal. The buyer needs to arrange customs clearance and onward transport.
DAP *(delivered at place) ...* *named place of destination*	The seller pays all costs of carriage to the named place (eg the buyer's premises), *excluding* costs related to import clearance, customs duty, VAT and so on. The seller also assumes all risks up to the point at which the goods are ready for unloading by the buyer. The buyer carries out all customs formalities, unless the contract states otherwise. (This is similar to a previous term called 'DDU': delivered duty unpaid.)
DDP *(delivered duty paid) ...* *named place of destination*	The seller is responsible for delivering the goods to the named place in the buyer's country (eg the buyer's premises), and pays all costs in bringing the goods to that destination, *including* all import duties and taxes. If the seller cannot obtain an import licence, this term should not be used. DDP represents the ultimate extension of responsibility to the supplier – with the advantage that capital costs are tied up until payment is received. The corresponding advantage for buyers is that they know exactly what they are paying, particularly if quoted in local currency.

Chapter summary

- It is important for buyers to have a working knowledge of commercial law, and particularly of the nature and role of contracts.
- There are five essential elements of a binding contract: agreement; consideration; intention to create legal relations; contractual capacity; and correct form.
- A contract may be vitiated by misrepresentation, mistake, duress or undue influence, or illegality.
- Important distinctions relating to the terms of a contract are between express and implied terms, and between conditions and warranties.
- The 'battle of the forms' arises when a buyer and a supplier each attempt to contract on their own standard terms.
- Model form contracts are published by trade and professional bodies. They save time and cost in the development of legal contracts.
- Express terms are explicitly set out in the contract; other terms may be implied into the contract by statute or custom.
- For buyers, the most important implied terms are those in the Sale of Goods Act 1979.
- The Unfair Contract Terms Act 1977 and Consumer Rights Act 2015 limit the ability of a contracting party to exclude its liability for breach of contract.
- Express terms will usually cover such provisions as time of performance, price, passing of title, passing of risk, and payment. There may also be clauses relating to liquidated damages, *force majeure*, confidentiality, intellectual property, indemnities and dispute resolution.
- There are particular legal difficulties concerned with international trade. The Uniform Law on Sales, the Uniform Law on Formation, and the use of incoterms, can help to mitigate these difficulties.
- Arbitration is the most common method of dispute resolution in international trade.

5

Self-test questions

Numbers in brackets refer to the paragraphs where you can check your answers.

1   What are the five essential elements of a binding contract? (1.5)

2   What is meant by 'consideration' in the context of contract law? (1.8)

3   List the types of flaws that may vitiate a contract. (1.13–1.17)

4   Distinguish between conditions and warranties. (2.3)

5   What is meant by a standard contract? What is meant by a model form contract? (2.14–2.17)

6   List advantages and disadvantages of model form contracts. (Table 5.2)

7   How may terms be implied into a contract? (3.5)

8   Describe the contractual terms implied by Sections 12–15 SGA 1979. (3.9)

9   What limitations are imposed by the Unfair Contract Terms Act 1977 and the Consumer Rights Act 2015 in relation to a party's attempt to limit liability? (3.17)

10   Why do contracts often state that 'time)) is of the essence'? (4.3)

11   What is the general rule relating to the time when risk passes from supplier to buyer? (4.11)

12   What is meant by a *force majeure* clause? (4.17)

13   List some of the issues commonly causing difficulties in contracts relating to international trade. (5.3)

14   What is a bill of lading? (5.12)

15   What is meant by Incoterms? (5.19)

CHAPTER 6

Managing Non-Performance

Assessment criteria and indicative content

 Explain the recourses for non-performances in contract

- Vital and non-vital contract terms
- Identifying non-conformances/breach of contracts
- Assessing damages
- Limits of liability
- Procedures for termination

Section headings

1 Performance and non-performance of contract
2 Vital and non-vital contract terms
3 Identifying non-conformances
4 Remedies for breach of contract
5 Limitation of liability
6 Termination of contract

Introduction

In Chapter 5 we focused on the applicable law and legal principles defining 'performance of contract', including the different express and implied terms with which both parties to a contract must comply.

In this chapter we go on to look at the equally important issue of non-conformances with contract terms – and what can be done about them.

We start by outlining the various ways in which contracts can be performed – and the different ways (including breach and frustration) by which they can be *not* performed.

We then work our way systematically through four closely related issues. Firstly, the distinction between 'vital' and 'non-vital' contract terms, which determines the remedies available in the event of breach of contract. Secondly, how a buyer can identify whether a breach of contract has in fact occurred. Thirdly, what recourses and remedies are available in the event of a breach of contract. And fourthly, the extent to which it is valid or invalid for a buyer or supplier to attempt to exclude or limit its liability, if it is threatened with legal action for a breach of contract.

Finally, we look briefly at the contractual aspects of termination of contract.

In this chapter we are still mainly exploring the *legal* aspect of these topics. The closely related issues of practical compliance monitoring and relationship management will be discussed in Chapters 9 and 10 respectively.

In this chapter, the law of England and Wales is used as exemplar of the relevant legal rules.

1 Performance and non-performance of contract

1.1 There are various ways in which a contract may terminate or come to an end.

- **Performance.** A contract is considered as discharged by performance when both parties have complied fully and exactly with the terms of the contract, and have no further obligations under it.
- **Agreement.** The parties may agree to terminate unfulfilled obligations, accepting partial performance of the contract.
  - The contract itself may set out *conditions* under which it will be discharged, in which case no new consideration is required for its application. One example is a contract for the sale of land 'subject to planning permission', so that if planning permission is refused, the contract is discharged (a 'condition precedent': a term preventing the contract taking effect *unless* a specified event occurs). Another example is giving notice of termination of employment (a 'condition subsequent': a term permitting discharge on the happening of a specified event).
  - Otherwise, any agreement to discharge or end the contract will be a new contract, requiring some consideration. If both parties have remaining obligations to perform, each party's promise to release the other from those obligations will be the consideration. If one party has performed all its obligations but the other has not, there may need to be further consideration (eg in the form of a cancellation fee). The courts may also award a supplier some payment for partly-fulfilled work or deliveries, on an equitable *quantum meruit* (how much is it worth?) basis.
- **Breach.** Breach of contract is the inexcusable failure by a party to a contract to fulfil some or all of his obligations under it. If one party commits a breach of contract, the other may in some cases choose to treat the contract as being at an end, so that his own obligations are discharged: for example, if the work hasn't been done, the buyer doesn't have to pay. He may, alternatively, sue for various remedies, including damages. We will discuss these matters separately below.
- **Frustration.** In certain cases, a contract may become 'impossible' to perform, and is therefore considered discharged. An example might include situations where events beyond the control of either party make it impossible to perform the contract, or where circumstances have changed so radically that performance would be completely different from the original intention of the contract.

1.2 We will look at ways of determining whether a contract can be considered to have been 'performed' or not (dealing with performance, breach and frustration), in Section 3 of this chapter.

2 Vital and non-vital contract terms

Conditions and warranties

2.1 Usually, each term of a contract can be classified as either a 'condition' or a 'warranty'.

- A **condition** is a vital term of the contract, breach of which may be treated by the innocent party as a substantial failure to perform a basic element of the agreement. (Don't be confused by the use of the word in the formula 'terms and conditions'.)
- A **warranty** is a less important or non-vital term which is incidental to the main purpose of the contract. Breach of a warranty does not constitute a substantial failure of performance. (Don't be confused by the use of the word 'warranty' for a type of guarantee.)

2.2 The contract may expressly declare that a given term is to be a condition: one important example is when the *time of performance* is declared to be 'of the essence of the contract' (so that late delivery would be considered a breach of condition, rather than a breach of warranty).

2.3 However, the mere use of the word 'condition' or 'warranty' is not of itself conclusive, and whether a term is one or the other may have to be decided by the court in the event of a dispute. In fact, the courts have tried to avoid too rigid a classification of terms on these lines and have recognised the existence of 'innominate' (unnamed) or intermediate terms (discussed below).

Why does it make a difference?

2.4   As we will see in Section 4 of this chapter, the *recourses* (options for getting help or resolution) and *remedies* (means of compensation or redress) for breach of a contract term are different, depending on whether it is a condition or a warranty.

2.5   In the case of **breach of a condition**, the innocent party has a choice of treating the contract as repudiated (or ended) and claiming damages for any loss suffered – as an alternative to merely claiming damages for the breach. In other words, the breach is serious enough to terminate the agreement. For example, James may buy a washing machine from Bernard, with the intention of using it in his laundrette. If the washing machine is seriously defective:

- James can choose to *repudiate* (deny) the contract, in which case he can refuse to accept the machine and seek a refund of the purchase price: effectively, putting both parties back to where they were before the contract was ever made. James may also claim damages for profits lost until the machine can be replaced.
- James may, alternatively, decide to *affirm* the contract. He may decide to keep the washing machine (after it has been overhauled by a mechanic), or may seek an order from the court for 'specific performance' (ie forcing Bernard to provide a working washing machine, as contracted). In either case, he can also claim damages for the inconvenience, repair expenses and loss of profits.

2.6   In the case of **breach of a warranty**, however, the whole agreement need not collapse: the innocent party may therefore claim damages for the breach, but cannot repudiate the contract. If the washing machine supplied to James works – but looks shoddy, say, owing to damage to the exterior casing caused during delivery – he must accept the machine, but may claim for damages, perhaps in the form of a partial refund of the purchase price (usually by mutual agreement between the two parties).

2.7   Compare the following two cases.

- In *Poussard v Spiers* (1876), a soprano (Madame Poussard) agreed to sing in a series of operas for an impresario (Spiers). When she failed to appear on the opening night, Spiers refused her services for subsequent nights, and she sued him for breach of contract. The court held that the obligation to appear on the opening night was a condition of the contract. Since Madame Poussard was in breach of this condition, Spiers was entitled to treat the contract as being at an end, and was therefore not himself in breach by cancelling the rest of her contract.
- In *Bettini v Gye* (1876), a tenor (Bettini) agreed to sing in a series of concerts and to attend six days of rehearsals beforehand. When he failed to appear for the first four days of rehearsals, Gye refused his services for the balance of the rehearsals and performances, and Bettini sued him for breach of contract. The court held that the obligation to appear for rehearsals was only a warranty, so Bettini's breach did not entitle Gye to treat the contract as ended. Gye was accordingly in breach of contract when he cancelled the rest of his contract.

Intermediate or innominate terms

2.8   A term may be neither a condition nor a warranty (an intermediate term) or may not be *identified* as a condition or warranty (an innominate term) at the time the contract is made. In such cases, the courts will consider the effect of a breach of that term. If the consequences of breach are serious, remedies may be granted *as if* it were breach of a condition. If the consequences are less serious, then the innocent party can only obtain remedies for breach of warranty.

2.9   In the case of *The Hansa Nord* (1976), citrus pulp pellets were sold for £100,000. One of the stated conditions of the contract was 'shipment to be made in good condition'. On arrival, not all the pellets were in fact in good condition, and their market value was reduced by £20,000. However, even if all the goods had been sound, their market value, which had fallen between sale and delivery, was only £86,000. The buyers rejected the goods.

The court held that the provision as to shipment in good condition was neither a condition nor a warranty, but an 'intermediate stipulation'. The effect of the breach was not sufficient to justify repudiation of the contract (rejection of the goods), so the buyers' only remedy was in damages (compensation for the difference in value of the sound goods and the defective goods).

3 Identifying non-conformances

The general rule on performance

3.1 The general rule is that a contract is discharged by performance only when both parties have complied completely, accurately and exactly with the terms of the contract.

In the case *Moore & Landauer* (1927), the contract was for tinned fruit to be delivered packed in cases of 30 tins each. The correct number of tins was delivered, but in cases varying between 24 and 30 tins each. The court held that the contract was not performed – even through the market value was the same. The buyer was entitled to reject all goods and not pay.

3.2 You might already be able to see how the general rule could lead to injustice. It is therefore subject to *exceptions*, some of which have been imposed by the common law and some by equity to make the rule fairer.

- It has sometimes been held that if a single price has been agreed for performance of the contract (an 'entire contract'), no part of the price is payable unless and until the entire contract is performed: *Cutter v Powell* (1795). However, some contracts may be intended to be **divisible or severable** into distinct and separate obligations, and in such a case, each individual contract may be discharged separately. In a contract to deliver a consignment of goods by instalments, for example, the buyer may agree to pay for each instalment when delivered. If the first instalment delivered conforms with the terms of the contract, the buyer cannot refuse to pay for it on the grounds that the second delivery is defective in some respect, although payment for the second instalment may be validly refused.

- One party may be prevented from fully carrying out its contractual duties as anticipated because of some **act or omission by the other party**. In such cases the party partially implementing the agreed terms may sue on a *quantum meruit* ('as much as is merited') claim or for damages for breach of contract, in order to recover compensation for the amount of work actually completed. *Quantum meruit* is a claim for the value of work done or services rendered (partial performance), rather than for the full contract price.

  In the case of *Planché v Colburn* (1831), Planché agreed to write a book for a series to be published by Colburn, but the series was discontinued before completion of the work. The court held that the original contract was discharged by the publisher's breach – but the author could recover reasonable remuneration for work carried out so far, on a *quantum meruit* basis.

Acceptance of partial performance

3.3 Where a party accepts the benefit conferred on him by the other party's partial performance, the court may infer a promise to pay for the benefit received, and grant the other party a right to recover a reasonable price on a *quantum meruit* claim. For example, a seller may agree to deliver forty bottles of a specified wine to a buyer. If only twenty bottles are tendered, the buyer may refuse to accept delivery; but if he *accepts* the twenty bottles, he must pay a reasonable price for them.

3.4 However, if a party has no choice but to accept partial performance, then no payment can be claimed. In the case *Sumpter v Hedges* (1898), Sumpter contracted to erect buildings on Hedges' land, but abandoned the work partially completed. Hedges completed the work himself, using materials which Sumpter had left behind. Sumpter sued on a *quantum meruit* to recover compensation for the value of the work done prior to his abandoning the job. The court held that Sumpter could *not* recover payment for his work, since

Hedges had not voluntarily accepted partial performance: he had no option but to complete the work himself, or employ another builder to do so. However, Sumpter was allowed to recover the value of the *materials*, because it was open to Hedges to choose whether or not to use them in completing the work.

Substantial performance

3.5 A party who has *substantially* performed his contractual duties in the manner stipulated may recover the agreed price, *less* a deduction by way of a claim for damages in respect of duties *not* properly executed. This is another exception to the rule of full performance.

In the case of *Hoenig v Isaacs* (1952), an interior decorator agreed to decorate and furnish the defendant's flat for a sum of £750, payable 'as the work proceeds, with the balance on completion'. When the job was done, and the client had moved in, he complained of bad workmanship and would not pay the £350 balance. The court held that in a contract for work and labour for a lump sum, the client *cannot* repudiate liability on the grounds that the work, when it has been substantially performed and when he has taken the enjoyment of it, is 'in some respects not in accordance with the contract'. The defendant had to pay for the work, *less* a sum in damages for breach of warranty.

3.6 If the defects are so extensive that it cannot be said that the contract has been 'substantially' performed, however, then no part of the contract price can be recovered.

Frustration of contract

3.7 As we saw earlier, the general rule is that, unless otherwise agreed, a party who fails to perform his contractual obligations is in breach of contract and liable for damages – whatever the excuse for non-performance. In the case *Cutter v Powell* (1795), Cutter was deemed to have failed to perform his complete contract (as a merchant seaman) because he *died* before arrival at the end of the voyage for which he had been contracted. You might notice that this is a little harsh.

3.8 The doctrine of frustration was designed to reduce the severity of the general rule, by allowing for genuinely good excuses for non-performance. Here are some examples.

- Destruction of the contract subject matter. In *Taylor v Caldwell* (1863), a music hall was hired – but burnt down before the date of the concert.
- Non-occurrence of the event on which the contract was based. In *Krell v Henry* (1903), a room was hired to enable people to observe the coronation procession of Edward VII – but the procession was cancelled owing to the King's illness.
- Incapacity to provide personal performance: eg frustration of an employment contract by reason of the death of the employee.
- Extensive interruption which makes further execution of the contract impracticable or different from that originally agreed. (This does not include circumstances where a contract merely becomes more difficult or expensive to perform, or where a party has undertaken to do something which he later finds he cannot achieve.)

3.9 The position of the parties in a case of frustration is governed by the Law Reform (Frustrated Contracts) Act 1943. All sums paid under the contract must be repaid, while sums payable (whether overdue or due in future) cease to be payable. If one party has received some benefit under the contract, however, he must pay a fair sum for it. The contract itself may contain a provision (known as a *force majeure* clause) setting out how frustration will be dealt with.

3.10 The purpose of *force majeure* (major force) clauses is to release the parties from liability in circumstances where their failure to perform a contract results from circumstances which were unforeseeable, for which they are not responsible, and which they could not have avoided or overcome. Examples of such circumstances include 'act of God'; flood, earthquake, fire, storm and other natural physical disasters; war, revolution, riot or civil disorder; general industrial disputes (not limited to the employees of the supplier or its subcontractors); and so on.

3.11   A *force majeure* clause should (according to the CIPS model clause):

- State the events that will constitute *force majeure*, as relevant to the industry or market
- Oblige either party to notify the other if *force majeure* events have occurred which may materially affect the performance of the contract
- State that a party will not be considered in default of its contract obligations, as long as it can show that full performance was prevented by *force majeure* events
- Provide for the contract to be suspended for up to 30 days, if performance is prevented by *force majeure* for this period
- Provide for the termination of the contract, by mutual consent, if the *force majeure* event continues to prevent performance for more than 30 days (with provisions for transfer of work done so far, in return for reasonable payment).

Breach of contract

3.12   A breach of contract occurs:

- When a party fails to perform an obligation under the contract: is in breach of a condition; improperly repudiates (ends) the contract; or prevents completion of the contract on his own side or by the other party, during performance. These are examples of **actual breach.**
- When, before the time fixed to perform an obligation, a party expressly or by implication repudiates the obligations imposed on him by the contract: ie shows an intention *not* to perform. This is called **anticipatory breach.**

3.13   Unlike frustration, breach of contract is an unjustified failure to perform all the terms of the contract. There are various remedies for breach of contract, depending on whether the breach is actual or anticipatory, and whether a condition or warranty is breached. We will discuss these next.

3.14   Meanwhile, bear in mind that the legal aspects are not the *only* factor in identifying non-performance of a contract. The buyer (or contract manager) will also have to monitor and interpret a range of financial, technical and performance data to establish whether the supplier is complying – or likely to comply – with price, time and delivery, quality and other express and implied terms; whether the goods delivered conform to specification; whether services comply with agreed service levels and so on. These aspects of contract administration and performance management are discussed in detail in Chapter 9, on contract management.

4   Remedies for breach of contract

4.1   If one party commits a breach of an essential term of a contract (known as a 'condition'), or a substantial breach of an intermediate term, or totally renounces the contract, the breach does not automatically terminate the contract. However, the injured party *may* choose either of the following options

- Treat the contract as terminated (discharged) and claim damages for any loss suffered (the technical term is **repudiation** of the contract). So for example, breach of a condition by a seller (eg delivery of an item that does not work) discharges the buyer from his duty to pay for the goods. The injured party should inform the party in breach of the decision to repudiate the contract; a silence may be construed as waiving his right to do so.
- Treat the contract as still operative (**affirming** the contract), but claim damages for any loss suffered. Both parties continue to be bound by the contract, since it is still operative.

4.2   If one party commits a breach of a less important term (or 'warranty'), which is incidental to the main purpose of the contract, the contract automatically stays in force, but the injured party may claim damages.

4.3 In the event of an anticipatory breach (where the other party repudiates the contract in advance of performance), the injured party also has a choice of action.

- He can, by notifying the other party of his decision, accept the other party's repudiation, treat the contract as immediately discharged (**accepting** the breach) and sue for breach of contract, even if the date for performance has not yet arrived: *Hochster v De La Tour.*
- He can affirm the contract, in the hope that performance will in fact be rendered, waiting until the time for performance arrives before he can sue. The party in default can escape liability if he in fact performs the contract at the due date – or if his obligation to do so is meanwhile discharged (eg by frustration or *force majeure).*

4.4 In appropriate cases, the party who has suffered a breach of contract may have any of the following 'remedies' in law.

- *Damages*: financial compensation for losses suffered as a result of the breach. This is the normal remedy and by far the most common.
- *Specific performance*: the court orders the defendant to carry out his obligations under the contract, if damages would not be an adequate remedy (eg if the claimant wanted to buy a particular piece of land).
- *Injunction*: the court orders a person to do something (mandatory injunction) or not to do something (prohibitory injunction), in order to avoid a breach of contract. An example may be an injunction restraining a supplier from breaking an exclusivity contract.
- *Quantum meruit*: a remedy available when a contract has been partly performed, entitling a party which has provided a benefit, or performed work, to be paid a fair amount for it.

Damages

4.5 The purpose of *damages* is to put the injured party into the position it would have been in if the contract had been properly performed: they are a 'compensatory', not a 'punitive' (or punishing) remedy. So if a seller has failed to deliver goods, for example, the buyer's measure of damages will be the difference between the agreed contract price and the price the buyer needed to pay in order to get the goods elsewhere at prevailing market price.

4.6 As a proactive form of dispute and relationship management, the parties may agree a sum to be paid in the event of breach of contract – or they may not discuss this point at all.

- Where the contract does not make any provision for damages, the court will determine the damages payable. Such damages are referred to as 'unliquidated damages'.
- Where the contract provides for the payment of a fixed sum on breach, this is known as a 'liquidated damages' clause.

Unliquidated damages

4.7 In assessing unliquidated damages, the court will take into account two main questions.

- The 'remoteness' of damage, or what losses should be included in the claim?
- The 'measure of damages', or what level of damages will compensate the claimant?

4.8 The concept of the **remoteness of damage** acknowledges that some losses are too 'remote' (not sufficiently close or directly attributable to the breach of contract) to be recovered.

4.9 In the leading case *Hadley v Baxendale* (1854), a carrier was given a mill-shaft to deliver to a plant manufacturer as a model for making a new shaft. The carrier was delayed in delivery and – unknown to him – the mill stood idle during the period of delay. The court held that the carrier was not liable for the loss of profit: without inside knowledge, the carrier could not be expected to realise that delay would keep the mill idle. The case give rise to the general principles that losses to be compensated should be:

- Losses that may fairly and reasonably be considered to arise naturally ('in the usual course of things') from the breach of contract: this is 'normal loss' for which 'general damages' may be awarded
- Losses that could reasonably be supposed to have been foreseen by both parties, when the contract was made, as the likely result of breach: 'abnormal losses' for which 'special damages' may be awarded.

4.10   The **measure of damages** is the amount which will, so far as money can, put the claimant in the position in which he would have been, had the contract been performed as anticipated. For example, if a buyer bought goods for £50 which the seller refused to deliver, the buyer's damages would be the cost of his acquiring the same goods from someone else. So if he had to pay £60, his damages would be £10 (plus recovery of the £50, if he had already paid that to the seller). If a buyer refused to accept goods, the seller's loss would be the difference between the contract price and the price he can actually sell the goods for, to other buyers. If the claimant has suffered no actual loss, he will be awarded only 'nominal' damages.

4.11   The courts will also take into account the responsibility of the claimant to take all reasonable steps to **mitigate (or lessen) the loss** caused by the breach of contract. Compensation will not be awarded for any damage incurred which the claimant had a reasonable opportunity to avoid.

4.12   In the case of *Brace v Calder* (1895), Brace was employed by a partnership for a fixed period of two years. The partnership dissolved after only five months and Brace was offered identical employment with the re-formed partnership. He refused, and sued for wages for the remainder of the two-year contract – but the court held that he had not taken reasonable steps to mitigate his loss (by taking the alternative employment), and he was awarded only nominal damages.

4.13   Recovery of damages in contract is usually for financial or economic loss (eg loss of profits) but other types of loss are also recoverable (eg personal injury and property damage).

Liquidated damages

4.14   If a contract clause provides for a fixed sum of damages on breach of contract, and if the clause is a genuine attempt at estimating the loss in advance of the breach, it is defined as a liquidated damages clause, and will be valid and enforceable by either party – regardless of the actual damages suffered as a result of the breach.

4.15   A liquidated damages clause is used to guarantee the buyer damages against losses arising from a supplier's late or unsatisfactory completion of a contract – and to motivate the supplier to perform the contract. Such clauses are often used in large contracts (eg for construction works or capital equipment).

4.16   The clause specifies the damages which will be payable for breach, at a predetermined amount (eg £x per day late) which is designed to be a *genuine estimate of the damage or loss which would be caused by the non-performance of the contract*. It will be enforceable if a breach occurs, usually without action in the courts: if both parties have agreed to the clause, the buyer can simply deduct the damages from its payment to the supplier in breach.

4.17   Even if the actual damages suffered are greater than the liquidated damages provided for in the contract, the claimant can only claim the liquidated amount. In the case *Cellulose Acetate Silk Co v Widnes Foundry (1933)*, a contract for the building of a factory contained a clause providing for payment of a fixed sum in compensation for each day's delay in completion of the work. The work was finished late, and the claimants sued for losses considerably greater than those envisaged when the contract was made – but the court held that the claimants were entitled only to the contracted rate of damages.

Penalty clauses

4.18   If a liquidated damages clause is framed as a disincentive or deterrent to breach of contract, it may be defined as a 'penalty clause' (regardless of the name given to it in the contract.) Such clauses are not enforceable in law: they are void in the event of breach. The injured party will have to prove the actual loss suffered in court, and unliquidated damages will be assessed and awarded by the court.

4.19   So when would a court regard a liquidated damages clause as a penalty clause? Generally, a clause will be presumed to be a penalty clause if it does *not appear to be a genuine attempt to estimate the potential loss*, eg if:

- The sum stipulated appears unreasonably large. (A valid liquidated damages amount *may* be larger than the loss actually suffered, as long as it is a genuine attempt to pre-estimate the loss.)
- A single sum of damages is payable on the occurrence of one or more breaches, not distinguishing between breaches that are trivial and those that are serious
- A sum is stipulated for breach by non-payment – but is greater than the amount of the payment owed.

4.20   In the case of *Dunlop Pneumatic Tyre Co v New Garage* (1915), the claimant supplied tyres to the defendants. The defendants agreed that for any of a number of specified breaches, they would pay Dunlop £5 per tyre sold in breach – and subsequently sold tyres at below the listed price, which was one of the breaches mentioned in the contract. The court held that the stipulated sum was for liquidated damages. The figure of £5 represented a rough and ready estimate of the possible loss which the claimants might suffer. Moreover, although the sum was payable on the happening of a number of different types of breach, the range of breaches was very limited and they were all of similar severity.

Specific performance

4.21   In relation to specific performance, the courts observe the following principles.

- If damages are an adequate remedy (as in the case of most sales of goods), the courts will not order specific performance.
- If the courts could not adequately define or supervise performance (as in the case of a construction contract, say), they will not order specific performance.
- The courts will not order specific performance in contracts for personal services. This is because it would be unreasonable to compel one party to continue personal relations with another if they are unwilling to do so.
- If damages are not adequate, and performance is fair and reasonable, as in the sale of unique goods or land, the courts may order specific performance.

Quantum meruit

4.22   It is worth noting that *quantum meruit* is intended as compensation for work done on a provisional basis. It is not intended to alter an agreed price, when extra work has been done. In the case of *Gilbert & Partners v Knight* (1968), Knight employed a firm of surveyors to supervise building work for a fee of £30 – but the surveyors did more supervision than asked for, and submitted an account for £30 *plus* £105 for the additional work. The court upheld Knight's refusal to pay the extra: the original contract had a fixed payment, and was still in existence.

Statutory remedies for the buyer

4.23   The Sale of Goods Act 1979 provides for a number of remedies for the buyer, depending on the nature of the seller's breach of contract.

- If the seller fails to make delivery (ie the buyer receives no goods at all), the buyer may recover damages for economic loss: s 51. The measure of damages will generally be the amount by which the market price, at the time when the delivery was due, exceeds the contract price: ie the extra amount the buyer has had to pay to source the goods elsewhere.

- In a contract for specific goods, where the goods are of unique value (so that damages would not be adequate redress), the buyer make seek an order of the court for specific performance: s 52.
- Where there is a breach of warranty (ie the buyer has accepted goods, but they are not in accordance with the contract), the buyer may set off the breach in a reduction of the price, *or* claim damages: s 52. The measure of damages may be the difference in market value between goods of contract quality and the goods actually delivered – or the cost to the buyer of remedying the defect in the goods.
- If title to the goods has already passed to the buyer, but the seller retains possession unlawfully, he may sue the seller for the 'tort' of wrongful detention of goods, under the Torts (Interference with Goods) Act 1977.

Statutory remedies for an unpaid seller

4.24 The Sale of Goods Act 1979 provides for a number of remedies for an 'unpaid seller': a seller who has not been paid the whole agreed price. In such a case the seller has remedies against the goods (to retain possession of the goods until he is paid) and against the buyer (to sue for payment).

4.25 Remedies against the goods include the following.

- The right of **seller's lien** (ss 41–43): the right of an unpaid seller still in *possession* of goods in respect of which the price is owing, to *retain* them until the price has been paid, or his debt secured or satisfied
- The right of **stoppage in transit** (ss 45–46): the right of an unpaid seller to require a carrier in possession of the goods *not* to deliver to the buyer, by giving notice of his claim to the carrier in possession before transit is completed – or by taking actual possession of the goods.
- The right of **resale** (s 48): the right of a seller to resell the goods, if the buyer expressly or by his conduct repudiates the contract (and therefore relinquishes his rights to the goods).

4.26 Note that these remedies apply where property or title in the goods has passed to the buyer, though the seller has not yet been paid. Where the seller retains the property in the goods, such remedies do not apply, because the seller has the right to retain or recover the goods by right of ownership (eg in the case of a retention or Romalpa clause, discussed in Chapter 5).

4.27 Remedies against the buyer include the following.

- **Action for the price** (s 49). The seller may sue the buyer for the price where the property in the goods has already passed to the buyer and the buyer fails to pay the price in accordance with the contract. He may also sue for the price if the price is due but unpaid on a date specified in the contract – regardless of whether the goods have been delivered, or property in the goods has not yet passed to the buyer.
- **Action for damages** for non-acceptance (s 50). If the buyer wrongfully neglects or refuses to accept or pay for the goods, and the property has not passed, the seller can sue for damages for loss resulting from the breach of contract.

5   Limitation of liability

5.1 The term 'exclusion clause' is applied to contract clauses which:

- Totally exclude one party from the liability which would otherwise arise from some breach of contract (such as the supply of goods of inferior quality); or which
- Restrict or limit liability its in some way; or which
- Seek to offer some form of 'guarantee' in place of normal liability for breach of contract.

5.2 Such clauses used to be very common in printed contracts and conditions of sale put forward by manufacturers, distributors and carriers of goods. However, the tendency of modern statutes is to limit the use of exclusion clauses – especially in dealings involving private citizens or consumers, who frequently do not read or understand the effect of the 'small print' put before them for acceptance.

5.3   To be valid, the exclusion clause must first pass a basic test, in two parts.

- The clause must be **incorporated into the contract**.
  - If a person signs a contract document in which the clause is included, he will generally be considered to have agreed to it (even if he did not read the document: *L'Estrange v Graucob*, 1934). If the document is not signed, the person is not bound, if it can be shown that he did not know that the document contained terms of the contract, or that reasonable notice of those terms was not given to him.
  - An exclusion clause cannot be introduced into a contract *after* it has been made, unless the other party agrees: *Olley v Marlborough Court,* 1949.
- The clause must be constructed in a **clear and precise** way.
  - The party relying on the clause must prove that, properly construed, it relates directly to the loss or damage suffered by the other party. In the case *Andrew Bros (Bournemouth) Ltd v Singer & Co Ltd* (1934), for example, a contract for the sale of 'new cars' contained a clause exempting the seller from liability for breach of all terms implied by common law, statute or otherwise. One of the cars was not new – and the court held that the exemption clause did not protect the seller, because there had been a breach of an *express* term, whereas the clause referred only to implied terms.
  - If there is any doubt as to the clause's meaning and scope, the clause will be interpreted against the party who is seeking to rely on it as a protection against his legal liability.

5.4   The clause must also pass the further test of compliance with the Unfair Contract Terms Act 1977 and the Consumer Rights Act 2015, which – as mentioned in Chapter 5 – restrict the extent to which a party can exclude or limit its liability for *negligence* and *breach of contract.*

5.5   In regard to **negligence**:

- A person in business cannot exclude or restrict his liability for death or personal injury resulting from negligence, and any clause purporting to do this is unenforceable.
- A person in business cannot exclude or restrict liability for negligence causing loss (other than death or personal injury), unless the exclusion clause is 'reasonable'.

5.6   In regard to **breach of contract**, any term purporting to exclude or restrict liability in a standard term contract (whereby one party deals on the other party's written standard terms of business) or in a consumer contract (between a business and a consumer for the sale of goods for ordinary private use) is effective only if it is 'reasonable'.

5.7   The burden of proving **reasonableness** of the exclusion clause is on the party wishing to rely on the clause to limit its liability. The term's inclusion must be fair and reasonable, in the light of the circumstances which were, or ought reasonably to have been, known to or anticipated by the parties when the contract was made. Relevant circumstantial factors include the following.

- The strength of the bargaining positions of the parties relative to each other
- Whether the buyer received an inducement to agree to the term
- Whether the buyer knew (or ought to have known) of the existence and the extent of the term, on the basis of trade custom or previous dealings with the seller
- Whether it was reasonable to expect, when the contract was made, that it would be practical for the buyer to comply with any conditions attached to the term (ie where the seller's liability would be excluded or restricted if the buyer did not comply with the stated condition)
- Whether the goods were manufactured, processed or adapted to the special order of the customer.

6   Termination of contract

Contract clauses for termination

6.1   It is important for a clause to be expressly written into a contract concerning the timing, circumstances and methods by which the contract can be terminated by either party, if required. This enables each party to 'get out of' a contract which is no longer satisfactory – while protecting the rights of the other party.

6.2   A **duration clause** might set out the contract period, with a specified commencement and expiry date. For example: 'The contract period shall be from 1 January 20XX ('the commencement date') until 31 December 20XX ('the expiry date') inclusive.'

6.3   A **termination clause** might set out the circumstances in which either party may terminate the contract immediately upon written notice to the other party (eg in the case of going into liquidation).

6.4   A **break provision** is sometimes incorporated into contractual provisions for termination. This is a somewhat stringent clause, inserted by buyers, which gives them the right to cancel the contract regardless of whether any breach has occurred. Since such an arbitrary clause would be construed as 'unreasonable' under the Unfair Contract Terms Act 1977, it should at the very least state that the buyer will pay for goods and/or services which have been wholly or partly provided prior to termination, as well as for the cost of materials and other resources bought in and which cannot now be used.

6.5   There might also be a **transition clause**, ensuring a smooth transition from the current supplier to any new supplier who may have been awarded the business for a new contract period. Such a clause should stipulate that the outgoing supplier will co-operate during the handover arising from the completion or earlier termination of the contract: giving access to documents and other information, returning assets, and taking no action to disrupt the handover.

Termination of relationship

6.6   The termination of supplier relationships (beyond the requirements of a particular contract), and the more 'relational' aspects of termination of contract, are discussed in Chapter 10 on supplier relationship management.

Chapter summary

- A contract may terminate through performance, agreement, breach or frustration.
- Breach of a condition entitles the injured party to repudiate the contract and sue for damages; breach of a warranty leads only to a claim for damages.
- Some terms (innominate terms) are recognised as being neither conditions nor warranties.
- 'Performance' of a contract means complete, exact and accurate performance.
- The doctrine of frustration of contract allows for genuinely good reasons for inability to perform contractual obligations.
- Breach of contract may be either actual or anticipatory.
- Remedies for breach include damages, specific performance, injunction, or quantum meruit.
- Where the contract provides for payment of a predetermined sum in the event of breach, this is referred to as 'liquidated damages'. Where it does not, the courts will determine the amount of damages ('unliquidated damages').
- SGA 1979 provides for specific remedies for an aggrieved buyer or seller.
- Contracting parties will often seek to limit their liability for breach of contract, but this is restricted by the Unfair Contract Terms Act 1977 and he Consumer Rights Act 2015
- A contract will usually include a term relating to the duration of the contract.

Self-test questions

Numbers in brackets refer to the paragraphs where you can check your answers.

1   List the different ways a contract may terminate. (1.1)

2   Distinguish between a condition and a warranty. Why is the distinction important? (2.1, 2.5, 2.6)

3   What is meant by an 'innominate term'? (2.8)

4   What is meant by 'partial performance', and what are its consequences? (3.3, 3.4)

5   What is meant by 'frustration of contract'? (3.8)

6   Describe the usual elements of a *force majeure* clause. (3.11)

7   What remedies may be awarded in the event of a breach of contract? (4.4)

8   What two issues must a court address in determining the amount of unliquidated damages? (4.7)

9   In what circumstances might a court rule that a liquidated damages clause is in fact a penalty clause? (4.19)

10   List statutory remedies for a buyer if a seller breaches the contract. (4.23)

11   Describe the common law test for validity of an exclusion clause. (5.3)

12   What are the limits on use of exclusion clauses imposed by the Unfair Contract Terms Act 1977 and the Counsumer Rights Act 2015? (5.5, 5.6)

13   What is meant by a 'break provision' in a contract? (6.4)

CHAPTER 7

Dispute Resolution

Assessment criteria and indicative content

 Explain the main approaches to conflict resolution in commercial contracts

- Negotiated settlements
- The mechanisms of alternative dispute resolution
- Other mechanisms for dispute resolution, adjudication, arbitration and litigation
- Contractual provisions for dispute resolution

Section headings

1 Contractual disputes
2 Negotiated settlement
3 Litigation
4 Arbitration and adjudication
5 Alternative dispute resolution (ADR)

Introduction

As we have seen, buyers and sellers arrange their dealings with each other in the form of contracts. As part of the contract, they aim to foresee and provide for the various eventualities that may arise in the course of their dealings – but of course this is not always possible. When things go wrong, both parties must come to some agreement as to the course of action to be taken. In the vast majority of cases, this is done by negotiation: the parties work towards a mutually satisfying (or compromise) solution to the problem.

To some extent the problem-solving process is regulated by the terms of the contract (since as we have seen, there may be a liquidated damages or *force majeure* clause) or by judicial precedent or statute. But to take advantage of these rules it may be necessary to have the matter resolved by a court through the process called litigation (bringing a law suit). This can be a time-consuming and costly procedure, and businesses often regard it as a 'last resort', in favour of other dispute resolution processes. We will look at a number of the options.

In this chapter, the law of England and Wales is used as exemplar of the relevant legal rules.

1   Contractual disputes

Why do contractual disputes arise?

1.1   It is worth recognising from the outset that a 'dispute' is a disagreement: it does *not* necessarily imply legal action – or any type of adversarial approach. A disagreement may arise within an amicable and constructive working relationship, over various matters.

- The interpretation of a contract term (eg has a *force majeure* event frustrated the contract or not?)
- Misunderstanding about requirements (eg what exactly has been specified in the contract?)
- Late delivery or payment, or quality problems
- The desire of one party to change or vary contract terms (perhaps because of changing requirements or circumstances), resisted by the other party.

1.2   Such disagreements will commonly arise in the course of contract management, and may be resolved quite informally: a phone call to the supplier to find out the reason for a late delivery, for example, and to obtain assurances that the problem will not happen again.

1.3   However, if a minor problem is not resolved to either party's satisfaction, it may escalate into a bigger problem.

- Failure to fulfil all the terms of a contract cannot be 'let slide': the other party may grow complacent and its performance may get worse over time.
- It may set a bad example to others, giving the impression that the organisation is 'soft' on contract management and performance.
- Persistent failure to meet contract terms may indicate the larger problem of a supplier (or buyer) who is unwilling or unable to perform as contracted, which may eventually result in a serious breach of contract.

1.4   In addition, as we have seen in the last two chapters, there may be some very serious 'issues' between parties, as a result of actual or anticipatory breach of contract, or where the conduct of one party makes it impossible for the other to fulfil its obligations under the contract. The delivery of defective goods, non-delivery, non-payment: these are all serious grounds for dispute, which may lead to a claim for damages or other remedies.

Approaches to resolving contractual disputes

1.5   In buyer-supplier relationships, supply contracts will often include clauses setting out the methods that will be used to settle disputes between the parties, and how they will be 'escalated' (taken further or to a higher level) if necessary.

1.6   In 2001, the UK Office of Government Commerce (OGC) produced guidance on dispute resolution. The guidance states that:

Dispute resolution techniques can be viewed as a continuum that range from the most informal negotiations between the parties themselves, through increasing formality and more direct intervention from external sources, to a full court hearing with strict rules of procedure.

1.7   OGC identify a sequence of escalating dispute resolution techniques.

- Negotiation
- Mediation
- Conciliation
- Adjudication
- Arbitration
- Litigation

What is at stake?

1.8   As we noted above, small problems may escalate into big ones, and big ones may be costly for an organisation in terms of its:

- Purchasing and production operations (eg a failure to get the right goods to the right place at the right time in the right quantity due to supplier non-compliance)
- Customer service and loyalty (eg a failure of availability or quality, due to supplier non-compliance)
- Cashflow and budgetary control (eg if a buyer fails to pay as contracted, or if a supplier varies the price or adds unforeseen charges)
- Reputation (eg if the organisation gets a reputation for breaking its promises, or as a poor payer or supplier, or as unfair, aggressive or litigious in dispute)

- Supply chain relationships (eg if supply chain partners are alienated by the organisation's conduct, or approach to disputes)
- Supply risk management (eg if the organisation can no longer rely on its suppliers to comply with contract)
- Contract management (eg if unnecessary purchasing time and resources are taken up in 'fire-fighting' contract disputes).

1.9 The choice of method of dispute resolution depends to a large extent on these factors. On the one hand, the need to manage risk and cost dictates that problems should be firmly dealt with, and that the organisation should 'win' its contract disputes. On the other hand, the need for ongoing relations with key suppliers dictates that problems should be handled positively and constructively, with the intention of coming to mutually acceptable solutions where possible.

2   Negotiated settlement

2.1 Two key approaches to dispute resolution are based on formal and informal communication between the parties involved, without outside intervention.

Consultation

2.2 Consultation is a form of 'issues' management, in which potential causes of conflict are discussed, and the other party has an opportunity to give its input, before the problem arises (or as soon as possible, once it has arisen). In the EU, for example, formal consultation is required with employee representatives about decisions likely to have a significant effect on employees' interests. A buyer may similarly consult formally or informally with suppliers about the need to vary the terms of a contract, for example, before it becomes an issue of potential dispute.

Negotiation

2.3 Negotiation is defined by Dobler *et al,* in the purchasing context, as: 'A process of planning, reviewing and analysing used by a buyer and a seller to reach acceptable agreements or compromises [which] include all aspects of the business transaction, not just price'. However, negotiation gurus Fisher and Ury (among others) point out that:

'Negotiation is a fact of life. Everyone negotiates something every day... A person negotiates with his spouse about where to go for dinner and with his child about when the lights go out. Negotiation is a basic means of getting what you want from others. It is a back-and-forth communication designed to reach an agreement when you and the other side have some interests that are shared and others that are opposed.'

2.4 Negotiation is summed up by Gennard and Judge *(Employee Relations)* as a process of:

- Purposeful persuasion: each party tries to persuade the other to accept its case or see its viewpoint *and*
- Constructive compromise: both parties accept the need to move closer to each other's position, identifying the areas of common ground where there is room for concessions to be made.

2.5 Negotiation is a useful approach to conflict or dispute resolution at any level and in a wide range of circumstances. As an official mechanism, it is often used:

- In industrial relations, for the resolution of collective disputes (between employees and their employer), the negotiation of collective agreements (on pay and conditions) and so on.
- In commercial relations, for the resolution of contract disputes (and other relational problems) with suppliers.

2.6   A negotiated approach can also have its own mini 'escalation' ladder. This might typically commence with buyer-supplier negotiation, and progressively escalate to a joint forum made up of senior management representatives from the concerned organisations.

Distributive and integrative approaches to negotiation

2.7   Distributive bargaining involves the distribution of limited resources, or 'dividing up a fixed pie'. One party's gain can only come at the expense of the other party: this is sometimes called a zero-sum game, or a win-lose outcome. In a contractual dispute, one party may impose a solution, 'get its way' or 'win the argument' – but at the expense of goodwill and collaborative and potentially value-adding future relations with the supplier.

2.8   Integrative bargaining involves collaborative problem-solving to increase the options available (or 'expanding the pie'), with the aim of exploring possibilities for both parties to find a mutually satisfying or win-win solution. This may also be called 'added value negotiating' (AVN): the aim is to add value to the solution, rather than extracting value from or conceding value to the other party.

2.9   The two approaches are reflected in very different negotiating tactics: Table 7.1.

Table 7.1 *Negotiating tactics*

DISTRIBUTIVE (COMPETITIVE) TACTICS	INTEGRATIVE (COLLABORATIVE) TACTICS
Presenting exaggerated initial positions or demands, in order to allow for expected movement and compromise	Being open about your own needs, and seeking to understand those of the other party: getting all cards on the table
Polarising conflicting viewpoints, in order to persuade opponents that their position is unrealistic	Collaboratively generating options, seeking to find those with genuine mutual or trade-off benefits
Withholding information that might highlight areas of common ground or compromise	Focusing on areas of common ground and mutual benefit, to keep a positive and collaborative atmosphere
Using all available levers to coerce, pressure or manipulate the other party to make concessions	Supporting the other party in accepting your proposals, with joint problem-solving, offering info or help with follow-up etc
Offering no concessions in return (unless forced to do so), even if they might be relatively low-cost to offer	Maintaining and modelling flexibility, by making and inviting reasonable counter offers, concessions and compromises

2.10   It is now generally recognised that integrative or collaborative negotiation is the most constructive and sustainable approach, where the key aim is to maintain ongoing positive working relations between the parties after the dispute is settled. However, there is still a place for 'hard bargaining' where the 'win' (issue or outcome) is more important than the relationship. An adversarial style may be used when a point is non-negotiable, when one party has high bargaining power over the other, or when gaining contract compliance (or redress for breach) is more important than developing the potential in a relationship.

Ethical or principled negotiation

2.11   In their classic text *Getting to Yes*, Fisher & Ury note that negotiation has traditionally depended on *positional bargaining*: each side takes a 'position' on an issue, arguing in its favour and attempting to get an outcome as close to that initial position as possible. People may bargain hard (taking up an extreme position and holding onto it, often eliciting an equally hard counter-response) or soft (making concessions readily in order to reach agreement, but often ending up with a negative result, since the initial position has been compromised). The focus on positions therefore fosters a win-lose or lose-lose outcome, and can be a time-consuming and relationship-damaging process.

2.12   In contrast, *principled* negotiation sees the parties as working collaboratively to attack a shared problem or to maximise a shared opportunity. Fisher & Ury advocate a style that is both hard (on the problem: deciding issues on their objective merits and standing up for your legitimate rights and interests) *and* soft (on the people: looking for mutual gains and insisting on fairness both in the debate and in the outcomes).

2.13   An approach to principled negotiation includes:

- Separating the people from the problem, in order to deal with substantive issues in a way that respects people and maintains positive relationships
- Focusing on reconciling interests (each side's need, concerns and fears) rather than positions. 'Behind opposed positions lie shared and compatible interests, as well as conflicting ones.'
- Generating a variety of ideas and options, rather than pushing for a pre-determined answer: expanding the pie before dividing it
- Insisting that the agreement reflect some objectively fair standard. Both parties may defer to a fair solution dictated by market value, legal or customary precedent, the principle of reciprocity, professional codes of practice, shared criteria (eg ethics or efficiency) and so on.

Beyond negotiation...

2.14   The OGC cites the following advantages of a negotiated resolution (compared to more formal, escalated routes): speed; cost saving; confidentiality (with no external involvement); preservation of relationships; range of possible solutions; and control over the process and outcome.

2.15   Unfortunately, agreement will not always be reached by negotiation. The other party may not see the disputed issue in the same light, or may have its own interests to protect by refusing to concede – or may be unable, for various reasons, to comply with the contract or give you the redress you require. If negotiation breaks down, or fails to reach a mutually acceptable conclusion, more formal means of dispute resolution may be required, bringing in a third party to facilitate further negotiation – or to decide the issue.

2.16   Negotiation may also be an inadequate method of conflict resolution where:

- Complex legal issues are involved, requiring the input of legal experts or the courts to decide (eg issues in the interpretation of contract terms)
- One party has a high degree of power, and a third party 'referee' may be required to ensure that the matter is conducted and resolved fairly
- The dispute involves international contracts. Differences in legal systems and jurisdictions – not to mention languages – may require third party involvement, for perceived impartiality and cross-jurisdictional recognition.

3   Litigation

3.1   Litigation is legal action to have a commercial or contract dispute resolved by the courts. Commercial cases in England and Wales are usually heard in a County Court or in the High Court (which is a lengthier and more formal procedure), with the option of appeal to the Court of Appeal if necessary.

3.2   The English system of litigation is essentially adversarial in nature. This means that there are two sides – the claimant and the defendant – who present cases, and who, by and large, control the course of the proceedings. The role of the judge and court has traditionally been fairly passive compared to the European inquisitorial system, where it is the judge who controls proceedings and the parties who present information. However, Civil Procedure Rules now allow judges to take more active control, so that the case can be dealt with more quickly and fairly (without time-wasting or manipulation by more powerful parties).

3.3   The main advantages of litigation are as follows.

- The procedure is designed to decide on the merits of the case, and the decision is therefore (in theory) fair and impartial
- The decision is legally binding, so the winning party has the full force of law on its side to impose the decision on the other party

- The drawbacks of litigation (discussed below) are such that the mere *threat* or option of litigation may be sufficient to influence the other party to fulfil its contract obligations, or to return to the negotiating table to resolve the dispute in some other constructive way.

Drawbacks of litigation

3.4 The litigation approach suffers from a number of disadvantages.

- Legal fees are costly (although the successful party may in some cases have its costs reimbursed by the court).
- The matter may not come to court for a long time – and then may not be resolved quickly, because of the nature of the system. This means not only that a solution will be a long time coming (which may be critical, eg if you need action, goods or payment from the other party), but that normal business activity may be disrupted in the meantime.
- The details of the conflict will be aired in public, possibly revealing confidential or reputation-damaging information.
- It is particularly complex in the case of international contracts, since the parties may operate in different legal jurisdictions, with different legal systems.
- The adversarial approach to resolving disputes almost certainly damages goodwill between the parties, and may be a barrier to an ongoing working relationship between them.

3.5 For these reasons, litigation is the method of 'last resort', particularly with important suppliers: even if it wins the case, the buyer may have 'lost' a valuable source of supply.

4 Arbitration and adjudication

4.1 Arbitration involves the appointment of a mutually acceptable independent person (or panel) who will consider the arguments of both sides, in formal, closed proceedings, and deliver a decision or judgement which is legally binding on both parties.

Contractual provision for arbitration

4.2 Because of the disadvantages of litigation, it is increasingly common for buyers and suppliers to treat court proceedings as a last resort, and to stipulate in their contracts that disputes must first be referred to arbitration: an **arbitration clause**. It is also usual for the arbitration agreement to contain *time limits* during which the arbitration must begin, in the event of a dispute.

4.3 An important part of such an arrangement is that both parties agree to be bound by the decision of the arbitrator, which can be enforced as if it were the decision of a court. Of course, this makes it important to choose someone suitable as arbitrator. In some cases, this means a person with legal experience, but often a specialised knowledge of the subject matter of the contract is more crucial. The arbitrator may be identified in the contract, or may be appointed once a dispute has arisen.

4.4 Unless the parties agree to the contrary, the arbitrator is obliged to give reasons for the award he eventually declares. It is regarded as a basic rule of justice that someone charged with making a binding decision affecting the rights of others should normally be required to justify the decision.

The legal framework surrounding arbitration

4.5 The law on arbitration agreements is contained in the Arbitration Act 1996.

4.6 The Act applies only to arbitration agreements set out in writing (as in most dealings between a commercial buyer and seller). It is based firmly on the principle of *party autonomy*: the parties in dispute are given maximum autonomy to decide how the arbitration should be conducted. They can tailor the arbitration to suit their own needs, determining for example how many arbitrators should hear their case, what procedures should be adopted, what powers the arbitrators should have and whether appeals can be made to the courts on points of law.

4.7 The courts are not allowed to *intervene* in the arbitral process unless it becomes clearly necessary to seek the court's assistance to move the arbitration forward, or if there has been a manifest injustice.

4.8 The courts do, however, have powers to *support* arbitral proceedings, for example by :

- Compelling the appearance of witnesses and the giving of evidence, if necessary
- Giving a ruling on a preliminary point of law, if it concerns a matter that substantially affects the rights of one or more of the parties
- Enforcing the award made by the arbitrator. If the award is challenged by one or other of the parties (eg on the grounds of irregularities in the proceedings or injustice in the award), the court may remit the award (refer it back to the arbitrator for reconsideration) or – in exceptional cases – set it aside.

Advantages of arbitration

4.9 Arbitration has significant advantages over litigation.

- The proceedings are held in private, avoiding negative publicity and public disclosure of sensitive information.
- The process is less confrontational than litigation, which may be important if the parties wish to maintain positive ongoing trading relations.
- It is intended as a single process (avoiding the appeals that tend to draw out litigation).
- It is often speedier and less expensive than litigation.
- The arbitrator may be selected for specialist knowledge, as well as legal expertise.

4.10 However, the preference for arbitration is not entirely clear-cut in all circumstances. If the parties choose litigation, at least once the procedure is complete the outcome is final, whereas arbitration may be subject to intervention by the courts – although this should happen only exceptionally. The powers of arbitrators are less extensive than those of judges, which can mean a greater possibility of delay in arbitral proceedings.

Arbitration in international contract disputes

4.11 Arbitration is the most commonly used form of dispute resolution for international contract disputes, which are rendered much more complex by parties being under different legal regimes and jurisdictions.

- It is highly flexible, with provision for arbitration in any country, in any language and with arbitrators of any nationality. This increases the likelihood of genuine neutrality, so that no party is unfairly disadvantaged by the location of the proceedings, the language used, the procedures applied and so on.
- It is widely accepted internationally. More than 140 countries have now acceded to the 1958 United Nations Convention on the Recognition and Enforcement of Foreign Arbitral Awards, known as the New York Convention. This enables an award made overseas to be enforceable in the UK – and *vice versa*.

4.12 There are well established frameworks for international dispute arbitration, using:

- The International Chamber of Commerce (ICC) court of arbitration, or
- The United Nations Commission on International Trade Law (UNCITRAL) arbitration code
- The London Court of International Arbitration
- The American Arbitration Association (AAA).

4.13   For any arbitration proceedings the enforcement of any award is of critical importance. Clearly if you cannot enforce an arbitration award its value is meaningless. In international trade a frequent question arises in this regard: is an award made overseas enforceable in the UK, and similarly is an award made in the UK enforceable overseas?

Adjudication

4.14   Adjudication is a process whereby an expert third party, appointed by agreement between the parties in a dispute, hears arguments and makes a decision. However, compared to arbitration, it:

- Is less formal (and therefore potentially less costly and time-consuming)
- Focuses on the facts of the dispute, rather than points of law
- Is less clearly binding and free from intervention by the courts (unless the contract provides for the expert determination to be final and binding).
- May be likened to 'negotiation with a referee present'.

4.15   In a formal legal sense, the term 'adjudication' is used almost exclusively in the UK for dispute resolution under the Housing Grants, Construction and Regeneration Act 1996 (HGCRA). Construction contracts must include a provision for adjudication, with the adjudicator giving a decision within 28 days of referral. The adjudicator's decision is binding *until* a final determination is reached by agreement, arbitration or litigation – or the parties may take the adjudicator's decision as final.

5   Alternative dispute resolution (ADR)

5.1   Litigation, arbitration and adjudication are all essentially adversarial, and tend to result in 'win-lose' solutions, which are potentially damaging to ongoing relationships; all are costly and time-consuming; and all ultimately take the power of decision away from the parties concerned. There has therefore been a growing interest in methods of what is called 'alternative dispute resolution (ADR)' or 'effective dispute resolution' (EDR): attempts to reach less adversarial, more empowering solutions.

5.2   There are two main forms of ADR or EDR: conciliation and mediation.

Conciliation

5.3   Conciliation is a process where conflicts or grievances are aired in a discussion, facilitated by an impartial conciliator, whose role is to manage the process and make constructive suggestions (and *not* to make a judgement for one side or the other).

- There is negotiation towards a mutually acceptable position – and, if possible, a 'win-win' outcome.
- The conciliator is not a 'referee' but a 'dispute resolution coach'.
- The decision reached is not legally binding (unless expressed in a contract).

Mediation

5.4   Mediation may follow conciliation, if a voluntary settlement has not been reached. It involves the appointment of an independent person (or panel) who will consider the case of both sides and make a formal proposal or recommendation (not binding on either party) as a basis for settlement of the dispute. It is possible to distinguish between:

- Facilitative mediation, where the mediator assists the parties' own efforts to formulate a settlement; and
- Evaluative mediation, where the mediator additionally helps the parties by introducing a third party view over the merits of the case or of particular issues between the parties.

5.5   This is the most common form of ADR in commercial disputes. In the public sector, the OGC advises that mediation should be seen as the preferred dispute resolution route, where traditional negotiation has failed to provide a solution. OGC survey findings indicate that more than 75% of commercial mediations result in a settlement, either at the time of the mediation or within a short time thereafter.

5.6   The Centre for Effective Dispute Resolution (CEDR) Model Mediation Procedure provides clear guidelines on the conduct of a mediation and requires the parties to enter into an agreement based on the Model Mediation Agreement. This will deal with points such as the nature of the dispute, the identity of the mediator, and where and when the mediation is to take place.

5.7   The mediator's role is to facilitate negotiations between the parties. OGC offers the following advice in relation to the role of the mediator.

- The mediator will not express views on any party's position, although he/she may question the parties on their positions to ensure they are being as objective as possible about the strengths and weaknesses of their own and the other party's/parties' legal and commercial stances.
- The mediator will try to get the parties to focus on looking to the future and their commercial needs rather than analysing past events and trying to establish their legal rights.
- It is essential that the mediator has mediation training; it is not essential that the mediator has experience, or even knowledge, of the subject matter of the dispute.

5.8   The format of the mediation process is somewhat flexible but will normally follow the following stages.

- Opening joint meeting where each party briefly sets out its position
- A series of private and confidential follow-on meetings between the mediator and each of the teams present at the mediation
- Where applicable, joint meetings between some or all members of each of the teams
- Signing of written terms of settlement (if reached).

5.9   The mediating team should be kept as small as possible, but must include a lead negotiator for each party. It is important that, where possible, the nominated lead negotiators have the necessary authority to settle on the day without reverting to others not involved in the mediation.

Contractual provision for mediation

5.10   A mediation clause in a contract may stipulate that in the event of a dispute:

- The parties will meet in a good faith effort to resolve the dispute, within a defined period (eg 10 days) of a written request by either party.
- If the dispute is not resolved at that meeting, the parties will attempt to settle it by mediation in accordance with the CEDR Model Mediation Procedure.
- Neither party may commence any court proceedings or arbitration until it has attempted to settle the dispute by mediation and either the mediation has terminated or the other party has failed to participate in the mediation.

Advantages of ADR

5.11   ADR/EDR attempts to overcome the drawbacks of adversarial, formal dispute resolution mechanisms. It is based on an idea that there should be no 'winners' and 'losers' in a commercial dispute. It is non-adversarial, speedy, confidential, and inexpensive – and can often avoid the bad feeling that may ruin future business relations.

5.12   In both conciliation and mediation, the settlement is designed by the parties, rather than imposed by a third party. Imagine a case where a buyer claims that certain products were defective and the supplier disputes the point. A court, adjudicator or arbitrator might find in favour of the supplier, leaving the buyer no alternative but to pay up without compensation. A mediator, or the parties themselves with a conciliator, is more likely to suggest a solution such as the buyer being allowed a better price on future supplies, say, in part compensation. This may represent a compromise acceptable to both sides, which will help to preserve the relationship.

5.13   The key benefit of involving a neutral third party is that it removes emotional and personal elements from the process, and refocuses the negotiation on the commercial issues related to the dispute.

5.14   However, there are some *disadvantages*.

- ADR clauses in standard contracts may not always be enforceable.
- Unlike litigation and arbitration, the results of an ADR process are not binding. If the parties have no incentive to settle, they will not do so unless they see it to be in their own self-interest.
- An ADR procedure may still wind up in arbitration or in court – having wasted time and money.

Chapter summary

- If a contractual dispute arises it is preferable, if possible, to seek a resolution without resorting to legal action or confrontation.
- Negotiation may be a fruitful means of resolving disputes. Modern thinking favours integrative negotiation over distributive negotiation.
- There are some advantages to litigation (especially its finality), but usually the disadvantages (cost, publicity, damage to relations etc) will be greater.
- It is increasingly common to agree that arbitration will be used before any legal proceedings have begun.
- Arbitration is particularly common in international trading agreements.
- Two main forms of alternative dispute resolution are conciliation and mediation.

Self-test questions

Numbers in brackets refer to paragraphs where you can check your answers.

1 Why is it important to resolve even minor contractual disputes? (1.3)

2 List the possible adverse consequences of a contractual dispute. (1.8)

3 Distinguish between distributive bargaining and integrative bargaining. (2.7, 2.8)

4 List typical tactics involved in (a) distributive and (b) integrative bargaining. (Table 7.1)

5 List the drawbacks of litigation. (3.4)

6 How may the courts support arbitration proceedings? (4.8)

7 Explain the process of adjudication. (4.15)

8 What is meant by 'mediation'? (5.4)

9 What are the possible disadvantages of alternative dispute resolution? (5.14)

CHAPTER 8

Assessing Contractual Risks

Assessment criteria and indicative content

 3.1 Assess the main types of contractual risks

- Risks that can impact on contracts, such as internal, market, economic, legal, ethical sourcing and performance based risks
- The role of information assurance
- The assessment of contractual risks

Section headings

1. Risks impacting on relationships
2. Internal and external risks
3. Legal and performance-based risks
4. Reputational and relationship risks
5. Information risks
6. Assessing contractual risks

Introduction

In this chapter we turn from the legal aspects relating to the performance of contracts to the more practical, operational and organisational aspects of contract management. We will devote Chapter 9 to detailed exploration of the various tasks and activities involved in the contract management process, and how they are typically allocated as responsibilities.

In this chapter, however, we begin by considering why contract management is necessary at all. As we saw in Chapter 5, the role of a contract is to set out the roles, rights and obligations of both parties in a transaction or commercial relationship. You might think that once contracts are signed, therefore, the buyer can simply say: 'The supplier will now do *that*'.

In fact, of course, things are not always so simple. As we saw in Chapter 3, there are many complex factors in the supply environment (both internal, external and relational) – any of which may intervene to delay, disrupt or derail contract performance. The discipline of contract management (monitoring progress and compliance to ensure that both parties fulfil their contracted obligations effectively and efficiently) is specifically designed to manage a range of what may be broadly identified as 'contractual risks': that is, risk factors raised by a particular contract, or risks which may *prevent* the contract from being successfully performed.

We will look at a number of key categories of risk in the internal, external and relational environments of supply, which may impact on performance of a contract and/or a supplier relationship. We will then briefly recap some techniques and tools for assessing the probability and impact of contractual risks, which you might use in the course of contract management – and the analysis of exam case studies.

1 Risks impacting on relationships

1.1 Increasingly, managers are urged not to be afraid of risk and uncertainty: they are a feature of the modern environment – and they can stimulate innovation, creativity and learning, without which the organisation may struggle to adapt and thrive. However, it is also accepted that risk must be managed, in order to reduce unacceptable impacts on the organisation and its stakeholders.

1.2 Contract management is, essentially, a form of risk management. It is designed to minimise the risk of loss or damage to the organisation and its owners or investors as a result of contract non-performance – and the risk of the organisation having to curtail or cease its activities owing to supply failure or disruption, lack of resources or breakdown in supplier relationships.

1.3 This is an ongoing challenge for the purchasing profession, because risk and vulnerability are highly fluid, dynamic and complex: new risks are constantly emerging – and risks change their severity and priority as circumstances change. Globalised, multi-tiered supply chains also create particular points of vulnerability – and challenges in monitoring and managing risk.

1.4 In Chapter 2, we emphasised the importance of the identification and assessment of risk and vulnerability (points of weakness that lead to risk) in prioritising strategic areas for supplier relationship management: identifying high-risk supply items and supply chains or suppliers. Here, we look in more detail at this process, with the more operational aim of prioritising areas for contract management attention.

Contractual risks

1.5 Contractual risks may be defined as:

- **Risks 'in' a contract or commercial relationship**: that is, factors *raised by* the contract or relationship itself. Certain generic risks are typically raised, for example, by inherently high-risk sourcing approaches such as outsourcing, single-sourcing arrangements, long-term partnership agreements and international sourcing. Specific risk factors may also be raised by specific contracts: for example, a contract for IT systems development using newly designed software by a small start-up supplier would raise risks in relation to the supplier's lack of a track record, the supplier's financial stability and capability, technology teething problems, user learning curve, capital investment – and the possibility of project failure.
- **Risks 'to' a contract or commercial relationship**: that is, factors *impacting on* a contract or relationship, which may jeopardise effective or efficient performance. Such factors need not be directly related to the contract itself, but may arise from the internal, external or relationship environment in which the contract is to be performed.

1.6 Either type of risk may be classified in a number of ways, according to the area or activity affected by the category of risk (eg reputational risk or supply risk), or the area or activity from which the risk arises (eg economic risk, technology risk, political risk or environmental risk). Some commonly used risk classifications, relevant to contract management, are listed in Table 8.1. You might be able to see how each category of risk would be exacerbated by an additional risk factor: poor supplier relationship, contract, project and risk management...

Table 8.1 *Some examples of risk classifications*

RISK	COMMENTS
Supply risk	Arising from supplier failure (eg as a result of financial instability, excessively 'lean' supply chains or cashflow problems exacerbated by buyer non-payment); supply failure (eg as a result of industrial action, weather events, transport problems or damage to supplies in transit); the length and complexity of supply chains (long lead times, transport risks); and so on.
Compliance risk	Exposure of non-compliant or illegal activity by the organisation or its supply chains, incurring reputational, operational and financial penalties
Reputational risk	Exposure of unethical, socially irresponsible or environment-damaging activity by the organisation or its supply chain, potentially damaging the organisation's image, brand and credibility in its customer, investor, labour and supply markets
Economic or financial risk	Risk of economic loss, as a result of poor investment or financial management, loss of sales (eg due to supply failure) or cost blow-outs (eg due to post-contract price or cost variances), or macro-economic factors (such as exchange rate fluctuations or rising costs of finance)
Market risk	Economic or supply risk arising from factors or changes in the external supply market, such as rising commodity prices, resource scarcity, the pace of technological change, or high or growing supplier power (eg with few suppliers, or supply market consolidation). There may also be product market (or 'marketing') risk, as a result of falling demand, product obsolescence or competitor initiatives (resulting in loss of competitive advantage).
Environmental risk	Risks of disruption or delay to supply, or rising supply costs, arising from factors or changes in the external environment of STEEPLE factors
Operational risk	Risks of operational failure, quality defects, health and safety incidents, transport failures or equipment breakdowns (eg resulting from failure to secure supplies or failure to enforce health and safety policies or maintenance schedules)
Technological risk	Risks of operational problems, and resulting economic losses, due to technology obsolescence, systems or equipment failure, data corruption or theft, new technology 'teething troubles', systems incompatibility (eg where buyer-supplier systems need to be integrated) and so on.

1.7 We will look briefly at some of the key categories of risk mentioned in the syllabus, highlighting their potential impact on contract performance and supplier relationships – and therefore their relevance and priority for contract management.

1.8 Bear in mind that the exam may require you to identify, discuss or explain such risks, from a theoretical point of view – but it may equally require you to:

- Identify such risks from the data provided in case study scenarios
- Analyse or evaluate the importance (likelihood and impact) of such risks on a case study organisation or specific contract, from data provided.

1.9 It may therefore be helpful to keep the basic risk categories and examples in mind, as a checklist for risk assessment (and structured analysis) in a case study question.

2   Internal and external risks

Internal risks

2.1 Internal risks arise from within the organisation (or, in this context, within the supply chain) and its processes. Examples of internal risks include: technology, equipment or systems breakdown (eg through lack of maintenance, incorrect usage or lack of contingency planning); human error and inexperience (eg lack of training or supervision); malicious activity (eg fraud, sabotage, theft, data theft or unethical conduct); security risks (unprotected or unauthorised access to facilities, data or assets); lack of internal controls (eg financial controls, security systems and risk management) and workplace hazards (risk of accidents and ill health); poor employee relations (lack of industrial action); business or financial risk as a result of poor management (uncontrolled costs, poor planning, poor relationship management and so on); or loss of key personnel and knowledge.

2.2 Contract performance (and organisational objectives) may also be put at risk by a number of internal factors relevant to contract and supplier relationship management.

- Lack of risk assessment and management in relation to contracts and supply chain relationships
- Poorly developed (unclear, under-specified or over-specified, non-value-analysed, overly prescriptive) specifications of requirement, KPIs, or improvement or service level agreements
- Undisciplined or poorly conducted appraisal, pre-qualification and selection of suppliers
- Over-reliance on single suppliers
- Unclear roles and responsibilities for contract performance (and/or contract management) and lack of governance structures
- Poor internal stakeholder relationships and communication on issues relating to contract performance (eg collaboration with users on specifications and performance management)
- Poor supplier relationship management, resulting in supplier-related risk, conflict risk, reputational risk and possibly supply risk arising from unfavourable customer status
- Lack of effective, integrated and secure information systems for monitoring and managing supplier performance and contract administration

2.3 The key point about internal risks is that they should be *controllable* by the organisation, its managerial processes (such as risk assessment, monitoring and supervision) and internal controls (policies, rules, checks and risk management measures).

External environmental risks

2.4 External risks are risks arising from factors in the external macro environment (STEEPLE factors) or micro environment (industry, market and competitive environment) or the organisation or supply chain. STEEPLE factors may present a wide range of risks to the **contract performance** of the supplier or buyer, for example by:

- Creating barriers to clear specification, negotiating, contracting and contract management (eg in international contracts, with language and cultural differences)
- Disrupting or delaying supply (eg in the case of supplier failure, industrial action, import or export restrictions, materials shortages or transport delays due to weather)
- Raising market prices (eg because of supply shortages or exchange rate fluctuations) or incurring extra costs (eg because of the need for insurance or alternative transport arrangements)
- Causing damage to, or deterioration of, goods at source (eg in the case of disease or damage to crops) or in transit (eg because of weather factors or extra handling requirements)
- Creating difficulties in payment (eg in international contracts, owing to currency and trust issues)

We discussed a range of such possibilities in Chapter 3 under the various STEEPLE categories (a structure which you will find helpful when discussing external risks in exam questions). The role of contract management is to assess and respond to such risks, in order to 'assure' efficient and effective contract performance as far as possible.

2.5 In addition, external macro-environment factors may directly impact on **supplier relationships**, perhaps acting as a constraint on relationship development or leverage: Table 8.2. You may be able to think of other examples relevant to your own work organisation or industry, or one with which you are familiar. (This too is useful preparation for the exam, which often asks you to contextualise your answer to an organisation described in a case study, or an organisation of your choice.)

Table 8.2 *STEEPLE factors affecting relationships*

FACTORS	EXAMPLE
Socio-cultural	• Cultural differences between parties (especially in international relationships) creating miscommunication or conflict • One party adapting to changing social values (eg equal opportunity, the environment) and another not – creating incompatibility
Technological	• One party developing new technologies, creating compatibility issues • One party pressuring another to adopt EDI or other systems • Products or processes (on which relationships were based) becoming obsolete owing to technological change
Economic	• Economic downturn or recession creating price or profit pressures • Exchange rates and wage costs making UK suppliers uncompetitive
Environmental	• Weather and resource availability affecting supplier performance • Pressure to develop 'green' practices (eg renewable materials, recycling), for which one party may have less capability
Political	• Export or import policies changing supply availability and market dynamics
Legal	• Compulsory competitive tendering in the public sector, making it difficult to develop long-term relationships • Tendency to use relationship-damaging litigation to settle disputes
Ethical	• Unethical treatment of one party by the other (eg forcing prices down or up exploitatively, fraud, breach of confidentiality) • A buyer's reputation is damaged by association with a supply partner 'caught' in unethical conduct (eg fraud, worker exploitation) • Buyer pressure to raise ethical standards, which may be costly for the supplier (eg higher wages, investment in health and safety)

Supply market risks

2.6   The workbook *Understanding Supply Chain Risk* (Cranfield School of Management/Department of Transport) identifies a series of generic questions that should be considered when looking at market-based supply risk.

- Is the supply chain dependent on dominant or specialist suppliers, where failure to supply could disrupt output?
- Are any suppliers, particularly critical suppliers, in potential financial difficulties that could interrupt output?
- Do any suppliers have extended lead times that potentially impact on inventory or customer service?
- Is there a record of poor quality from any suppliers, and are there risks that could arise as a result?
- Are there any suppliers who have poor schedule compliance, and if so, are they among the suppliers on whom we depend?
- What is the state of the supply market? Is our company taking a large slice of the supply? Are there any tight spots in the supply market that might disrupt output?
- Are there measures of performance in place with suppliers, providing a platform for a risk management and performance improvement programme?
- Do suppliers in the market have the capacity and capabilities to plan and fulfil demand? Are they using systematic, good-practice methods or working hand to mouth?

Financial or economic risks

2.7   Financial risks may be *internal,* arising from the organisation's financial structures and transactions. Here are some examples.

- Lack of price or cost analysis in setting or negotiating prices for a contract
- Lack of budgetary or cost control and management through the life of the contract, leading to cost blow-outs and lost profits

- Poorly designed or implemented financial controls and procurement or payment procedures, leading to the risk of financial fraud
- Financial penalties incurred as a result of poor contracting, or contract non-compliance (eg interest on late payments to suppliers)
- High capital investment in a contract or project, accompanied by inadequate investment appraisal, lack of whole-life costing, or high costs of loan finance.

2.8 Financial risks may also be *external,* resulting from factors such as the following.

- Macro-economic factors, such as: business cycles (eg economic recession, creating low demand, poor credit availability, supplier instability); fluctuating commodities prices; availability and costs of finance (interest rates); and fluctuating exchange rates (in international transactions)
- The financial strength, stability and general 'health' of suppliers.

2.9 The risks of supplier financial instability – particularly for critical supplies or supply partners – is a major focus of contract and supplier management. A variety of tools is available for monitoring and assessing the financial stability and strength of prospective suppliers and existing vendors (in order to minimise the risk of their unexpectedly going bust and disrupting supply). Information for this analysis is largely available in the published financial statements of public, private and not-for-profit organisations.

2.10 Examples of the kind of thing a sourcing or contract manager might be looking for include signs that a supplier:

- Is not making much profit, is experiencing falling profit margins, or is making a loss, which suggests that it is operating inefficiently (revenue is too low or costs are too high) – and that it may run out of finance to continue or develop the business
- Is not managing its cashflow (the balance and timing of cash coming in and going out), or is experiencing a strong cash 'drain' from the business, making it difficult to meet its short-term debts and expenses
- Has more loan capital (borrowed from lenders) than share capital (invested by owners), incurring high finance costs (interest payments) and the obligation to repay the loan – a particular risk in periods of 'credit crunch'.

2.11 An article in *Supply Management* (6 February, 2006) identified the following additional signs of supplier financial difficulty (other than poor financial ratios or posted losses), which a contract or supplier manager is well placed to pick up on.

- Rapid deterioration in delivery and quality performance
- Senior managers leaving the business within a short period of time
- Changes in the auditors and bankers of the firm
- Adverse press reports
- Very slow responses to requests for information
- Problems in the supply chain (and/or changes in subcontractors)
- Chasing payment before it is due

3 Legal and performance-based risks

Legal and compliance risk

3.1 We have already considered legal aspects of contracts with suppliers, in Chapters 5–7. Legal, contract and compliance risks may arise from factors such as the following.

- **Poor compliance management**, leading to the risk of non-compliance (and related penalties, sanctions and reputational damage) with law and regulation eg on labour rights, environmental protection or health and safety – and related penalties, sanctions and reputational damage.
- **Poor contract development and contracting processes**: ambiguous terms, lack of adequate

protections for contractual risks (ensuring that remedies are available); unenforceable terms (eg unlawful or unreasonable limitation of liability; penalty clauses instead of valid liquidated damages clauses); lack of supporting documentation (eg specifications, KPIs or service level agreements) to specify performance expectations; lack of supplier incentives to promote committed performance; lack of provision for dispute resolution, contract termination, transfer and so on.

- **Unmanaged battle of the forms**, so that there is ambiguity about which set of standard terms governs the contract, or the set of standard terms used unfairly disadvantages one party.
- **Poor contract administration and change control**, eg: unauthorised or uncontrolled changes to contract; lack of version control; or lack of communication of contract changes to relevant stakeholders.
- **Lack of adequate protection of intellectual property**, assigning and protecting rights of ownership (and licence for usage) of documents, drawings, computer software and work specifically prepared or developed in performance of the contract, or used in the performance of the contract. Protections may be secured within the contract (using IP clauses), as well as statutory provisions (such as registration of designs, patents, trademarks and copyright).
- **The assignment of liability** for problems such as injury, economic loss, damage to property, or negligence of the supplier's personnel – especially if the supplier is providing services at the premises of the buyer (or downstream customers). The buyer will usually wish to confirm that the supplier has the ability to pay compensation in the event of problems, and will usually make it a requirement of the contract that the supplier has the necessary insurances to cover such events: eg employer's liability insurance (employees who sustain injury, illness or incapacity as a consequence of their employment); public liability insurance (claims made by third parties for personal injury or damage to property); professional indemnity insurance (where a failing by the supplier results in economic loss to the buyer) or product liability insurance (injury or damage to property arising from the use of goods supplied, repaired or tested by the supplier).
- **Liability for health and safety risk** arising in performance of the contract. It is common for buyers to use contract terms to remind suppliers of the statutory requirements imposed on the parties by the Health and Safety at Work Act 1974; of the supplier's responsibility for compliance; and of the supplier's duty to ensure that staff working at the premises of the buyer (or the buyer's customers) comply with the health and safety requirements of those premises. A buyer may also require the supplier to indemnify it against any liability, costs, losses or expenses sustained by the buyer if the supplier fails to comply with the legislation.
- **Costs and relational damage arising from commercial or contractual disputes** with suppliers. According to a research study (reported in *Supply Management*, 18 October 2007), only 12% of risk management policies have detailed information on how to resolve conflict – and nearly two-thirds of organisations have no training programmes on dispute avoidance. Meanwhile, commercial disputes cost businesses £33 billion per year in the UK. The most common cause of disputes is poorly written contracts, so clear contracting procedures are a good start to risk mitigation. There should also be plans for how disputes will be handled, avoiding the costs of litigation (eg by alternative dispute resolution or arbitration, as discussed in Chapter 7).

Performance-based risks

3.2   Performance-based risks are basically supply risks, arising from suppliers' reliability and performance – *and/or* from the buyer's contract, project and supplier management policies and practices. They refer to risks arising in the performance of a contract (or project) which:

- Jeopardise its successful performance (eg causing cost blow-outs, schedule delays or breaches of contract) or
- Create other risks for the organisation and supply chain (eg poor cost management, or buyer non-payment, leading to supplier failure; or poor ethical conduct by the supplier leading to reputational damage for the buyer).

3.3 An exam case study scenario may well highlight practices, plans or progress indicators which raise the risk of contract non-performance, if the emerging variance is not corrected before it continues or escalates. You should look out for any data that appears to indicate a mis-match (variance or non-conformance) between the supplier's stated plans or claims, or measured current progress, and specified or agreed targets or indicators, such as:

- Agreed milestones and progress measures (schedules, critical path charts, project stage reviews)
- Key performance indicators, standards and targets
- Product or service specifications (including agreed tolerances and permitted variances)
- Agreed service levels or improvement targets
- Agreed cost budgets or targets.

3.4 Performance-based risks include factors such as the following.

- The capacity and capability of prospective suppliers
- The capacity and capability of contracted vendors
- The percentage of supplier capacity utilised by the current contract and other customers (vulnerability to being over-stretched)
- The likelihood of unanticipated demand (over-stretching capacity)
- Supplier lead times for delivery and whether there is any 'slack time' or flexibility in the schedule
- Supply risks affecting the supply chain or individual suppliers, and the effectiveness of risk management and contingency planning
- The accuracy and clarity of specifications, contract terms and buyer expectations
- Vulnerabilities in supply chain quality assurance (especially if tolerances are tight)
- Accuracy of scheduling and forecasting
- The quality, reliability and transparency of data shared between contract participants and stakeholders (supporting risk-managed decision-making)
- Cost management; internal or external factors impacting on costs; and what price arrangements have been agreed (eg cost-plus or fixed-price contracts)
- Project and contract management effectiveness, to monitor and manage all these elements

Risks in international sourcing

3.5 International sourcing and trading imposes a distinct set of risks for businesses. Depending on the particular circumstances, they may include:

- Socio-cultural differences (including business customs, consumer behaviour, communication and negotiation styles, management styles, and social values) – creating potential barriers to communication, and difficulties in attempting to transfer marketing, sourcing and managerial strategies across cultures
- Language barriers – with potential for misunderstanding (in a legal sense, affecting the validity of a contract, as well as in general communication)
- Legal issues, such as which nation's legal rules apply in determining contract disputes
- Logistical and supply risks, arising from long-distance supply lines, long lead times for supply; the risks of loss, damage or deterioration of goods in transit; and the potential ambiguity of the passing of risk and title, and responsibility for insurance, in such circumstances
- Exchange rate risk, due to potential fluctuations in foreign currency values during the contract period (requiring measures such as forward exchange contracts)
- Payment risk, due to limited direct contact between the parties, different legal systems, and the possibility of currency restrictions
- Difficulties of monitoring and assuring quality, environmental and ethical standards in overseas supplier and contractor operations (especially in areas where local standards, regulation and legislation are less stringent) – creating quality, compliance and reputational risk.
- General STEEPLE factor risks in the overseas environment: political instability; economic instability;

protectionist policies (tariffs, quotas etc); poor technological infrastructure; poor education and training infrastructure; and so on.

4 Reputational and relationship risks

Ethical sourcing and reputational risks

4.1 'Ethics' are simply a set of moral principles or values about what constitutes 'right' and 'wrong' behaviour in a given society, market or organisation.

4.2 Ethical, sustainable or responsible sourcing policies at the level of corporate ethics (or corporate social responsibility) may cover a range of matters, depending on the ethical risks and issues raised by the organisation's activities and markets. Here are some examples.

- The promotion of fair, open and transparent competition in sourcing (and the avoidance of unfair, fraudulent, manipulative or coercive sourcing practices)
- The use of sourcing policies to promote positive socio-economic goals such as equal opportunity and diversity in the supply chain; support for local and small-business suppliers; and minimisation of transport miles (to reduce environmental impacts and carbon emissions)
- The specification and sourcing of ethically produced inputs (eg certified as not tested on animals; drawn from sustainably managed or renewable sources; or manufactured under safe working conditions)
- The selection, management and development of suppliers in such a way as to promote ethical trading, environmental responsibility and labour standards at all tiers of the supply chain (eg by pre-qualifying suppliers on CSR policies, ethical codes, environmental management systems, reverse logistics and recycling capabilities, and supply chain management; and incentivising, monitoring and developing supplier ethical performance)
- A commitment to supporting the improvement of working terms and conditions (labour standards) throughout the supply chain, and particularly in low-cost labour countries with comparatively lax regulatory regimes
- A commitment to supporting sustainable profit-taking by suppliers (eg not squeezing supplier profit margins unfairly) and to ensuring that fair prices are paid to suppliers back through the supply chain, particularly where buyers are in a dominant position (eg in developing and low-cost supply markets)
- Adherence to the ethical frameworks and codes of conduct of relevant bodies such as the International Labour Organisation (ILO), Fair Trade Association or Ethical Trading Initiative, the International Standards Organisation guidelines on Corporate Social Responsibility (ISO 26000: 2010), or the Codes of ethics/conduct of relevant professional bodies (such as CIPS)
- A commitment to compliance with all relevant laws and regulations for consumer, supplier and worker protection

4.3 In addition, a range of ethical issues may be raised by day-to-day contract management and supplier relationship management. Some of the key ethical issues typically provided for in codes of ethical conduct for procurement and contract management professionals include the following.

- The provision of fair, truthful and accurate (not false or misleading) information. This makes unethical, for example, the practice of deliberately inflating estimates of future order sizes in order to obtain a price that would not be offered if the true usage patterns were admitted.
- The confidentiality of information, where appropriate. Confidential information obtained in the course of business should not be disclosed without proper and specific authority, or unless there is a legal duty to disclose it: for example, if there is suspicion of money laundering or terrorist activity.
- Fair dealing with supply chain partners. A temptation may be offered, for example, where a supplier makes an exploitable error in a quotation or invoice; where there is potential to delay or dispute an agreed payment; where quotations are sought from suppliers where there is no intention to purchase; or where some vendors are favoured over others in a tender situation. Deception or unfairness in such

8

situations may be perceived as unethical and potentially damaging to ongoing trading relationships.

- Hospitality and gifts. It is a key principle of purchasing ethics not to offer or accept gifts or inducements which may – or may be *perceived* to – influence the recipient's decision-making. A related principle is that purchasing professionals should not use their position for personal gain, eg by accepting inducements to award contracts or divulge confidential information. The purchasing department may well have specific guidelines on accepting business gifts and hospitality.

4.4 Ethical sourcing, trading and supplier management are important to the management of compliance, reputational and performance-based risk, for a number of reasons.

- Unethical conduct leads to poor relationships with stakeholders who have been badly treated – which in turn may result in poor customer status with suppliers, poor supplier motivation and performance, and increased risk of conflict and disputes. Exploitation, abuse and disappointed expectations will inevitably lead to broken relationships or reciprocal 'corner cutting' by suppliers.
- Poor stakeholder relationships, as a result of unethical conduct, also represent loss of the opportunities, value and profits that might arise from positive relationships, in terms of committed performance, innovation, collaboration and synergy and so on. Lack of capability to seize such opportunities is a source of long-term business and competitive risk.
- Poor treatment of employees and suppliers may make it difficult to attract, retain and motivate them to provide quality service and commitment – particularly in competition with other employers and buyers in the market.
- Unethical conduct may lead to increased regulatory, media and pressure group scrutiny – increasing reputational and compliance risk.
- Exposure of unethical conduct may result in reputational damage, damage to the organisation's product or employer brand, loss of goodwill (from customers, employees and supply chain partners), lost sales – and perhaps even consumer boycott.
- Illegal behaviours create additional compliance and legal risk – including penalties and sanctions for non-compliance (financial penalties, rectification orders, costs of litigation and damages, reputational damage through 'name and shame' schemes and so on).

4.5 There may be costs and challenges involved in ethical sourcing and supplier management: major organisations such as Nike, Vodafone and Marks & Spencer, for example, have taken on the responsibility of educating, monitoring and managing overseas suppliers, to ensure that they treat their workers fairly and observe environmental standards. However, *failure* to do this is now regarded as a business risk, with significant potential costs. One high profile example was the reputational damage suffered by social charity Oxfam, when it became known that overseas suppliers of its 'Make Poverty History' wristbands were in fact themselves exploiting their workers. Another example is the public pressure applied to the popular Apple brand, following the exposure of exploitative working conditions in the factories of some of its major Chinese assemblers.

Relationship risks

4.6 A further key category of business and supply risk – and one particularly relevant to this module – is the nature, structure and management of relationships with suppliers.

4.7 Different risks attach to different types of relationship, sourcing approaches and supply chain configuration decisions. There are particular risks, for example, arising from the following scenarios.

- **Sole sourcing arrangements** (where there is only one supplier available in the supply market) and **single sourcing arrangements** (where the organisation chooses to use only one supplier for a given requirement) – because of the extent of the buyer's dependency on one supplier, and vulnerability to risks of supplier (and possibly therefore supply chain) failure, complacency or leverage. This was discussed in Chapter 1.
- **Outsourcing arrangements** – because the organisation is effectively replacing its own assets,

resources, knowledge and competencies with those of an external contractor, and perhaps rendering itself vulnerable to reputational, performance and marketing risk by having the contractor deliver services to customers on its behalf. There may also be risks related to loss of control, intellectual property and confidential data sharing. This was discussed in Chapter 1.

- **Long-term partnership relations** – because the organisation is effectively 'locked in' to a long-term collaborative relationship with a partner who may turn out to be under-performing, incompatible, strategically divergent and/or complacent (in the absence of competition, or continuous improvement agreements). The potential value of partnership may not be realised – or may be lost as internal and external changes erode its rationale. Collaboration may itself pose risks to confidential data and/or intellectual property. This was discussed in Chapter 1 – and will be explored further in Chapter 10 on relationship management.
- **Supplier tiering** (an approach to structuring the supply chain whereby the buying organisation develops partnership relations with a few lead providers or 'first tier' suppliers, who take responsibility for managing the lower levels or tiers of the supply chain) – because of the 'distance' this causes between the buyer and lower tiers, in terms of performance and CSR monitoring and management. There may be insufficient supply chain transparency to enable the buyer to 'drill down' to lower levels – and it may not be able to rely on the supply chain management and quality or CSR assurance of the lead provider.

Risks of supplier switching

4.8 One sourcing policy issue related to supplier relationship strategies is the extent to which the buying organisation is prepared to engage in supply switching: that is, 'dropping' an existing supplier, or deciding not to renew a supply contract, in favour of a new or alternative supplier. This will be relevant in contract management, where contracts are reviewed with a view to renewal or termination.

4.9 There may be a range of reasons for changing or switching suppliers, including: problems with the performance or reliability of the existing supplier; a new supplier offering a more competitive bid (eg a better solution or better value), when an existing contract comes up for renewal; or a situation where low-risk, widely-available, standardised items are sourced through arms' length, transactional purchasing approaches – making opportunistic switching easy, and taking advantage of price competition.

4.10 Contract managers need to be aware, however that switching suppliers causes upheaval and cost (identified as 'switching costs') – especially where strong relationships have been established, and relationship-specific plans and investments made. Some of the costs and risks of switching are summarised in Table 8.3.

4.11 Here are some key issues for contract managers if switching does take place.

- The need for early flagging of contracts up for renewal, so that buyers can discuss renewal and switching options with key stakeholders (including users who may have feedback on the impact of supplier performance and risk)
- The need for proactive transition planning and risk management, including contract clauses and supplier KPIs providing for transition and hand-over to new suppliers.

8

Table 8.3 *Costs and risks of supplier switching*

RISKS OF SUPPLIER SWITCHING	COSTS OF SUPPLIER SWITCHING
• The new supplier may fail to perform (eg if it made exaggerated claims to win contract...) • Process incompatibility (eg if integrated systems and relationship-specific modifications were made with the old supplier) • Cultural or inter-personal incompatibility (eg where patterns of understanding and behaviour developed in the old relationship) • Loss of knowledge (eg where collaborative processes with the old supplier were undocumented) • Learning curve: time for the new supplier to achieve peak performance, teething problems • Exposure to new or unfamiliar supply risks (political instability, labour unrest, CSR issues, exchange rate risk, transport risk) • Exposure of intellectual property, confidential data (without trust having yet been built up) • Problems of adversarial hand-over from the old supplier to the new: trouble accessing designs, documents, assets, work in progress etc.	• Identifying and qualifying new suppliers • Initiating and administering tendering exercises or other sourcing and contracting processes • Settlement of not-yet-delivered items from old supplier; settlement of outstanding claims; payment of 'exit' (eg early cancellation) fees • Change of internal systems and processes to align with the new supplier • Familiarising and training the new supplier in systems, procedures and requirements • Contract development and contract management (perhaps with more intensive monitoring and contact in the early stages of the relationship) • Risk mitigation measures (eg insurances) and corrective measures (eg re teething problems)

Power and dependency issues in supply chain relationships

4.12 Power is the ability of an individual or group to exercise influence over others. It is an aspect of any relationship – not just obvious ones such as leader-subordinate or buyer-supplier. It also applies to inter-organisational relationships, as well as interpersonal ones.

4.13 Power may take various forms in buyer-supplier relationships.

- It may be applied directly and transparently – through tactics such as competitive leverage, hard negotiation, strong leadership, logical persuasion or the offering of incentives.
- It may be built into a situation or context ('structural power'), as in the case of legal obligations on organisations, buyers who are dependent on suppliers (or *vice versa*) or employers who control the rewards of their employees.
- It may arise from different sources of power: organisational or legal authority (eg the power given by a senior management position or agreed contract terms); valued expertise (eg the power of a specialist adviser); or control over resources (eg the power of a buyer to withhold valued business from suppliers, or the power of a supplier to control access to essential supplies).

4.14 Coercive, arbitrary, unfair or abusive exercise of power in supplier and customer relations (as in interpersonal relations) is generally discouraged on several grounds.

- Firstly, it may be unlawful (eg unfair treatment of suppliers in a public sector tender situation, under EU public procurement directives) or unethical (eg abuse of the buyer's position of influence for personal gain, under the CIPS Code of Conduct).
- Secondly, it is generally counter-productive. Such forms of power may secure short-term compliance, but they generally also cause resentment, resistance and loss of potential for more constructive long-term relationships.

4.15 This is one reason why adversarial relationships, based on overt competitive leverage, are not considered suitable for all supply situations. They are rarely likely to achieve long-term best value for money, or potential for mutually satisfying partnerships.

4.16   Cox *et al* depict the relationship between power and dependency in supply chains in a simple matrix: Figure 8.1.

Figure 8.1 *The power/dependency matrix*

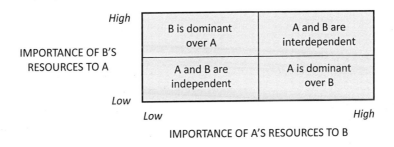

4.17   Broadly speaking, each party will wish to avoid a situation where the other party is dominant, because a position of dominance and dependence may easily be exploited. A dominant supplier may threaten to cease supply unless the buyer accepts a price increase, or a change in specification. A dominant buyer may squeeze the supplier's profit margins excessively (as major supermarkets are periodically accused of doing to grocery suppliers, for example). Independence (neither party needs the relationship) and interdependence (both parties need the relationship) create a more equal balance of power and risk.

4.18   The dangers of over-*dependency* are obvious enough. (What happens if our partner finds a better deal elsewhere? What choice do we have but to meet its increasingly costly demands?) But there are also dangers in having an over-*dominant* position. Many buyers are reluctant to take too much of a supplier's output, or to insist on relationship-specific adaptations – even though the supplier might be keen to get more business: firstly, out of an ethical desire to avoid exploiting a situation (and perhaps being responsible for the supplier's collapse if the business is later withdrawn); and secondly, because a less dependent supplier will be more attuned to a diverse customer base, and may therefore have more to offer.

4.19   Interdependence creates the need to secure long-term collaboration and commitment, usually by means of some form of partnership arrangement.

Exit strategy

4.20   As part of the risk assessment of a contract, it is important to identify where early contract exit or termination may be required, and how this will be managed. This is an issue relevant to ethical contract management – and to broader relationship and performance-based risk, because the buying organisation cannot afford to get 'trapped' in contracts or long-term relationships with under-performing or incompatible suppliers.

4.21   There should be a clear understanding of the circumstances in which a contract can be terminated (other than those mandated by contract law, such as breach or frustration of contract: discussed in Chapter 6); what processes should be followed; and what notice given. Ideally, there should also be provision for review, feedback and learning from the 'failure' of the contract – and for keeping the door open to future relations, where possible (eg with clear parameters for the changes and improvements required).

4.22   Particular consideration will have to be given to the social and economic impacts of termination of contract on dependent suppliers, and their workforces and communities. Corporate social responsibility policies may address areas such as the discouragement of supplier dependency, phased withdrawal of business, and the performance management procedures and other options (such as supplier development) to be explored prior to termination.

5 Information risks

5.1 Information risks are relevant to contract and supplier management in two main ways.

- Data security, knowledge management, and information technology systems risks represent a key category of business risk, which must be managed.
- Effective contract and supplier relationship management depends on the gathering, use and sharing of appropriate, well-structured, relevant and reliable (risk-managed) data and information.

5.2 Data security, knowledge management and IT risks include the following.

- The theft of hardware or software
- Unauthorised access to confidential or commercially sensitive data (eg through 'hacking')
- Industrial espionage, data fraud and data theft
- Data corruption (due to error, damage, computer viruses or sabotage)
- Hardware breakdown, damage or obsolescence
- Systems failure, and associated data loss (hence the need for all data to be 'backed up' to external hard-drives or servers, and the rise in the use of 'cloud' computing using external servers)
- Input or transcription errors in processing market, supplier, contract or project management data
- Lack of systems integration and compatibility (eg between buyer-side and supplier-side systems and protocols)
- Lack of controlled data management (eg controls over contract changes or the alteration of data held in shared databases)
- Compliance risk in regard to law and contractual provisions on issues such as data protection (secure storage and relevant use of personal data by corporations), intellectual property (protecting the rights of owners of designs, patents and copyrights) and confidentiality (preventing the unauthorised disclosure of commercially or personally sensitive data)
- Risks to the organisation's intellectual property, as a result of sharing proprietary processes and designs with supply chain partners (without adequate IP protections such as patents, registered design rights and trade marks, copyright protection – and contractual provisions to penalise abuse of these)
- Risks to the confidentiality of the organisation's sensitive commercial data, as a result of sharing it with supply chain partners (without adequate controls and contractual provisions such as confidentiality agreements)
- Turnover of key personnel and/or the outsourcing of organisational activities, and the resulting loss of potentially value-adding knowledge and information.

The role of information assurance

5.3 Information assurance (IA) is the practice of managing risks related to the use, processing, storage, and transmission of information or data and the systems and processes used for those purposes. It is related to the field of 'information security' (a branch of computer science aimed at the protection of information systems and their contents, mainly by applying security controls and defences against malicious attacks). However, information assurance embraces a wider range of issues.

- Corporate governance: compliance with regulatory standards, internal controls and auditing in regard to data protection, IT systems and fraud prevention
- Contingency, business continuity and disaster recovery planning in relation to key systems risks (data loss, security breaches, systems breakdown)
- Strategic development and management of IT systems to fulfil the current and future needs of the organisation (and supply chain), while minimising risk, through areas such as systems integration, compatibility, flexibility and security.

5.4 A typical IA project will involve the following steps.

- Systematic risk assessment: identification of information assets to be protected; identification of vulnerabilities in information assets and systems; identification of threats capable of exploiting or damaging the information assets; probability and impact analysis of identified risks
- Risk management planning: proposing counter-measures to 'treat' identified risks, including prevention, detection and response to threats. These may include technical tools such as access control systems; password protection and user IDs; firewalls and anti-virus software; data encryption; data back-up protocols; the use of 'cloud' computing services; employee training in data security awareness; or the resourcing of specialist IT security departments or incident response teams. Proposed plans are tested for feasibility and analysed in terms of costs and benefits.
- The risk management plan is agreed, implemented, tested and evaluated, often by means of systematic audit. Performance data is gathered and reviewed on an ongoing basis, so that the risk management plan can be continually revised in the light of performance gaps or emerging risks, as required.

Information-related risks

5.5 As information and knowledge become increasingly systemised and transparent, so they become more vulnerable. A number of risks may arise from knowledge and information systems, including the gathering of information in supplier databases; the sharing of intellectual property and confidential data with suppliers in the course of collaboration; and the management of relationships via a corporate extranet, negotiations and so on.

5.6 Here are some of the information-related risks which might arise in contract and supplier relationship management – or which might be managed *through* them.

- Risks to the organisation's intellectual capital from unauthorised access to intellectual property (eg patents, designs or prototypes) and sensitive commercial data (eg on competitive plans or risk assessments) – perhaps as a result of industrial espionage, hacking or phishing
- Risks to the organisation's intellectual capital and commercial advantage due to misuse of data by parties with whom it was shared (eg a supplier's breach of confidentiality, or the sharing of data with competitors) – and corresponding risks of liability if the buying organisation breaches the confidentiality, or misuses the intellectual property of a supplier
- Risks to the integrity and security of data, through a range of factors including software corruption; computer viruses; input or transcription errors; and deliberate fraud (eg the falsification of orders and invoices) – exacerbated by poor house-keeping and internal controls
- Risks to the integrity and value of contract data through lack of effective change control protocols (resulting in multiple conflicting versions)
- Risks and inefficiencies in the design and implementation of management information systems, extranets, contract databases and other relevant systems: eg inefficient storage and retrieval protocols; lack of integration and compatibility with supplier systems; teething problems; and systems breakdown
- Turnover of key personnel and loss of their intellectual property (where relevant) and/or knowledge of the organisation's procurement needs, contract histories and supplier relationships
- Loss of organisational knowledge, information and capabilities through the outsourcing of functions to external suppliers.

5.7 With the increasing use of the internet, extranets and intranets in supply chain relationship management, it is ever more crucial to exert control over the corporation's information assets, knowledge and intellectual property.

5.8 A range of measures may therefore be put in place, as part of an information assurance plan, in areas such as the following.

8

- Ensuring that all buyer-side and supplier-side information systems are subject to robust access controls (eg passwords, user IDs and firewalls) – and that 'human mediated' information exchanges, such as negotiations, are subject to appropriate confidentiality guarantees
- Rules and protocols for the secure use of information systems (eg the use of firewalls and anti-virus software, and the training of staff in security awareness)
- Protocols for the backing-up of stored data, to prevent loss due to systems failure or data corruption (eg use of 'cloud' computing, regular back-ups to external servers or hard drives and so on)
- Systems maintenance, contingency planning and back-up systems, to minimise loss in the event of systems breakdown (or hardware theft)
- Database management, ensuring that useful information and knowledge is captured and maintained, and obsolete information is deleted or archived
- Protocols and controls over contract changes, variations, versions and updating (with authorised individuals having controlled rights to make amendments and administer versions)
- Internal controls, checks and balances to prevent misuse of data or funds and fraud: examples include authorisations and sign-offs; reconciliation of contracts, delivery notes and invoices; and separation of duties (eg the same person does not authorise ordering and payment)
- Intellectual property protection, through the use of registered design rights, patents and copyrights; and appropriate contractual clauses to control access to intellectual property (eg via exclusive or non-exclusive licences) and to protect ownership rights (eg who will own IP generated in the course of the contract)
- Confidentiality of commercially sensitive data exchanged in the course of the contract (eg using confidentiality and non-disclosure clauses in contracts, training staff in confidentiality, and publishing and enforcing ethical codes)
- Training staff in the requirements of relevant legislation (including intellectual property law, data protection and freedom of information)
- Documentation of best practice, supplier relationship histories, learning from contracts – and other value-adding knowledge and information – to support organisational learning and prevent loss of data through personnel departure or outsourcing.

Reliability of information

5.9 It is also worth noting a more general sense of the term 'information assurance': that is, the need to 'assure' the quality, validity or reliability of information for contract and relationship management, through robust processes for gathering, checking, verifying, analysing and interpreting supplier, supply market and performance data.

5.10 One obvious example is the need to verify supplier capability and performance data supplied by suppliers themselves in self-appraisal questionnaires (eg for pre-qualification or vendor rating).

6 Assessing contractual risks

6.1 Risk management may be defined as 'the process whereby organisations methodically address the risks attaching to their activities with the goal of achieving sustained benefit within each activity and across the portfolio of all activities' (Institute of Risk Management).

6.2 While our focus here is on assessing contractual risks, with a view to monitoring and managing them through the contract management process, it may be worth having an overview of the process of risk management in general. The process of risk management is often portrayed as a cycle: Figure 8.2.

Figure 8.2 *The risk management cycle*

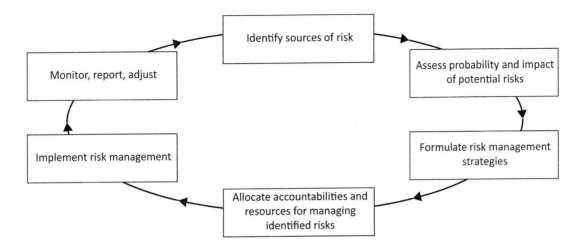

Risk identification

6.3   Risk identification is the process of seeking to identify potential problems or areas of uncertainty: in other words, asking 'what could go wrong?'

6.4   At the level of contractual risk, this may be done by processes such as:

- Environmental scanning, STEEPLE factor analysis and contract or supplier SWOT analysis (discussed in Chapter 3)
- Formal risk analysis exercises (for high-value contracts in volatile or vulnerable environments)
- Monitoring risk events affecting current contracts and projects
- Critical incident investigations (investigating the causes of major or unexpected variations or contract problems)
- Process audits (checking the effectiveness of quality and performance management processes for contracts, say)
- Consulting with key stakeholders (including users and supplier) and industry experts
- Employing third party risk management consultants

6.5   In an exam case study, of course, you will merely have to *recognise* potential contractual risks (such as the categories discussed in this chapter) from available data.

6.6   Risk identification should be an ongoing process, as the organisation's contractual risk profile may continually change, presenting new risks or turning slight risks into potential crises (eg if they attract media or regulatory scrutiny). A comprehensive list of identified risks should be compiled in a **risk register** (discussed below) for major contracts.

Risk assessment or evaluation

6.7   Risk assessment is the appraisal of the probability and significance of identified potential risk events: in other words, asking 'how likely is it and how bad could it be?' As we saw in Chapter 2, risk is often quantified using the basic formula: *Risk = Likelihood (Probability) x Impact (Adverse Consequence).*

- **Risk likelihood** is the probability of occurrence, given the nature of the risk and current risk management practices. This may be expressed as a number between 0 (no chance) and 1 (certainty) or as a percentage (100% = certainty), a score (1–10) or a rating (Low–Medium–High). The more likely the risk event is to occur, the higher the overall level of risk, and the higher priority risk management will be.
- **Risk impact or consequence** is the likely loss or cost to the organisation or the likely level of impact on its ability to fulfil its objectives. The severity of impacts may be quantified (eg in terms of

estimated cost or loss), scored (1–10), or rated (Low–Medium–High). Even if assessed as improbable, high-impact events should be the subject of detailed contingency planning as part of contract management, so that the organisation can respond effectively to the event if it occurs.

6.8   In Chapter 2 we saw how this analysis might be quantified in tabular format.

Supply chain (or value stream) mapping

6.9   Another technique that may be used for risk identification and assessment is the mapping of the supply chain or value stream (discussed in Chapter 3). Research from Cranfield University (*Creating Resilient Supply Chains*) argues that 'the current understanding of supply chain risk is under-developed' and that a systematic approach is needed to identify business, supply and contractual risks arising from failure within the supply chain, at some point in the flow of value towards the customer, or at some 'linkage' point in the chain.

6.10   Supply chain or value stream mapping is a technique that provides a time-based representation of the process involved as goods, materials, information and other value-adding resources move through the supply chain. The map (eg a network diagram or flow chart) shows the time taken at the inter-connection (linkage) and movement points within the chain. This enables organisations to determine:

- The inter-connecting 'pipeline' of suppliers through which value-adding elements must travel to reach the end-user
- The transport links by which value-adding elements are passed from one 'node' to another in the chain
- The amount of work in progress and inventory stockpiled at each stage in the pipeline
- The time it would take to source replenishment from various points in the pipeline in the event of disruption.

6.11   The Cranfield researchers argue that the information gained from such an analysis can assist in identifying areas of contractual and supply risk, and planning actions such as:

- Consulting and collaborating with supply chain partners to manage areas of identified vulnerability
- Strengthening relationship and contractual protections at vulnerable linkage points or supplier relationships
- Monitoring and managing first-tier suppliers' management of lower tiers of the supply chain, to reduce vulnerabilities at lower tiers
- Determining alternative sources of supply
- Holding additional buffer or safety stocks ('just in case' inventory)
- Formulating contingency plans for alternative transport arrangements in areas vulnerable to disruption.

Progress monitoring tools

6.12   A number of progress monitoring tools are used in contract and project management, to 'keep track' of performance against agreed plans and milestones, to identify:

- **Points of vulnerability** (such as deadlines in delivery or production schedules for which there is no 'slack time', or processes for which zero-defect tolerances are essential to assure quality)
- **Process, project or contract variances**: price, schedule or output variances – outside planned, specified or contracted parameters or tolerances – which indicate a failure of process control, with the risk of unacceptable variation, escalation or failure.

6.13   We will look at progress, project and performance monitoring techniques, and tools such as budgetary and cost control, Gantt charts, network diagrams and critical path analysis (CPA) in Chapter 9, where we discuss the use of data relating to the performance of contracts.

Risk register

6.14   A 'risk register' is a concise, structured document listing all the identified risks for a business, project or contract, together with columns for:

- Description of the type and nature of the risk
- Probability of the risk event occurring (expressed as an appropriate rating, or described briefly)
- Impact, cost or consequences if the risk event occurs (expressed as an appropriate rating or described briefly)
- Identified possible responses (mitigation or contract management) actions
- The risk owner: an identified individual or position with lead responsibility for its management
- Regularly updated information on the current status of each risk (response actions put in place and whether they are effective) – with the date of latest update.

6.15 A risk register provides project sponsors and contract managers with a documented framework from which risk status can be reported. It also provides a tool for communication about risk issues with key internal and external stakeholders (including suppliers). You might use a simple risk register format in an exam, to structure data on contractual risk, as the basis for a contract management strategy.

Risk management strategies

6.16 Identifying and quantifying vulnerability allows an organisation to prioritise planning and resources for contract management to meet the most severe risks, and to set defined risk thresholds at which contract management action on an issue will be triggered.

6.17 Risk management strategies ('what can we do about it?') are often classified as the Four Ts.

- *Tolerate* (or accept) the risk: if the assessed likelihood or impact of the risk is negligible
- *Transfer* or spread the risk: eg by taking out insurance cover, or not putting all supply eggs in one basket (ie dual or multi-sourcing) – or using contract terms to ensure that the costs of risk events will be borne by (or shared with) supply chain partners (eg by clarifying liability for risks at all stages of the contract, using liquidated damages clauses, insisting on supplier insurances or sharing responsibility for risk monitoring as part of the contract management process)
- *Terminate* (or avoid) the risk: if the risk associated with a particular contract is too great, and cannot be reduced, the organisation may consider not entering into that contract (if that option is available) or re-negotiating the contract to avoid the risk. So, for example, a supplier contract may not be renewed on the basis of poor industrial relations or non-improving quality assurance
- *Treat* (or reduce) the risk: take active steps to manage the risk in such a way as to reduce or minimise its likelihood or potential impact, or both. This may involve measures such as: supplier monitoring and performance management; codes of conduct; supplier certification or pre-qualification; critical incident and/or variance reporting and analysis; contingency and recovery planning (eg alternative sources of supply); and so on

6.18 In any case, the organisation will need to make contingency plans in regard to high-impact risks: alternative courses of action, alternative sources of supply, workarounds and fallback positions ('What will we do if…?').

Monitoring, reporting and review

6.19 Monitoring, reporting and review ('What happened and what can we learn?') is an important part of risk management, in order to:

- Ascertain whether the organisation's contract risk profile or exposure is changing, and identify newly emerging or escalating contractual or relationship-related risks
- Give assurance that the organisation's risk management processes are effective, by demonstrating effective avoidance or mitigation of risks
- Indicate where contract risk management processes need improvement, or where lessons can be learned from critical incidents and contract problems.

Chapter summary

- Risks in a contract are factors raised by the contract itself; risks to a contract are factors impacting on it.
- One classification of risks distinguishes between: supply risk; compliance risk; reputational risk; economic or financial risk; market risk; environmental risk; operational risk; technological risk.
- Internal risks arise from within an organisation and its processes. External risks arise from factors in the macro environment.
- Legal and compliance risks include: poor compliance management; poor contract development processes; unmanaged battle of the forms; poor contract administration and change control; inadequate protection of IP; etc.
- Performance-based risks are a particular concern in international trade.
- Modern thinking emphasises the importance of ethical trading. Failure to achieve this leads to reputational risks.
- Particular types of contractual arrangement (eg sole sourcing, outsourcing etc) give rise to particular types of risk.
- It is important for buyers to manage issues of power and dependency in supply relationships.
- Information risks relate to data security, knowledge management etc. Information assurance is the process of managing risks related to information.
- A standard model of risk management features six stages: identify risk sources; assess probability and impact; formulate risk management strategies; allocate accountabilities; implement strategies; monitor, report and adjust.
- A risk register logs all potential risks in a structured way.

Self-test questions

Numbers in brackets refer to the paragraphs where you can check your answers.

1   What is the purpose of contract management? (1.2)

2   Give possible examples of (a) supply risk and (b) market risk. (Table 8.1)

3   List internal factors that might put contract performance at risk. (2.2)

4   Give examples of how STEEPLE factors might affect supplier relationships. (Table 8.2)

5   Describe factors that might give rise to legal and compliance risk. (3.1)

6   Describe factors that might give rise to performance-based risks. (3.4)

7   List particular risks that might apply in international sourcing. (3.5)

8   Give examples of ethical and sustainable sourcing policies. (4.2)

9   What adverse consequences might arise from failure to adopt ethical sourcing policies? (4.4)

10   List the costs and risks of supplier switching. (Table 8.3)

11   List the kinds of risks that might apply to data security, knowledge management and IT. (5.2)

12   List measures that might be adopted as part of an information assurance plan. (5.8)

13   What are the stages in a risk management cycle. (Figure 8.2)

14   What is meant by 'supply chain mapping'? (6.9, 6.10)

15   List typical contents of a risk register. (6.14)

8

CHAPTER 9

Contract Management

Assessment criteria and indicative content

3.2 Interpret financial, technical and performance data relating to the performance of contracts

- Data that relates to the performance of contracts
- Interpreting data relating to the performance of contracts
- Contract administration

3.3 Assess the responsibilities for contract management

- Responsibilities for contract management: procurement or non-procurement role
- Contract implementation plans and ongoing demand management
- Planning and governance for contract management
- Resources required for contract management

3.4 Explain the main responsibilities of a contract manager

- Performance management and ensuring compliance to agreed standards
- Payment responsibilities
- Risk assessment and management
- Contract development
- Relationship management

Section headings

1. The contract management process
2. Planning and governance of contract management
3. Responsibilities of the contract manager
4. Contract administration
5. Contract performance data

Introduction

In Chapter 5 we introduced the concept of contract management as the management of buyer- and supplier-side activities, in order to ensure that both parties fulfil or 'perform' the terms of the commercial contract between them.

In this chapter we focus in more detail on the operational processes of contract management. We have already looked at some of the legal aspects of contract performance and non-performance (in Chapters 5–7) and at a range of risk factors which may jeopardise successful contract performance (in Chapter 8). Here, we go on to explore the activities involved in contract management, how responsibilities for contract management are allocated, the responsibilities of a contract manager (or contract management team), and how a range of data can be used to manage contract performance (or interpreted in an exam case study to draw conclusions about contract performance and the need for problem-solving and adjustment).

1   The contract management process

1.1   We saw in Chapter 5 that the role of a contract is to set out the roles, rights and obligations of both parties in a transaction or commercial relationship. We also noted – in Chapters 5–8 – that there is a large number of ways in which either party may struggle or fail to perform its obligations under the contract, due to misunderstandings or disputes, performance problems, intervening risk factors or *force majeure* events.

1.2   Once contracts are signed, therefore, it is *not* as simple as saying: 'The supplier will now do *that*.'

- There will be obligations and actions to be followed up on either side (for example, instalment payments made for stages of completion, or shared responsibility for risk and quality management activities).
- If risk events or contingencies arise, the contract may (or may not) lay down what happens next.
- If the supplier shows signs of struggling to conform with contract requirements or agreed standards (falling behind schedule, say, or delivering higher than agreed levels of defective items, or seeking price variations), remedial or corrective action may have to be taken: expediting or 'chasing' progress, say, or monitoring and controlling processes more closely.
- If performance fails to conform to agreed terms and standards, there will be a variety of options for pursuing the dispute, enforcing the terms of the contract or gaining remedies (such as reducing payment, or suing for damages).
- Circumstances and requirements may change over the life of the contract, and contract terms may have to be re-negotiated, agreed and amended accordingly.

Handling all these issues is an ongoing process through the life or duration of the contract: basically, to 'stay on top of' contract performance and compliance. This is the process of contract management.

1.3   Contract management is a process designed to ensure that both parties to a contract meet their obligations, and that the intended outcomes of a contract are delivered. It also involves building a good working relationship between the buyer and supplier, continuing through the life of a contract.

1.4   Contract management can represent a considerable investment for both the buyer and the supplier. Most emphasis in the procurement literature is typically given to the procurement process, leading up to contract award. This is, of course, an important part of the overall procurement cycle – but it may only represent a fraction of the costs and benefits that accrue over the life of the contract. Many of the added value outcomes of commercial relationships (eg systems integration, collaborative cost savings and continuous quality improvements) are achieved as a buyer and supplier work together *after* the contract has been awarded, for its entire duration – and, potentially, beyond (as we will see in Chapter 10).

Laying the foundations

1.5   The process of contract management should begin as early as possible. From the first stages of evaluating prospective suppliers, there should be emphasis on avoiding misunderstandings, managing expectations, ensuring process capability and minimising the risk of problems. Well-drafted procurement specifications and constructive negotiations are equally important in this context. In some cases, this approach is formalised in a system of early supplier involvement (ESI), which we discussed in Chapter 4.

1.6   Early discussions and negotiations with suppliers should not be confined to the terms and conditions of the purchase contract or partnership agreement. It helps to look behind the agreed terms, so that each party knows how the other is operating in order to achieve the requirements. This could involve discussion and clarification of any or all of the following matters.

- Timetable of stages in the operation
- Staff planning: grades of staff, estimated number of hours, arrangements for supervision etc
- Rules and procedures relating to site conditions, operations and safety issues

- Invoicing and payment procedures
- Buyer's responsibilities to provide designs, tools, facilities etc
- Supplier's responsibilities for reporting on progress
- Procedures and timetable for review of progress; and so on

1.7 Once the contract has been awarded, the buyer accepts the following ongoing responsibilities.

- **To maintain regular contact with the supplier**, to check on progress and ensure that any issues or problems are discussed. We cover various structures for doing this in Section 2 of this chapter.
- **To monitor the supplier's performance against the agreed terms and standards**, to ensure that they are being fulfilled. It is the supplier's responsibility to ensure that contractual agreements are fulfilled to the agreed standard – but as we have seen, this does not mean that buyers can simply sit back and hope for the best. A contract manager (or management team) must take an active and proactive 'interest' in contract performance, as discussed in Section 3 of this chapter.
- **To motivate the supplier**. A supplier may be motivated by the thought of losing repeat business if performance is poor, but buyers may introduce more positive incentives and rewards for suppliers who achieve consistently high performance. Supplier motivation is often carried out in the wider context of supplier relationships – beyond any individual contract. We will therefore discuss it in this wider context, in Chapter 10.
- **To work with the supplier to solve any performance and relationship problems**. We discussed the nature and resolution of contract disputes in Chapter 7, but there may also be times when suppliers run into difficulties and require help in problem-solving or resourcing solutions. Buyers should be ready to accept that their own firm's success depends on the supplier's ability to perform. This important issue is also generally considered in the wider context of supplier performance management – beyond any individual contract – and will be discussed in this context in Chapter 11, under the heading of 'supplier development'.

1.8 The key processes and activities involved in contract management are summarised in Table 9.1.

Benefits of effective contract management

1.9 Many of the cost savings and improvements available from contract and supplier management are achieved by how buyer and supplier work together *after* the contract has been awarded. If contracts – and contract performance – are not proactively or effectively managed by the buying organisation the following adverse outcomes may occur.

- The *supplier* may be obliged to take control of contract performance and problem-solving, resulting in unbalanced decisions that do not serve the buyer's interests.
- Decisions may not be taken at the right time (or at all) to protect or optimise performance.
- Buyer and/or supplier may fail to understand their contractual obligations and responsibilities, creating poor conditions for performance.
- There may be misunderstandings and disagreements, and too many issues may be escalated inappropriately, damaging the relationship.
- Progress may be slow (because un-expedited) or there may be an inability to move forward.
- The intended benefits from the contract may not be realised.
- Opportunities to *improve* performance, add value and secure competitive advantage (the over-arching goals of contract management, as discussed in Chapters 3 and 4) may be missed.

Table 9.1 *Key elements of contract management*

ELEMENT	COMMENTS
Contract development	The formulation of a legally binding agreement, setting out detailed terms and conditions of business, and the specification of requirement.
Contract communication	Copies of the contract documentation and delivery plans (and notification of any changes, as they are incorporated) should be distributed to those involved with managing them on a day-to-day basis.
Contract administration	The implementation of procedures, by buyer and supplier, to ensure that contract obligations are fulfilled. This may include procedures for: • Contract maintenance, updating and change control: ensuring that changes to the contract are agreed, authorised, accurately documented and implemented by both parties, and ensuring that all versions and related documents (such as budgets and service level agreements) are consistent • Budgeting and monitoring of costs and charges • Ordering and payment procedures • Management reporting
Managing contract performance	• *Risk management*: collaborating with users and suppliers to identify potential risks or barriers to performance, so that they can be managed or mitigated • *Performance monitoring and measurement*. Service level agreements (SLAs) and KPIs may be used to express the desired outputs from the contract. These documents will form an operational tool (usually more flexible than the contract itself) with which buyer-side and supplier-side contract managers can monitor performance on a day-to-day basis. • *Continuous improvement planning*. Buyer and supplier may work collaboratively over the life of the contract to set periodic improvement targets, solve performance issues, identify emerging opportunities and so on. The contract may need to be revised to reflect new targets and agreements – or may make a general provision for improvement planning. • *Supplier motivation*: incentives and rewards for performance, or sanctions and penalties for non-compliance. • *Performance management*: problem-solving and corrective action in the event of progress or performance shortfalls; pursuing dispute resolution procedures (as set out in the contract); pursuing remedies to mitigate loss or damage as a result of breach of contract or non-compliance. Supplier performance will be managed both on a contract basis (via contract administration) and on an 'aggregate' basis (over all the contracts placed with that supplier): we will discuss performance management in this wider context in Chapter 11.
Relationship management	Developing the working relationship between the purchaser and supplier, through regular contacts, communication and information sharing; developing and applying supplier incentives; managing and resolving conflicts; developing approaches to collaboration and mutual support; and so on. This activity may be carried out both on a contract basis (optimising the relationship for the performance of a particular contract) and on an 'aggregate' basis (optimising the relationship for future contracts and business development): we will discuss relationship management in this wider context in Chapter 10.

Contract renewal or termination	Towards the end of the contract period, the buyer's contract manager(s) should review both (a) the success of the contract and relationship and (b) the status of the supply need.
	  If an ongoing need remains, the contract has been satisfactorily fulfilled by the current supplier, and there is no immediate value to be added by supplier switching (eg to take advantage of a more innovative supply solution) or being re-opened to competition (eg to take advantage of competitive pricing), the contract may be renewed.
	  If the need has been met, or has changed, or if the current supplier's performance has been unsatisfactory, the contract may be terminated (as discussed in Chapter 6).

1.10   On the other hand, there are benefits of positive and proactive contract management.

- Improved risk management in developing and managing contracts (particularly in dynamic supply environments where minimal inventory is held, putting pressure on reliable, risk-managed supplier performance)
- Improved compliance and commitment by the supplier
- Incentives and momentum for ongoing relationship and performance improvement
- Added value (arising from efficient contract administration and performance).

1.11   There are, however, several reasons why organisations may fail to manage contracts successfully. Some possible reasons include the following.

- The role and value of contract management may be poorly understood or underestimated eg in traditional industries where large buffer stocks are held (theoretically minimising the risk of being let down by a supplier – but in a very inefficient way).
- Contracts may be poorly drafted, failing to identify foreseeable risks and issues, leaving 'loopholes' and areas of misunderstanding, or failing to take into account the needs of key stakeholders (such as users, implementers and budget-holders).
- Inadequate resources (personnel, information systems, time, skills development) may be assigned to contract management.
- The wrong people may be assigned to contract management, leading to lack of rapport or interpersonal conflict between buyer and supplier teams.
- The buyer may fail to develop effective performance measures, or to monitor and review performance.
- The focus may be solely on current arrangements, rather than what is possible or the potential for improvement and relationship development.
- There may be inadequate procedures for contract administration (eg for payment of supplier invoices, or for incorporating changing requirements and implementing version control).
- There may be inadequate co-ordination of cross-functional contract administration responsibilities, causing problems (eg failure to pay or disputes over inspection responsibilities).
- Both parties may have failed to evaluate likely risks, contingencies and changes, when developing contracts: contracts may fail to manage or mitigate risk, or may be inflexible and unreasonable in the light of changing conditions.

2   Planning and governance of contract management

Governance for contract management

2.1   The term 'corporate governance' refers broadly to the rules, policies, processes and organisational structures by which organisations are operated, controlled and regulated, to ensure that they adhere to accepted ethical standards, good practices, law and regulation.

2.2   Governance mechanisms such as defined responsibilities and accountabilities, formal communication and reporting channels, policies and procedures, are arguably essential for any commercial activity. However, it may be argued that governance is particularly important in contract management, because individuals responsible for developing and managing commercial contracts:

- Operate in a cross-functional and cross-organisational role, which requires robust mechanisms for co-ordination, communication and control
- Operate in a 'stewardship' role, responsible for the custodianship of finance and assets which are owned by the shareholders (or other funders and owners of the business)
- Potentially control very large sums of organisational funds
- Are faced by many opportunities to commit financial fraud or to misuse systems or information for personal gain, in the course of sourcing and contract management (eg confirming delivery quantities which may cover theft, stock under- or over-valuation, or over-invoicing; or authorising of payments, which may cover misappropriation of funds)
- Are responsible for the standing, credibility and reputation of the organisation in its dealings with supply chain partners.

2.3   We will look at some options for the governance of contract management, focusing on the issue raised by the syllabus: the need to clarify responsibilities for contract management. The terminology of the syllabus may be subject to confusion here. In the exam, make sure you distinguish between questions about:

- **Responsibilities for contract management** – ie *who* (what function, team or individual) has lead responsibility for managing a given contract; and
- **Responsibilities of a contract manager** – ie *what* does a contract manager do, or what is the scope of the contract manager's role?

The assessment criterion 'Explain the main responsibilities of a contract manager' is actually addressing the latter question, not the former...

Contact and communication structures

2.4   There are various ways of allocating and structuring contact between a buying organisation and its suppliers, for the purposes of contract management. One of the first questions to ask is: how many contacts or 'touch points' there should be between the buying and supplying organisation.

- When a buyer wants to get in touch with a supplier, does he have one contact to deal with (say, an account manager) – or a directory of different contacts for different purposes?
- Are other people in the buying organisation (eg user departments, the accounts department, goods inwards) also in contact with the supplier at relevant points – or are all contacts channelled through the buyer, vendor manager or contract manager (the buyer-side equivalent of an account manager)?
- Will contract management be primarily a procurement role – or a non-procurement role?

2.5   In general, it is good to co-ordinate or centralise contacts. A **single point of contact** (SPOC) approach means that a supplier appoints a designated supplier-side contract manager or account manager as the single communications interface with the customer – and a corresponding buyer-side designated buyer, contract manager or vendor manager is the 'gatekeeper' controlling all dealings with the supplier organisation. This has certain benefits, especially for relatively small, centralised operations.

- People know who their contact is.
- There is added value in a 'one stop shop' level of service, rather than being handed from department to department.
- There is less likelihood of inconsistent or conflicting requirements or information being communicated by different contacts.
- There is greater ownership and accountability for contract and relationship management.
- Repeated contact with the same person enables familiarity and trust to be built up over time, as the foundation for a deepening relationship.

2.6   However, 'contacts' may perform a range of different roles in the wider context of supplier relationship management: early supplier involvement in product and service development; contract negotiation; performance monitoring and management; more specific delivery or payment chasing; problem-solving and dispute resolution; feedback-seeking and feedback-giving; business networking; relationship development and partnering; and so on. Some of these contacts will involve different functions, business units or operating sites, and it may be inefficient to route all communication, for all purposes, through a single point of contact. As the complexity of markets, organisations, supply chains and products and services increases, a SPOC approach becomes increasingly difficult.

2.7   The alternative of *decentralised* contact, via **multiple touch points**, allows certain benefits.

- Diverse inputs to supplier relationships for different purposes and at different levels of expertise (so that a supplier can talk to a commodity specialist, designer or engineer, quality manager, logistics or inventory manager, legal or contracts expert or finance person according to the issue arising)
- Avoidance of communication 'bottlenecks' where a single contact is overburdened
- Better relationship, knowledge and service continuity, if a contact leaves or is unavailable

2.8   Cannon *(Procurement Policy, Strategy and Procedures,* 2005) argues that different functions may have responsibilities in contract management activity.

- Legal and finance specialists, providing technical advice on contract development and compliance
- The finance or accounts function, analysing costs, managing budgets, and processing invoices and payments
- Internal customer or user functions, liaising with the supplier on operational issues such as delivery schedules and quality management

- The procurement department, involved in commercial decisions, negotiating and contracting, interpreting the contract, and managing contract performance and supplier relationships

2.9 Other business processes creating 'touch-points' for contract management might include the following.

- **Business reviews** – key suppliers are invited to participate in business review meetings both to enrich the quality of communications and to assist in supplier planning for the future.
- **Steering committees** – key suppliers are invited to sit on company steering committees in relation to supply chain development. The objectives here are to take advantage of the supplier's technical expertise, to provide balance by bringing in external input, and to promote supplier buy-in for change management and continuous improvement initiatives.
- **Performance measures** designed clearly but giving due attention to the 'voice of the supplier' in their formulation. Buyers try to achieve a two-way performance philosophy to achieve supplier buy-in.
- **Multi-functional teamworking** – supplier participation, either through formal team membership or through less formal support and involvement, can potentially achieve greater team effectiveness via higher quality of information exchange between the team and key suppliers.
- **New product development** – early supplier involvement (ESI) is a customer-supplier interface technique where the supplier's knowledge and technology are integrated into the company's new product considerations. The objective of ESI is to reduce project cost by achieving right-first-time and the achievement of decreased time-to-market targets.

2.10 In order to get the best of both worlds, and minimise the drawbacks of each, the best approach may be **co-ordinated decentralisation**. In other words, you set up multiple contact points and communication channels – but you ensure that coherent and consistent messages are being given across them all, by setting up efficient cross-functional information sharing and relationship management systems: cross-functional purchasing teams, cross-organisational new product development teams and project steering committees, and database information management systems.

Procurement or non-procurement role?

2.11 The procurement function should be involved in *developing* supply contracts, where appropriate in collaboration with relevant operational or user departments and other expert stakeholders (such as the engineering, legal and finance departments).

2.12 However, it need *not* be the case that procurement retains responsibility for ongoing contract management.

- Governance and communications efficiency may dictate that the lead responsibility for contract management should reside in the function which will require most collaboration, co-ordination and information exchange with the supplier (in order to avoid delays and misunderstandings from routing of communications through a 'third party' gatekeeper).
- There may be a need for specialised knowledge and expertise to manage technically specialised, complex contracts: operational users, or specialist support functions, may have a better appreciation of supply risks, quality, service and cost issues, and technical terminology than procurement specialists.

2.13 So, for example, procurement may hand over post-award management of a contract to develop and install IT systems to the IT manager, or to managers of the departments or business units in which the system will be installed and operated (or both, in a contract management team). Similar logic might be applied to contracts to supply specialised components and subassemblies (managed by the operations function); HR services such as recruitment and selection, or training and development (managed by the HR function); security, catering or cleaning services (managed by the facilities manager); and so on.

2.14 Alternatively, a team of contract managers (especially for a complex project, for example) may be attached to a project planning department or project management team.

The contract manager

2.15   The appointment of a dedicated 'contract manager' is a common approach to structuring and co-ordinating contact between the buyer and supplier, for the purposes of managing a particular supply contract. The role of the contract manager is broadly to ensure that both parties to a contract fulfil the terms of their agreement over time. We will discuss this role, and its typical responsibilities, in the following section.

The account manager

2.16   Another way of structuring contact in longer-term relationships (beyond the scope and duration of a particular supply contract) is to use 'account managers': individuals either on the buyer or the supplier side, or both, who are responsible for managing and co-ordinating the overall relationship on behalf of their organisation.

2.17   Account management had its roots in customer relations, where the marketing organisation nominated individuals to manage relationships with key account customers: you might be familiar with this in banks and advertising agencies, for example. The concept is now being applied to supplier relations as well (for 'key' suppliers, as identified by segmentation and prioritisation tools: discussed in Chapter 2).

2.18   The role of account manager (who may be called a 'vendor manager', on the buyer side) will typically include the following tasks.

- Managing all aspects of the relationship between the supplier and the buyer, and between the supplier and the buyer's internal customers: acting as liaison between them
- Managing project and relationship processes (contact structures; cross-functional teamworking; communication channels; collaborative planning, decision-making and conflict resolution mechanisms and so on)
- Acting as a single point of contact and information for all internal and external stakeholders in the relationship
- Acting as a champion of the relationship to senior management (eg recommending the supplier for projects, reporting on the relationship to senior management or securing executive sponsorship of a partnership)
- Ensuring delivery of goods and services according to agreed terms and standards (perhaps liaising with a contract manager)
- Managing the development of the relationship through maintaining rapport, developing trust, and proactively managing tensions and conflicts
- Encouraging the supplier to adhere to agreed standards or KPIs, and to seek ongoing improvements in performance through the duration of the relationship (eg initiating and gaining supplier buy-in to cost reduction, continuous improvement or innovation programmes)
- Monitoring, reviewing and drawing learning from the relationship

2.19   An account manager therefore requires a range of skills and attributes such as: knowledge of the products or services purchased; knowledge of the customer or supplier and its transaction history; an understanding of contracts; project management skills; and good interpersonal and networking skills.

2.20   The benefits of customer or supplier account management include the following.

- Better control over the performance of contracts, and changes to plans and specifications
- Maintaining communication during the supply relationship, with potential to develop goodwill, trust and deepening collaboration over time
- Greater responsiveness and speed of problem-solving, with a single 'hub' for contact with the organisation who is familiar with the account and its potential issues
- Added value through planned improvements and well-managed relationships and work flows

- The ability to anticipate performance and relationship problems early, and to deal with them before they become serious.

2.21 Account management represents an extra level of investment, and will therefore not be necessary or viable for all supply chain relationships. It is generally applied only to key account customers (high value, high frequency, high status); strategic or critical supplies (as identified by the Kraljic matrix); strategic or critical suppliers (as identified by Pareto analysis or relational competence analysis); or relationships which require improvement or development (as identified by the supplier preferencing matrix).

Executive sponsors

2.22 To further reinforce the interface with key suppliers some organisations have introduced the role of 'executive sponsors'. Typically (but not exclusively), the executive sponsor is a senior executive within the buyer organisation who has overall executive responsibility for relationship development between the organisation and nominated key suppliers.

2.23 The executive sponsor, who is typically from outside the procurement function, will oversee cross-functional activity, as well as specific key-supplier development projects being managed by the procurement function. From the supplier's perspective, executive sponsors provide a high-level point of contact within the buyer organisation – demonstrating the commitment of the buyer organisation, and the value it attaches to the relationship with the supplier.

2.24 Ideally, there should be a strong executive-level alliance between the respective organisations, to support strategic relationships and projects. Buyer-side and supplier-side executive sponsors will meet at least quarterly to review the progress of a key supplier development initiative and its success in achieving the agreed relationship objectives.

2.25 The main responsibilities for the executive sponsor's role are as follows.

- Coordinate internal and external interactions with key suppliers and take on responsibility for overall supplier performance and relational development.
- Ensure the alignment of organisational strategic objectives with supplier development objectives across all touch-points. This should introduce business consistency in dealings with key suppliers thereby enhancing trust, and increasing the willingness of suppliers to invest in the relationship.
- Actively promote the relational alliance concept within both buyer and supplier organisations.
- Review achievements related to mutually established key initiatives that are required to bring added value to the relationship and ensure that expectations are being met.
- Resolve relational barriers – conflicting requirements will inevitably arise within such relationships from time to time. When the respective core teams cannot resolve these conflicts, executive sponsors should help reach an acceptable solution.
- Input suggestions and recommendations for future relationship development.

3 Responsibilities of the contract manager

Resources for contract management

3.1 For smaller contracts, a single individual may be sufficient to carry out all contract management responsibilities. For larger contracts, a contract management team may be required. It will be necessary to assess the management structures proposed for each contract to be managed, and ensure adequate staff resources are available to make them work.

3.2 The size of the contract management team may have to change over the life of the contract, since the early stages are often more demanding in terms of management time.

Responsibilities of the contract manager

3.3 The main operational responsibilities of a contract manager (or contract management team) on the **buyer's side** are as follows.

- To act as a single point of contact for all commercial and legal correspondence relating to the contract
- To maintain the specification of contract performance measures (eg SLAs or KPIs)
- To monitor contract performance and report on overall service levels
- To represent the buyer's interest to the supplier
- To oversee operation and administration of the contract
- To determine and take remedial actions, in agreement with the supplier, on any problems that arise
- To negotiate remedies with the supplier, in the event of breach of contract terms
- To escalate contract disputes to higher levels, if necessary
- To maintain revised and updated contract specifications
- To advise and support operational managers in other functions, to whom day-to-day management and monitoring of contracts which affect them may be devolved (as discussed earlier).

3.4 The main responsibilities of the contract manager on the **supplier side** are as follows.

- To monitor contract performance
- To identify and manage exceptions
- To represent the supplier's interests to the buyer
- To respond to changing customer needs
- To determine and take remedial actions, in agreement with the buyer, on any problems that arise
- To negotiate remedies with the buyer, in the event of a breach of contract terms
- To escalate contract disputes to higher levels, if necessary
- To operate and administer the contract to the specification.

3.5 Like an account manager, an effective contract manager requires a range of project management, administrative, decision-making, problem-solving and interpersonal skills (communicating, negotiating, managing conflict). He or she also requires detailed knowledge of contract development, performance specification and measurement, budgeting, purchasing – and the organisation's particular policies, procedures, systems and documents for each of these tasks.

3.6 We have already explained the core processes involved in contract management (in Table 9.1), but it may be worth gathering together some points on the specific responsibilities mentioned in the syllabus.

Contract development

3.7 Contract development involves the negotiation, formulation and agreement of contract terms, and associated documentation, such as:

- A product or service specification, or other description of the business need (such as a request for quotation or invitation to tender)
- Service level agreements and other agreements (eg on continuous improvement targets)
- Pricing and delivery schedules
- Documentation requirements (eg health and safety records, details of supplier staff, use of subcontractors, quality and other standards certifications)
- Supplier incentives and performance measures (KPIs), for performance management

3.8 As discussed in Chapters 5–7, the terms of the contract should include exact product or service specifications; agreed levels of service; pricing mechanisms; timetables for delivery; supplier incentives and performance measures; communication channels and dispute resolution procedures; contract change control procedures; agreed termination and handover strategies; and all other requirements.

3.9 Contract negotiation should **support ongoing contract management** by clearly identifying mutual rights and obligations, and working methods.

- A copy of the contract document should be given to those involved with managing it on a day-to-day basis.
- A register should be kept of each copy issued, and these should be version-controlled to ensure that amendments and updates are properly incorporated into all copies.

Contract administration

3.10 Contract administration is concerned with the operational relationship between the buyer and the supplier; the implementation of procedures defining the working methods and practices between them; and the smooth operation of routine administrative and clerical functions supporting contract performance.

3.11 The importance of buyer-side and supplier-side contract administration procedures to the success of the contract, and to the relationship between them, should not be underestimated. Clear administrative procedures ensure that all parties to the contract understand who does what, when, and how.

3.12 Contract administration will also require appropriate resourcing and governance. If the responsibility is shared across a contract management team, it is important that all members of the team deal promptly with contract administration tasks, particularly during the early stages of implementing new contract arrangements.

3.13 Some key contract administration issues are discussed in Section 4 of this chapter.

Risk assessment and management

3.14 As discussed in Chapter 8, a range of risks may require assessment and management, as part of the contract management process.

- Risk factors *raised by* the contract or relationship itself. Certain generic risks are typically raised, for example, by sourcing approaches such as outsourcing, single-sourcing arrangements, long-term partnership agreements and international sourcing. Specific risk factors may also be raised by specific contracts or contract partners.
- Risk factors *impacting on* a contract or relationship, which may jeopardise effective or efficient performance. Such factors may arise from the internal, external or relationship environment in which the contract is to be performed.

3.15 We will not repeat the material covered in detail in Chapter 8: you should recap our coverage there, if necessary. The point is that contract managers may have a responsibility to:

- Identify and evaluate contractual risks, collaborating with specialist risk managers and other stakeholders (including suppliers and users) where required
- Develop and maintain risk registers relevant to a given contract
- Monitor contract performance and environmental risk factors through the life of the contract, in order to have 'early warning' of identified – and newly emerging – risks
- Use contract development procedures to minimise vulnerabilities as far as possible (eg by expressly defining requirements and terms, and building in contractual requirements for insurances, guarantees and indemnities, assignment of liability, remedies for breach such as liquidated damages, *force majeure* clauses and so on)
- Use contract management procedures (such as performance and progress reviews, information and feedback sharing, 'issues management' discussions and proactive conflict management) to control risks – and to minimise their impact if risk events do occur (eg avoiding the escalation of problems and disputes).

Performance management

3.16   The contract managers from both buyer and supplier organisations should meet on a regular basis to review performance, compliance with (or conformance to) agreed quality standards and service levels, and delivery of the contract-specified outputs and outcomes.

3.17   There may well be regular issues to discuss (eg customer feedback, complaints logs, progress against schedule), and these will be standing items on the meeting agenda. Other agenda items will probably relate to particular issues during the period under review. All meetings should be minuted, with clear action points allocated to named individuals from both the supplier and the buyer organisations. The action points should have dates for completion, and these should then be reviewed, and any problems highlighted at the next review meeting.

3.18   The monitoring and measurement of performance (in this context, mainly defined as conformance with contract terms, specifications, service level agreements and other elements of the commercial agreement) is important because it helps to ensure that contract outputs and outcomes are delivered – and that threats and problems are dealt with as they arise (and/or in any future contracts or improvement agreements).

3.19   The task of measuring and managing supplier performance commences with the negotiation and development of the contract. Clear and concise performance measurement methods and criteria (such as KPIs) should be jointly agreed. As with many business processes, supplier performance evaluation forms a repeating cycle, enabling buyers to provide regular feedback for performance adjustment, improvement target-setting, and decisions about contract renewal.

3.20   In a developed buyer-supplier relationship, suppliers will expect to be involved in regular performance reviews and ongoing discussions related to targeted areas for future improvement. This wider process of performance management within supply chain relationships – beyond the performance of a particular contract – is discussed in detail in Chapter 11.

Relationship management

3.21   Managing a supplier relationship requires a discrete set of responsibilities and activities that, for larger contracts, may be assigned to a nominated individual or team within the contract management structure. Even if responsibility for managing the *relationship* is given to the *same* individual or team responsible for managing the *contract*, it is important to ensure that the specific tasks of relationship management are carried out.

3.22   The approach to managing the relationship will vary depending on the type of contract. There is no one style that is appropriate for every contract, or for every provider. For some non-strategic contracts, a more tactical or even arms' length approach may be suitable. For long-term strategic contracts, the emphasis on building a relationship will be much greater. We discussed these points in detail in Chapters 1 and 2.

3.23   Contractual arrangements may commit the organisation to one supplier or a small number of suppliers to a greater or lesser degree, and for some time. Inevitably this involves a degree of dependency. The costs involved in changing supplier are likely to be high and, in any case, contractual realities may make it highly unattractive. It is in the organisation's own interests to make the relationship work, throughout the duration of the contract – and often, beyond. (The longer-term aspects of managing supplier relationships, beyond the scope and duration of any particular supply contract, are discussed in Chapter 10.)

3.24   The contract managers from both the buyer's and supplier's organisations need to set the stage early for working together in managing the performance of the contract. The relationship will be underpinned by the contract and service level agreement, but much will depend on the ability of the contract managers to communicate with each other, and to work as a team towards the delivery of the contractually agreed outputs.

3.25 However good the relationship between buyer and supplier, **problems** may arise. So procedures for handling these should be agreed; clear reporting and escalation procedures help keep the heat out of the relationship. The objective is a relationship in which purchaser and supplier co-operate to ensure that problems are recognised and then resolved quickly and effectively.

3.26 The contract must define the procedures for undertaking **corrective action** if, for example, target performance levels are not being achieved. The purchaser response to non-performance should be commensurate with the severity of the failure. For certain types of failure, as we saw in Chapter 6, the contract may specify the application of 'liquidated damages'; procedures are required to calculate these and to enforce them. Problems can arise in a number of areas and for a wide range of reasons: clashes of personality; slow or incorrect submission of invoices; slow payment of invoices; problems with contract administration procedures.

3.27 If a dispute cannot be resolved at the level where it arises, it will be necessary to involve a more senior manager. **Escalation procedures** should allow for successive levels of response depending on the nature of the problem and the outcome of action taken at lower levels. The levels for escalation should match those of the interfaces established between the buyer and the supplier to resolve the problem at the lowest practicable level. For more serious problems, the contract should specify the circumstances under which the organisation would have the right to terminate the contract. The contract manager must consult senior management and purchasing or contractual advisors as soon as this possibility arises.

3.28 Normally, most problems should be resolved before they become major issues; contract managers on both sides should meet regularly to raise any issues promptly as they occur. Where agreement cannot be reached, the purchaser and supplier should seek the assistance of mediators before resorting to legal action. The contract should specify the procedures for invoking a formal dispute resolution process, as discussed in Chapter 7.

4 Contract administration

4.1 The basic procedures that usually make up contract administration are as follows.

- Contract maintenance, document management and change control (discussed further below)
- Ordering procedures (eg under framework, systems or 'call off' contracts)
- Payment procedures (discussed further below)
- Budgetary control procedures (logging actual expenditures, costs and charges against budgeted estimates, in order to report budget variances)
- Resource management and planning
- Management reporting (eg on progress, or – by exception – on variances from the plan, schedule or contract)

4.2 These procedures – and others, where required – should be designed to reflect the specific circumstances of the contract and the two organisations involved.

Expediting

4.3 'Expediting' simply means 'assisting the progress' of something. If the buyer has any concerns about delivery (because the supplier is less than reliable, or because on-time delivery is critical), orders made under a contract may require expediting.

4.4 The term 'progress chasing' is sometimes used instead of 'expediting': usually meaning an enquiry into how progress is going, or (more often) where an order is when it is late. However, this is a reactive or 'fire

9

fighting' approach, focused on problem solving rather than problem avoidance. Expediting should ideally be a proactive role, as an ongoing part of contract management: taking planned steps to ensure that suppliers are able and on schedule to deliver as agreed in the supply contract.

4.5   Not all orders will be worth the effort and cost of expediting, so the first requirement will be to prioritise deliveries, identifying those for which:

- There is a higher risk of delivery problems (because the supplier is unknown to the buyer, or has a poor or variable delivery track record)
- The potential consequences of delivery problems are more severe (because the material is critical to production processes or schedules; or the organisation has low safety stocks; or because there are no alternative sources of supply or substitutes for the item concerned).

4.6   Expediting tasks may then consist of:

- Ensuring that delivery deadlines and specifications are clearly set out – and, if any changes are made, that these are clearly communicated and agreed
- Maintaining project and production schedules, and time-phased materials requirements (eg in a materials requirements planning system). A project expediter may maintain critical path network charts and/or Gantt charts showing the optimum and latest times at which supplies are required for each stage of the project (as discussed in the following section of this chapter). For regular supplies, a simple diary system may be sufficient to 'flag' which orders need to be expedited on a given day or week.
- Monitoring or enquiring about supplier progress at key stages (without 'micro-managing'), or developing a system of 'reporting by exception' (where the supplier notifies the expediter of any stage deadlines missed or potential problems identified)
- Working with suppliers to solve any identified problems. The expediter may have to persuade a supplier to give priority to the order or buying organisation; offer help with production difficulties; offer help in sourcing any materials or information which may be holding the supplier up; and so on.
- Requiring notification of despatch of goods, and using track and trace facilities (where available) to monitor their progress in transit
- Placing pressure on delinquent suppliers, where required: reminding them of late delivery penalties (eg liquidated damages clauses), say, or involving senior managers in problem-solving or enforcement discussions.
- Where necessary, using contingency plans to search for alternative suppliers, existing stocks or substitute goods to meet an emergency shortage due to delivery delay.

Document management and change control

4.7   Contractual relationships evolve and must respond to changes in the business environment. It follows that the contract document itself must be capable of development through formal change control procedures and by mutual consent, in response to changing requirements. It is preferable to update documentation systematically as changes occur, rather than relying on informal or oral agreements.

4.8   Keeping the contract documentation up to date is an important activity, but it should not be a burden. The effort required may be reduced by ensuring that the contract is sufficiently **flexible** to enable changes to the requirement and pricing mechanism (within agreed parameters) without needing to change the contract documentation.

4.9   Procedures should be established to keep contract documentation **up to date** and to ensure that all documents (and versions of documents) relating to the contract are consistent, or agree with each other. For a large or complex contract, or a situation where a number of service level agreements (SLAs) are covered, a formal document management procedure is critically important.

4.10 Applying **document management** principles involves:

- Identifying all documentation relevant to the contract (including contract documents, specifications, KPIs, schedules, SLAs, procedures manuals, ethical codes, CSR policies and so on)
- Implementing change control procedures, and ensuring no changes are made without appropriate authorisation
- Recording the status of all documents (current or historical, draft or final, approved or not-yet-approved and so on)
- Ensuring consistency across documents and document versions.

4.11 It is particularly important that variation or addition of requirements, post-contract, should be carefully controlled. In many cases, for example, orders for products or services may only be submitted through the contract manager. In other cases, especially where budgets and procurements are devolved, business managers may have authority to submit orders within specified budgetary and technical constraints. Formal authorisation procedures will be required to ensure that only those new requirements that can be justified in business terms are added to the contract.

4.12 Changes to the requirement, procedures or contracts may impact on supplier performance and add costs. The specification and management of change control is an important area of contract administration. Change control procedures should be included in the contract. The respective roles and responsibilities of both parties in the change control process must be clearly identified, along with the procedures for raising, evaluating, costing and approving change requests.

4.13 A single change control procedure should apply to all changes, although there may be certain delegated or shortened procedures available in defined circumstances (eg delegated budget tolerance levels within which a contract manager would not have to seek senior management approval). Flexibility should be built into this procedure to deal with emergency variations (eg additional, urgent requirements, or an agreement to pay instalments in order to support a supplier in cashflow difficulties).

Management reporting

4.14 Requirements for performance reports and management information should have been defined before and during contract negotiations, and confirmed during the implementation period of the contract. It is likely that information requirements will change during the lifetime of the contract, which should be flexible enough to allow for this.

4.15 Where possible, use should be made of the supplier's own management information and performance measurement systems. Information may be required about all performance measures or only about exceptions – that is, instances when performance differs from what was expected. 'Exception reporting' minimises the time the buyer needs to assess performance and ensures attention is focused on areas that need it most.

4.16 We will discuss the use of data relating to the performance of contracts in the final section of this chapter.

Payment responsibilities

4.17 Payment of the supplier, on agreed terms, in return for goods or services provided is a basic contract obligation for the buying organisation and – as we saw in Chapter 6 – the supplier has legal remedies for breach of contract by the buyer in the event of non-payment or late payment.

4.18 It is therefore a key responsibility of the contract manager to ensure that the relevant budget holder authorises and actions payment on agreed terms and schedules.

4.19 In a simple supply contract, administered by the procurement department, the supplier will send an invoice or request for payment. The buyer should check that it corresponds to the order or contract

9

(in regard to agreed price, instalment schedule and payment terms) and to relevant goods received documentation or service logs (to confirm that goods or services have been delivered as contracted), and then *either* query discrepancies with the supplier *or* authorise the invoice for payment and pass it to the accounts department for payment.

4.20 For more complex contracts, the contract manager may have to analyse a range of data on costs, pricing arrangements, consignment deliveries and related payment instalments – and so on. His role may be to verify payment eligibility, in order to advise the relevant budget holder that a payment can be authorised, rather than personally actioning payment.

4.21 Invoices should be paid within the period stated in the agreed terms of trade: often 30, 60 or 90 days. Credit periods are an issue for cashflow, for both the buyer and the supplier. The buyer may want to pay as late as possible, in order to retain cash (or earn interest on banked funds), but the supplier will want to be paid as early as possible, to obtain those same benefits – especially since it has already incurred the cost of supplying the product or service.

4.22 It is part of ethical trading to pay supplier invoices *on time, as agreed*. It also impacts on the buyer's standing as an attractive (or unattractive) customer for suppliers, and on the ongoing relationship with suppliers. An unjustly unpaid invoice may result in stoppage of supply until the matter is settled, and/ or the threat of legal action by the supplier. Repeated late payment or disputed payment of invoices can significantly damage the buyer's credibility, the supplier's loyalty and commitment (and therefore future reliability and quality), and in the worst case, the buyer's ability to find suppliers willing to do business.

4.23 Commercial payments are usually made by *electronic credit transfer*, through the banking system, which is safe and swift. (One disadvantage, however, is that payments tend to be handled on regular days of the month, on a payment cycle, which may represent a late payment for a supplier, or prevent the buyer from receiving an early payment discount.)

4.24 Another possibility is payment by *corporate credit card* or *purchasing card*, which allows the delegation of routine purchases to user-department staff, and is efficient in terms of invoicing and other transaction costs for low-value procurements (eg call-off orders or catalogue purchasing). However, this may also allow 'maverick' spending by non-purchasing specialists, unless safeguards are in place: eg spending limits on the use of cards, authorised supplier lists and so on.

Contract renewal or termination

4.25 Towards the end of the contract period, the contract manager from the buyer's organisation should be involved in a full end-of-project or end-of-contract review conducted by the business. If the business need still remains, then the contract management team is well placed, through its practical knowledge of the current operational requirements, to advise on any updating or modification to the specification of requirement. In most circumstances, it is inadvisable merely to re-use the same specification of requirement for a further contract (renewal) period, with either the existing or a new supplier.

Post-contract lessons management

4.26 The contract management team (or a cross-functional review team) should intentionally review the contract's history and outcomes, and gather feedback from a range of contract stakeholders on what went right and what went wrong in the performance and management of the contract; how things could have been done more effectively or efficiently; and what new knowledge or lessons have emerged from the contract and should be carried forward to future contracts and contracting processes.

5   Contract performance data

5.1   We will explore a wide range of data for 'supplier performance management' (that is, the monitoring and evaluation of performance within an ongoing supplier relationship, beyond the demands of a particular contract) in Chapter 11.

5.2   Here, we will merely highlight some of the specific data that may relate to the performance of a particular contract. Obviously, this will depend greatly on the nature and specifics of each contract. The assessment criterion in this area of the syllabus requires you – not to be able to identify, discuss or explain types of data – but to 'interpret financial, technical and performance data relating to the performance of contracts'. In other words, you may be given such data in relation to a case study scenario, and asked to interpret or analyse the data given, in order to identify:

- **Current variances** from agreed performance levels, standards, costs or schedules, which require joint problem-solving with the supplier to determine corrective action; other performance management techniques, such as the application of incentives and penalties to improve supplier performance; or – if satisfaction cannot be achieved by such means – the seeking of contractual remedies for non-performance of contract (as discussed in Chapter 6)
- Process inconsistencies (eg failure in quality assurance processes) or trends (such as escalating late deliveries) which indicate the **risk of future variances** from agreed performance levels, standards, costs or schedules (or escalation in current variances) if preventive or corrective action is not taken
- **Further information** that may be required in order to draw conclusions from the available data, for the purposes of problem solving and performance management. This too may form the basis of contract management action, in the form of process audits or reviews, or discussions with supplier-side contract manager(s).

Data relating to the performance of contracts

5.3   Depending on the nature and specifics of the contract, and related contract documentation, some of the data which might be utilised to monitor and evaluate contract performance is listed in Table 9.2.

Supplier reporting requirements

5.4   Dobler *et al* (*Purchasing and Materials Management*) suggest that, as part of pre-award discussions, arrangements should be made for the timely provision of performance information by suppliers, including (as relevant to the particular situation and contract):

- A project or contract organisation chart, clearly indicating accountabilities and contacts for contract management
- A project plan, identifying major milestones on a time-phased basis (including those of the supplier's major subcontractors)
- A funds commitment plan (for incentive and cost-reimbursement contracts), showing estimated financial commitments on a monthly and cumulative basis
- A human resources commitment plan (eg a Gantt chart showing resource allocations)

5.5   Periodic progress reports should also be requested for complex or long-term contract projects, including:

- A narrative summary of work accomplished during the reporting period (technical progress update, summary of work planned for the next reporting period, problems encountered or anticipated, corrective actions taken or planned, and a summary of any buyer-supplier discussions)
- A list of all action items, if any, required of the buyer during the next period
- An update of the milestone plan, showing actual progress against planned progress (eg in the form of a Gantt chart)
- An update of the funds commitment plan showing actual funds committed against the planned funds (eg in a budgetary control spreadsheet)

- A report on any significant changes in factors which could affect performance or increase risk (eg changes in personnel or machine maintenance schedules)
- Missed milestone notifications (or slippage in schedule or cost) and recovery plans.

Table 9.2 *Data relating to the performance of contracts*

Financial data	• Supplier quotations, bid documents, schedules of prices, fees and charges, payment terms – and other available statements of what 'the price' will include (or not include), how it will be calculated (eg on the basis of market prices), how much it will be (if fixed, agreed or quoted), and how and when it will be payable (eg credit terms and conditions, and the basis on which staged instalments will be paid). This data will be crucial in monitoring price variances or discrepancies, and in verifying amounts and schedules for authorising payment. • Supplier cost breakdowns (where available), suggesting cost escalation – which may (or may not) impact on prices and charges to the buyer, depending on the nature of the pricing agreement • Data indicating the financial status and stablity of the supplier (eg liquidity ratios, evidence of positive cashflows). This should be part of a pre-contract pre-qualification of the supplier, but may also be part of a contract management risk monitoring process (as discussed in Chapter 8) • Budgetary control data, showing actual costs and expenditures on the contract against budgeted estimates • Records or estimates of losses incurred as a result of delays, defects or other non-conformances, to support assessment of damages, losses to be deducted from the price (where relevant) and so on
Technical data	Product or service specifications – and details of the product or service actually supplied – may (depending on type and detail) include: • Functionality to be achieved, at specified levels, in specified circumstances and conditions (performance specification) or outputs to be delivered (output specification) • Design and engineering compliance (technical or design specifciations eg engineering drawings, designs or blueprints) • Chemical or physical properties, or materials included (composition specifications) – or not included (eg controlled or banned materials such as asbestos or lead paint) • Brand names and/or models to be supplied • Attributes to be reproduced (eg in specification by sample) • Tolerances (a range of 'leeway' within which variance from specification will be accepted): engineering tolerances may be very narrow, while service tolerances (eg answering calls 'within five rings' may be broader) • The market grade of supplies required (eg for commodities) • British or international standards applicable to the item (eg for dimensions, safety, methods of testing and other quality parameters) or requirements for the item – or the supplier and its processes – to be certified or accredited under relevant standards (such as ISO 9001 for quality management or ISO 14001 for environmental management) • Maintenance and reliability requirements (taking into account specification of conditions under which the asset will be installed and used etc) • Specification of packaging (including special arrangements for protection in transit, where required) • Information to be provided by the supplier for users, such as instructions, or advice on installation, operation and maintenance.
Performance data	• Delivery deadlines and schedules or agreements (eg for staged project milestones, or consignment deliveries) • Estimated lead times and project or production plans and schedules on which delivery deadlines are based. Monitoring these might indicate the risk of missed delivery deadlines, if intermediate milestones are missed, or there is schedule 'slippage'. • Project resource plans (eg Gantt charts), which may indicate potential bottlenecks, or vulnerable points at which the supplier does not have sufficient resources, capacity or capability to maintain the required rate of production • A wide range of data from supplier reporting, and buyer monitoring, of actual progress (compared with agreed plans and schedules) and performance (compared with agreed targets, standards and key performance indicators)

5.6 As with all facets of contract and supplier relationship management, such data – being costly to compile – should be required only where it can be justified by the significance of identified risks, the likelihood of avoiding slippage by using the required level of data, and a net saving (following cost/benefit analysis).

Chapter summary

- Awarding the contract is not the end of the buyer's responsibilities. Buyers must also manage performance to ensure successful completion.
- Key elements of contract management include: contract communication; contract administration; managing performance; relationship management; and contract renewal or termination.
- Buyers and suppliers must consider the relative advantages and disadvantages of 'single point of contact' and 'multiple point of contact'.
- The 'nuts and bolts' of contract management may not always be the responsibility of procurement staff. A range of different structures are possible.
- For larger contracts it is likely that contract management will be handled by a team rather than a single individual.
- Monitoring and measurement of performance may be by reference to contract terms, specifications, service level agreements etc.
- Relationship management is also important and goes beyond management of performance on a single contract.
- Contract administration involves a range of tasks such as expediting, document management, change control etc.
- Data relating to contract performance may include financial data, technical data and performance data (such as deadlines, resource plans etc).

Self-test questions

Numbers in brackets refer to the paragraphs where you can check your answers.

1   What are the ongoing responsibilities accepted by a buyer once the contract has been awarded? (1.7)

2   What are the benefits of effective contract management? (1.9)

3   List the key elements of contract management. (Table 9.1)

4   What is meant by a 'single point of contact'? (2.5)

5   Which functions in a buying organisation may have responsibilities in contract management? (2.8)

6   What are the benefits of supplier account management? (2.20)

7   List operational responsibilities of a contract manager on the buyer side. (3.3)

8   What is meant by 'contract administration'? (3.10)

9   What are escalation procedures in the context of contract management? (3.27)

10 List basic procedures involved in contract administration. (4.1)

11 Why is it important for a buyer to ensure on-time payment to a supplier? (4.22)

12 Give examples of (a) financial data, (b) technical data and (c) performance data relating to the performance of contracts. (Table 9.2)

CHAPTER 10

Supplier Relationship Management

Assessment criteria and indicative content

4.1 Compare contract management and supplier relationship management

- Definitions of contract management and supplier relationship management
- The management of individual contracts compared to the management of relationships with suppliers

4.2 Explain the main techniques for supplier relationship management

- Supplier selection
- Team selection and responsibility for supplier improvement
- Supplier performance measurement

4.4 Explain techniques for relationship improvement

- Relationship assessment methodologies

Section headings

1. Supplier relationship management
2. Selecting and managing new suppliers
3. Motivating and managing supplier performance
4. Assessing relationships
5. Managing relationship development and improvement
6. Managing relationship problems, decline and termination

Introduction

In this chapter we explore the processes involved in supplier relationship management.

We start by distinguishing supplier management and supplier relationship management – which deal with the management of suppliers and supply chain relationships – from contract management (covered in Chapter 9), which deals with the management of individual procurement contracts.

We then work through the relationship lifecycle (introduced in Chapter 1), and explore the issues, methodologies and techniques of managing: the selection and adoption of new suppliers; supplier motivation and performance management; the assessment of relationship progress and satisfaction; the management of relationship 'growth' (development and improvement); and the management of relationship problems, 'decline' and termination. Note again that these are broader concepts than the management of contracting, contract performance and risk, or contract disputes (discussed in Chapters 5–9): a long-term supplier relationship goes beyond the fulfilment of any particular supply contract or procurement exercise.

This chapter focuses on the management and development of supplier relationships. We will pick up the management and development of supplier *performance* in Chapter 11.

1   Supplier relationship management

Supplier relationship management and contract management

1.1   Chapters 5–9 of this Course Book have covered the syllabus sections on the performance and management of contracts. Although many of the same structures, techniques and methodologies will be used to manage suppliers and supplier relationships, it is important to distinguish clearly between 'contract management' and 'supplier relationship management'.

1.2   Broadly speaking, as the syllabus explains, contract management concerns the management of individual supply contracts – while supplier relationship management concerns the management of relationships with suppliers. This may seem obvious, but it has a number of implications.

- Supply contracts do not necessarily correspond in a one-to-one way with supplier relationships. A buying organisation may place only a few supply contracts, but may have a very wide supplier base – some of whom are currently under contract and some not. On the other hand, the organisation may have a small group of regular suppliers, and place a number of supply contracts with each of them, either concurrently or over time.
- Individual supply contracts may be of short duration, and are typically of fixed duration (subject to renewal). The relationship with the supplier, however, may be ongoing, open-ended and of long duration: in other words, the relationship will be continuous, with a view to placing a series of supply contracts with the supplier over time. Contract management will be relevant to arm's length and transactional sourcing approaches – whereas supplier relationship management will be a feature of longer-term, collaborative single sourcing and partnering approaches.
- The focus of contract management is specifically on ensuring the compliance of both parties with the agreed terms of the contract: hence our reference in preceding chapters to 'contract performance' (or non-performance). The focus of supplier relationship management is more broadly on appraising, accessing, developing, improving and leveraging the capabilities and performance of suppliers to contribute to the current and future strategic objectives of the buying organisation, such as profitability, customer value, competitive advantage (or market share), innovation, sustainability and business development. Where the focus of contract management is 'compliance', the focus of supplier relationship management is 'contribution'.
- The relationship management aspects of contract management are likewise focused on contract performance, and may therefore be largely limited (for short-term contracts) to aspects such as: communication and data sharing to support performance and compliance; maintaining mechanisms for collaboration and governance; resolving relationship issues and conflicts that would get in the way of contract performance; and managing contractual disputes. Supplier relationship management potentially has a much wider scope including: the decision of what kind of relationship is desirable or beneficial; the deepening of relationships and trust; negotiating relationship values; developing integration and compatibility; developing long-term partnering arrangements; and managing relationship change, decline and termination.
- The terms of a supply contract are (ideally) detailed and clear cut, as a guide to managerial decision-making and action, exception reporting, expediting and problem-solving. The terms and values of supplier relationships – even if based on a relationship charter or partnership agreement – are much less explicit, and may need to be negotiated (formally or informally) over time.
- Contract management, while important, is primarily an operational activity, whereas supplier relationship management is a tactical or (as a foundation for supply chain management) strategic activity.

Supplier management

1.3   The term supplier relationship management is often used interchangeably with the term 'supplier management'. The correspondence is highlighted by definitions of supplier management, as:

- 'That aspect of purchasing or procurement which is concerned with rationalising the supplier base and selecting, co-ordinating, appraising the performance of and developing the potential of suppliers, and where appropriate, building long-term collaborative relationships' (Lysons & Farrington)
- 'Managing the supplier in order to extract additional value and benefits as a result of the relationship' (CIPS).

1.4 The focus on the firm's suppliers and supplier relationships distinguishes supplier and supplier relationship management from related concepts such as:

- *Contract management,* which focuses on the management of a supplier's performance of a particular supply contract (as highlighted above), for the duration of that contract
- *Supply management,* which focuses on management of the operational aspects of the supply process and procurement cycle: ensuring that supplies flow efficiently into and through the organisation, and fulfilling the 'five rights of procurement'
- *Supply chain management,* which focuses on strategically integrating processes and relationships across the whole supply chain (as discussed in Chapter 4).

1.5 In this chapter we will look at a range of operational issues within an established relationship with a supplier, and how the supplier's co-operation can be secured: day-to-day supplier relationship management methodologies and techniques.

2 Selecting and managing new suppliers

Supplier pre-qualification

2.1 The purpose of supplier appraisal, evaluation or pre-qualification is to ensure that a potential supplier will be able to perform any contract or tender that it is awarded, to the required standard. Such a process adds value by avoiding the wasted cost, time, effort and embarrassment of awarding a contract (on the basis of lowest price) to a tenderer who *subsequently* turns out to lack capacity or technical capability to handle the work, or turns out to have systems and values that are incompatible with the buying organisation, or turns out to be financially unstable and unable to complete the work because of cashflow problems or business failure.

2.2 'Pre-qualification' in its broadest sense is the definition and assessment of criteria for supplier 'suitability', so that only pre-screened suppliers with certain minimum standards of capability, capacity and compatibility are invited or considered for participation in a given sourcing process. This may be carried out across a range of requirements: to prepare an approved supplier list, for example. Or it may be carried out on a procurement-specific basis, to pre-screen suppliers to receive an invitation to tender or to quote for a contract.

2.3 Having a list of pre-qualified suppliers reduces the investigations needed for individual tenders and purchases: the buyer already knows that any supplier on the approved list has been assessed as capable of fulfilling requirements. This may be particularly helpful where routine purchasing activity is devolved to user department buyers, who may not have the expertise to evaluate or select new suppliers for themselves: instead, they can choose from a list of suppliers pre-assessed and qualified by purchasing specialists.

2.4 Pre-qualification is also an important opportunity to embed qualitative selection criteria (such as social and environmental criteria, cultural compatibility or willingness to innovate) in the supplier selection process – without compromising clarity, fairness, competition and economic value in the final selection decision (which can be made primarily on the basis of quantitative criteria such as lowest price or best value).

10

Supplier appraisal

2.5　Whether or not a separate stage for supplier pre-qualification, screening or shortlisting is applied, there will be a need to appraise or evaluate potential suppliers, in order to assess their capability and suitability, prior to entering into negotiation or other processes for supplier selection and contract award.

2.6　Supplier appraisal may arise in several circumstances. A supplier may apply to be pre-qualified prior to being placed on a list of approved suppliers. Or a buyer may need to source something that has not been purchased before, or is not available from existing suppliers. In either case, the buyer's aim is to ensure that the potential supplier will be able to perform any contract awarded to it, to the required standard.

2.7　A full-scale supplier appraisal exercise is time-consuming and costly, so it may not be required for all new suppliers (eg for one-off, standardised or low-value purchases). According to Lysons, it will be particularly important for strategic or non-standard items; for major high-value purchases (eg capital equipment); for potential long-term partnership relations; for international sourcing and outsourcing (because of the risks involved); and for supplier development and quality management (in order to identify areas for improvement).

2.8　At the planning stage, purchasers will have to consider the following issues.

- The objectives of the appraisal (depending on the purchase situation, the importance of the purchase, the time and budget set aside for the process etc)
- The number of suppliers to be appraised
- The scale, rigour and formality of the process to be used (depending on the information already available, the importance of the purchase etc)
- The time set aside for the process (eg based on the location and feasibility of supplier site visits, the urgency of the purchase situation)
- The resources needed for the process (including personnel eg in a multi-disciplinary appraisal team, information and documentation)
- The likely perspective and response of the supplier(s) to the appraisal process
- Cost/benefit analysis: is the process worth carrying out?

What should be appraised?

2.9　A supplier appraisal may cover a wide and complex variety of factors that a buyer may consider essential or desirable in its suppliers. Criteria should be related to the requirements of the particular buying organisation and procurement type, but one generic model frequently referred to in the procurement literature is the '**10 Cs**', which we have adapted (from Ray Carter's original framework) as follows.

- *Competence* (or *capability)* of the supplier to fulfil the contract: whether it can produce the kinds of items, or deliver the kinds of services required; what management, innovation, design or other relevant capabilities it has
- *Capacity* of the supplier to meet the buying organisation's current and future needs: eg how much volume the supplier will be able to handle (its production capacity); and how effectively managed its own supply chain is
- *Commitment* of the supplier to key values such as quality, service or cost management – and to a longer-term relationship with the buying organisation (if desired)
- *Control* systems in place for monitoring and managing resources and risks; eg willingness to comply with procedures, rules or systems required by the buyer; quality or environmental management systems; financial controls; risk management systems and so on
- *Cash* resources to ensure the financial status and stability of the supplier: its profitability, cashflow position (whether it has working funds to pay its bills, buy materials and pay workers), the assets it owns, the debts it owes, how its costs are structured and allocated, and so its overall financial 'health'. These factors will reflect on the ability of the supplier to fulfil its contract with the buyer. They may

raise the risk of delivery or quality problems – and more drastic disruption to supply (and complex legal issues) if the supplier's business fails and it becomes insolvent. They will also impact on the prices the supplier will be able to charge.

- *Consistency* in delivering and improving levels of quality and service: eg a 'track record' of reliability, or 'process capability' (robust processes, quality assurance and controls)
- *Cost*: price, whole life costs and value for money offered by the supplier
- *Compatibility* of the supplier with the buying organisation: both cultural (in terms of values, ethics, work approach, management style and so on) and technological (in terms of processes, organisation and IT systems)
- *Compliance* with environmental, corporate social responsibility or sustainability standards, legislation and regulation
- *Communication* efficiency (and supporting technology) to support collaboration and co-ordination in the supply chain.

2.10   Information for supplier appraisal and pre-qualification may be acquired by various means: the use of appraisal questionnaires completed by suppliers; perusal of the supplier's financial statements and reports; checking the supplier's certifications, accreditations, quality awards, policy statements and so on; arranging to get references from existing customers; and checking product samples or portfolios of work.

2.11   Where potentially suitable suppliers have been identified on the basis of such methods, the buyer may use a supplier audit, site visit or capability survey to verify and deepen the data. Site visits are visits to the supplier's premises by a cross-functional appraisal team (eg with experts on purchasing, quality and engineering) which shares responsibility for the decision to approve or reject the supplier on the basis of their observations. A supplier visit can be used:

- To confirm information provided by the supplier in an appraisal questionnaire
- To observe and discuss, in greater detail, the supplier's premises, personnel, equipment, processes and outputs.

Supplier selection in the public sector

2.12   The EU Public Procurement Directives (and the Public Contracts Regulations 2015, which enact them into UK law) regulate the way in which suppliers are selected for procurements made by public bodies over a specified financial threshold.

2.13   Essentially, and subject to certain exceptions, public bodies must use open competitive tendering procedures: advertising an invitation to tender across the member states of the European Union, and giving all potential tenderers equal information about the contract, selection criteria and the weighting of any non-price criteria used (eg environmental or social sustainability). Detailed procedures for contract award ensure that contracts are let on the basis of open competition: buyers are generally obliged to select the lowest-price or 'most economically advantageous' tender (MEAT). Alternative procedures allow for some bidder pre-qualification (the restricted procedure) or for dialogue with prospective suppliers to develop more complex solutions (the competitive dialogue procedure) or for setting up partnerships, to innovate products etc which do not yet exist (the innovative partnership procedure).

Relationship implications of supplier appraisal

2.14   Sometimes an appraisal arises because a supplier has asked to be added to an approved supplier list, or has expressed an interest in a selective tender – and in such a case, it may be safe to assume that the supplier is highly motivated to take part in a pre-qualification appraisal process (such as self-assessment questionnaires, site visits and capability surveys).

2.15   However, if the initial approach or request for pre-qualification comes from the buyer, the response from potential suppliers will not necessarily be favourable. There may be reluctance on the part of suppliers for various reasons: Table 10.1.

Table 10.1 *Why suppliers may not welcome an appraisal*

REASON FOR SUPPLIER'S RELUCTANCE	STEPS A BUYER CAN TAKE
A particular supplier may not find the buyer's business attractive.	Estimate the likely attractiveness of the business to potential suppliers, using tools such as the supplier preferencing model.
Suppliers may have bad experiences of previous appraisals, with this or other buyers.	Emphasise that the appraisal process will be carried out fairly and transparently so that suppliers will not just be wasting their time.
Suppliers may be unsure of the selection process, perhaps suspecting that some other supplier has an 'inside track' or that the buyer is not serious.	Provide full information about how the selection process will work, and keep suppliers informed about progress through the various stages.
The timing of the proposed appraisal may be inconvenient.	Ensure that suppliers have adequate time to prepare for the appraisal, and avoid suggesting dates that will obviously coincide with suppliers' busy periods. Be sympathetic if a supplier suggests a different timetable.
Suppliers may believe that the process will be expensive and time-consuming (exacerbated by the fact that it may not lead to profitable business in the end).	Ensure that the exercise is streamlined as far as possible, consistent with obtaining the information required. Consider using trial orders as part of the appraisal.
Suppliers may be wary of sharing confidential information during the appraisal.	Be prepared to sign a confidentiality agreement.

Providing post-appraisal feedback

2.16   Under best practice supplier appraisal and selection procedures, the buyer should provide feedback to each supplier subjected to detailed pre-qualification or assessment. This will happen as a matter of course with the successful supplier, but even unsuccessful suppliers deserve to know how the buyer evaluated them, and what prevented them from achieving approved status or winning a contract.

2.17   A constructive feedback process will:

- Provide the supplier with helpful information to improve its performance and competitiveness for future business development
- Give suppliers some benefit, as a return on their investment in the appraisal process
- Leave suppliers with a positive impression of the buyer's appraisal and selection process, raising confidence and trust for future sourcing exercises or tenders (ie not deterring a potential supplier from bidding for future business for which it may be qualified)
- Help to preserve good relations between the buyer and a future prospective supplier
- Help to preserve the buyer's reputation in the supply market for fair, positive, ethical and transparent sourcing processes.

Supplier approval and managing new suppliers

2.18   Supplier approval is: 'the recognition, following a process of appraisal, that a particular supplier is able to meet the standards and requirements of the particular buyer. The approval may be for a one-off transaction or may mean that the supplier is put on a list of approved suppliers' (Lysons & Farrington).

2.19   In general, approval of a completely new supplier should only be for one year, subject to review. Suppliers that fail to meet performance standards should be removed from the database of approved suppliers, while those that consistently meet standards may be progressively upgraded from 'approved' to 'preferred' – perhaps even with potential to become a 'sole supplier' or 'supply partner'.

2.20   New suppliers will have to be supported through the early stages of the relationship. There will have to be frequent two-way communication, both to develop trust and to ensure that all necessary information has been shared to support initial performance. (Both sides may have much to learn about each other, and assumptions and expectations to manage.) Performance will be closely monitored in the initial stages, to ensure conformance to the immediate supply contract and specification, and to enable problem-solving and adjustment where required: a dedicated contract manager or liaison officer may be appointed in both organisations, to facilitate this process.

2.21   In order to manage the risk of the new relationship not working out, it may be possible to conduct trial or pilot projects, or short-term contracts, to test out the supplier without a longer-term initial commitment.

2.22   More complex issues, such as managing the handover of supply contracts from an outgoing supplier to a new one, should be beyond the scope of this syllabus, and will be covered in your later purchasing studies.

3   Motivating and managing supplier performance

Supplier motivation

3.1   'Motivation' is the process by which human beings calculate whether it is worth expending the energy and resources required to reach a particular goal. It is also the process by which one party influences or supports this kind of calculation in another, in order to secure their engagement and effort in pursuit of a goal. Leaders motivate their teams, for example, by offering praise, recognition and perhaps financial bonuses for high-level performance or improvement. Similarly, buyers can motivate suppliers by offering incentives for them to perform to the required standard, or to improve their level of service, or to add value in some other way.

3.2   Motivation can operate positively (the 'carrot' approach), by offering incentives and rewards which are valued by a supplier, and therefore make it worthwhile to put extra effort into attaining the desired behaviour or level of performance. It can also operate negatively (the 'stick' approach), by threatening sanctions or penalties which the supplier will think it worth the effort to *avoid,* by attaining the desired behaviour or level of performance.

3.3   You might wonder if supplier motivation is really necessary. After all, the buyer usually has an enforceable contract, or service level agreement, with which the supplier is legally bound to comply. Isn't this enough?

3.4   Contracts and contract management are part of the process of supplier motivation, because they are legally enforceable: they include sanctions and penalties for non-performance, which the supplier will wish to avoid. However, they only set a minimum level or 'floor' for compliance – and only address an individual contract or procurement exercise, not ongoing relationships. If the buyer wants the extra benefits of commitment, flexibility, innovation, proactive problem-solving, continuous improvement and co-operation – over and above what is expressly required by a given contract – he will have to make it worth the supplier's while. A purely compliance-based approach to motivation ('Do exactly what the contract requires or else!') creates a compliance-based approach to performance ('You'll get exactly what the contract requires – and no more!')

Improving supplier commitment and co-operation

3.5   One way of getting more out of supplier relationships is to improve supplier commitment, co-operation and loyalty. This can be done in a number of ways.

- Supplier motivation and performance management: using supplier incentives (for good performance) and penalties (for poor performance), based on clear, jointly agreed expectations, expressed in contracts, specifications, KPIs and/or service level agreements. (This is discussed in detail in Chapter 11.)
- Ensuring that there are meaningful incentives for performance and relationship improvement, and that the rewards (including informal recognition, thanks and praise) are given when earned
- Maintaining positive, relationship-building contacts and communications with suppliers, perhaps also

10

building on inter-personal co-operation and loyalty through the use of dedicated contacts such as account managers

- Securing the commitment and sponsorship of senior managers in both organisations, providing influential support for co-operation within the supplier organisation, and the potential for escalation of conflicts or disputes to higher levels
- Cultivating personal contacts and networks, building trust and goodwill on each side
- Ethical, constructive, collaborative and, where possible, 'win-win' negotiation to resolve relationship and performance problems; demonstrating willingness to understand the supplier's point of view on issues and in negotiations
- Being an attractive customer (or avoiding being an *un*attractive customer), by maintaining a sufficient volume of business to justify suppliers' investment in the relationship *and* by maintaining ethical, co-operative, efficient, professional and congenial dealings with suppliers. As we saw in Chapter 2, this may mean paying invoices on time, handling disputes fairly, sharing risks and gains equitably, allowing suppliers reasonable profit margins, sharing information appropriately and so on.
- Engaging suppliers in co-investment and co-development: collaborative product development, planning and training; systems integration; gain sharing; and so on – so that performance enhancement is a 'win' for the supplier as well as the buyer.
- Ensuring that the principles of reciprocity, mutual benefit or 'win-win' are observed as far as possible: that suppliers are always offered *something* in return for giving the buyer what it wants, to its long-term benefit

Supplier incentives

3.6   Incentives for suppliers to perform to the required standard, and/or to improve, are normally built into the contract and other performance management documents. The aim of such incentives is to motivate the supplier by offering increased profit, or some other desirable benefit, as a reward for improved performance or added value.

3.7   Here are some examples of supplier incentives, both financial and non-financial.

- Staged payments (so that the supplier only gets paid in full on completion of the project) or contingency payments (eg part of the payment is linked to results) or faster payment for early delivery (eg pay-on-receipt arrangements)
- Specific key performance indicators (KPIs) or improvement targets linked to recognition and rewards: extension of the contract or the promise of further business; inclusion on the approved or preferred supplier list; publicised supplier awards and endorsements; financial bonuses (eg for extra units of productivity, or for each day or week ahead of schedule); and so on.
- Revenue, profit or gain sharing (eg allocating the supplier an agreed percentage or flat fee bonus for cost savings). Where supplier improvements create added value, revenue or profit for the buyer, the 'gain' is shared: a 'win-win' outcome.
- The promise of long-term business agreements or increased business, or the award of 'preferred supplier' status. (As we saw in Chapter 2, however, this will only work if the buyer is also an 'attractive' customer – and remains so. The buyer needs to conduct itself ethically, constructively and co-operatively, otherwise the supplier's motivation calculation will work the other way: the extra business will not be worth the 'hassle' of dealing with an awkward, unethical, late-paying or litigious customer.)
- Guaranteed or fixed order levels, allowing the planning of investments and improvements by the supplier
- Opportunities for innovation: eg if the contract gives the provider the chance to implement or devise new solutions that will develop their business and reputation
- A capped price for the product or service that decreases year on year, motivating the supplier progressively to improve efficiency in order to preserve his profit margins
- The offer of development support (eg training or technology sharing)

- Supplier award programmes, giving high-performing suppliers public recognition
- Positive feedback sharing, praise and thanks from the buying team for a job well done. (The interpersonal aspects of motivation may not be *sufficient* to secure performance, but they do contribute meaningfully to it. Nobody likes their contribution to be ignored or treated with ingratitude.)

3.8   In order to be effective in supporting ongoing continuous improvement, it is important that incentives are:

- Balanced: they should not emphasise one aspect of performance at the expense of other, perhaps less visible, aspects. Otherwise, they might encourage corner-cutting on quality to meet productivity or cost reduction targets, say.
- Specific (so that it is clear when rewards have been earned) but not so narrowly defined that they stifle flexibility and innovation in pursuit of desired outcomes: focused on results, not on methods and means
- Fair and easy to administer. Performance criteria must be clear, and objectively measurable in a way that both parties can agree to. Rewards must be given when earned, consistently and without grudging.

Supplier penalties

3.9   An alternative approach to encourage suppliers to meet performance expectations is to use the threat or fear of being penalised for non-compliance with expectations. Here are some potential sanctions or penalties.

- The threat of reduced business for poor performance
- The threat of removal from the approved or preferred supplier list
- Publicised poor supplier gradings ('name and shame')
- Penalty clauses in contracts, entitling the buyer to financial damages in compensation for any losses arising from a supplier's failure to fulfil the contract.

3.10   While penalties support compliance with minimum standards of performance, they usually encourage only short-term improvements at best. Fundamental issues are often not addressed, and the relationship invariably suffers. The 'carrot' is generally acknowledged to be more effective than the 'stick' where the aim is long-term commitment, co-operation and improvement.

Supplier performance measurement and management

3.11   There are various good reasons to put effort into the formal evaluation of supplier performance. According to Lysons & Farrington, supplier performance appraisal can:

- Help identify the highest-quality and best-performing suppliers: assisting decision-making regarding: (a) which suppliers should get specific orders; (b) when a supplier should be retained or removed from a preferred or approved list; (c) which suppliers show potential for more strategic partnership relationships; and (d) how to distribute the spend for an item among several suppliers, to manage risk.
- Suggest how relationships with suppliers can (or need to be) enhanced to improve their performance (eg to evaluate the effectiveness of purchasing's supplier selection and contract management processes)
- Help ensure that suppliers live up to what was promised in their contracts
- Provide suppliers with an incentive to maintain and/or continuously improve performance levels
- Significantly improve supplier performance, by identifying problems which can be tracked and fixed, or areas in which support and development is needed.

10

3.12   Remember that supplier *appraisal* (pre-contract, for the purposes of supplier selection) is a somewhat different process from supplier *performance appraisal* (post-contract, for the purposes of management control). The former assesses a potential supplier's *capability* to fulfil the buyer's requirements; the latter assesses a current supplier's *performance* in fulfilling them.

3.13   We will discuss the process and techniques of supplier performance measurement, management and improvement in detail in Chapter 11: these are tools for improving supplier *performance,* or for supplier development, rather than a way of improving the relationship between buyer and supplier.

3.14   However, it should be noted that *constructively handled* performance measurement does:

- Encourage meaningful two-way dialogue and information exchange, which enhances relationships
- Require the giving of feedback, which creates opportunities for recognition and reward, and/or for constructive and collaborative problem-solving and supplier development
- Have the aim of improving supplier performance (and, where required, buyer support for performance improvement): this is an essential requirement for continuing and deepening the relationship, which will otherwise decline because of recurring problems and service gaps and loss of trust.

Trust in supply chain relationships

3.15   Trust means having confidence in the truthfulness, integrity, competence and reliability of another person or party – and acting accordingly (eg by delegating tasks to them, or proceeding with your own plans on the basis that they will do what they have said they will do). Trust is, in a sense, a gamble: you are giving a trusted party latitude to undertake actions, that – if they turn out to be untrustworthy – will pose a risk or cost to you. On the other hand, it is also a form of risk management, in that you *don't* give latitude or responsibility to parties whom you do not appraise as trustworthy.

3.16   Trust is a crucial pre-condition for open, honest communication – which in turn is the basis for positive and deepening collaborative relationships. In commercial relationships, trust is usually built up on objective factors such as reputation, testimonials from other satisfied partners, and a track record of dependability and fulfilled promises. There is also likely to be some form of risk management, in the event of trust being misplaced: however trustworthy two parties believe each other to be, they will form a written contract that defines – and enables them to enforce – their promises to each other, and that offers remedies in the event that either is let down by the other party.

3.17   Trust must be earned, on the basis of actions demonstrated consistently over time. Actions that build trust include: doing what you say you will do; not letting the other party down (eg through breach of contract, missed deadlines or undisclosed problems); showing that you understand and take into account the other party's needs and concerns; showing consistent integrity; maintaining the confidentiality of sensitive information; dealing openly and constructively with problems and disputes; supporting the other party in times of difficulty; demonstrating willingness to trust the other party (by sharing information); and so on.

3.18   You should be able to think of the opposite actions that undermine or break trust. Obvious examples include: breaching confidentiality agreements; failing to fulfil contract terms or promises; concealing information that would be important for the other party to know; offering misleading information to manipulate the other party; refusing to acknowledge responsibility for problems, and failing to address them; acting dishonestly (whether or not this impacts negatively on the other party); allowing fluctuations in quality or delivery performance; and so on.

4 Assessing relationships

4.1 Purchasing must assess whether and how far its relationship with a given supplier is satisfactory, in order to provide feedback for learning and adjustment. This may partly be done by supplier performance evaluation, on the basis that if the supplier is underperforming, there must be something wrong with the buyer-supplier relationship, or how it is being managed. However, aspects of the buyer-supplier relationship *itself* may be the subject of appraisal – or of procurement's own performance appraisal.

4.2 Evaluation will be concerned with key aspects of the supply relationship.

- Whether the relationship is being suitably managed, given its priority, importance and potential to add value (using relationship mapping models introduced in Chapter 2)
- Contract performance (in relation to volume, quality, on-time delivery, service levels, payment terms, dispute resolution and so on) and therefore the quality of contract management
- Operational efficiency, in terms of scheduling (and changes to schedules), specifications, communication and information-sharing and so on
- The quality of rapport, trust, communication and problem-solving built up between contacts in the two organisations
- The fair sharing of the risks, costs and rewards of doing business together
- How effectively, positively and collaboratively problems and disputes are resolved
- The extent to which the supplier demonstrates willingness to go beyond contract compliance to offer added value (eg through flexibility, responsiveness, service, preferential treatment, innovative supply solutions, knowledge sharing and so on)
- The willingness and potential for the relationship to develop further and to offer added value or competitive advantage for the supply chain.

Relationship mapping

4.3 Relationship mapping is a way of analysing, classifying and prioritising relationships: that is, deciding which relationships are most valuable and profitable for the organisation, and therefore worth concentrating investment of time and money in.

4.4 The best known form of relationship map in a purchasing context is **Kraljic's relationship matrix** or purchasing portfolio matrix (discussed in Chapter 2). This may be used to evaluate whether the organisation's relationship with a supplier is of the right type to 'fit' the profile of the type of goods being purchased, and whether resources are being efficiently deployed across the purchasing portfolio, to maximise relationship leverage.

4.5 The **supplier preferencing matrix** or 'supplier perceptions' matrix (discussed in Chapter 2) can be used to prioritise and evaluate relationships with (internal and external) customers: which customers are valuable and worthy of investment, and which can be exploited or terminated? It can also be used to assess the purchaser's own status as a customer to its suppliers: is it an attractive and valuable customer, or does it risk being exploited or terminated? Can it increase its attractiveness (by being more congenial to deal with, or offering benefits to suppliers) or can it increase its volume and value of business (eg by consolidating orders)?

4.6 The **relationship lifecycle** (discussed in Chapter 1) can also be used to evaluate relationship success in terms of stakeholder loyalty, commitment and retention – on the basis that stakeholders express their satisfaction or dissatisfaction 'with their feet'.

- *Relationship duration*: how long have suppliers, customers or other stakeholders remained in relationship with the organisation? (It must be doing something right!)
- *Retention rate*: what percentage of suppliers, customers or other stakeholders remain in relationship with the organisation after one year, two years and so on?

10

- *Defection rate*: what percentage of suppliers, customers or other stakeholders terminate relationship with the organisation in a given period?

Mapping purchaser-supplier satisfaction

4.7 Leenders, Fearon, Flynn & Johnson (*Purchasing and Supply Management*) point out that the assessment of a buyer-supplier relationship is not always clear cut. Different parties may have different perceptions of its effectiveness. In addition, while in simple transactions the buyer's assessment may depend on immediate rapport with the supplier's sales representative, in the case of a long-term partnership relationship, the assessment will be based on past and current performance *and* personal relationships *and* future expectations. And such assessments may change over time.

4.8 Leenders *et al* provide a framework for clarifying a current purchaser-supplier relationship. Supplier and purchaser each score the relationship from 1 to 10, according to how satisfied they are with it: Figure 10.1.

Figure 10.1 *A purchaser-supplier satisfaction model*

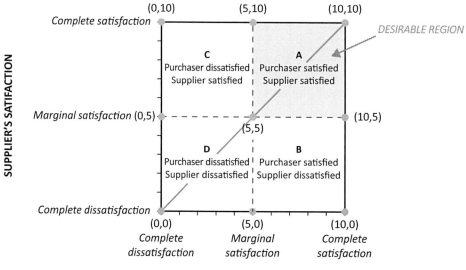

4.9 Looking at each quadrant of this model:

- In the bottom left quadrant, nobody is satisfied. Both parties will want to change the relationship – or to leave it.
- In the bottom right quadrant, the buyer is at least marginally satisfied, but the supplier is not – and in the top left quadrant, the positions are reversed. In either case, the dissatisfied party will be seeking to change or leave the relationship.
- In the top right (desirable) quadrant, both parties are relatively satisfied, although there may be room for improvement to reach the ideal situation of (10, 10), where both parties are perfectly satisfied with the relationship.

4.10 The diagonal line in the diagram is the line of 'stability' or 'fairness'. Movements up or down this line indicate equal improvement (or deterioration) for both parties. The further up the line the relationship is rated, the greater its overall stability (commitment, loyalty and likelihood of continuance), because there is less pressure for change from one party or the other.

4.11 Mapping a given supplier-customer relationship onto this grid gives both parties a starting point for improvement planning. It focuses attention on relationships which are least satisfactory, or most unstable (creating supply risk), and therefore have the most need of improvement and the most potential to improve. In addition, it may act as a starting point for dialogue about *why* one or both parties is dissatisfied, and what can be done to improve matters.

4.12 The next question to ask is: what techniques can be used to bring about change in an unsatisfactory relationship? Leenders et all distinguish between 'crunch' tools – negative measures that may lead to drastic change and possibly severance of the relationship – and 'stroking' tools (more positive, less severe approaches): Table 10.2.

Table 10.2 *Tools for moving positions*

BUYER-SIDE CRUNCH TOOLS	BUYER-SIDE STROKING TOOLS
Complete severance of purchases without advance notice	Granting of substantial volumes of business or long-term commitments
Refusal to pay bills	Sharing of internal information, eg on schedules
Refusal to accept shipments	Evidence of willingness to change behaviour
Use or threat of legal action	Rapid positive response to requests from suppliers, eg on discussing price changes
SELLER-SIDE CRUNCH TOOLS	SELLER-SIDE STROKING TOOLS
Refusal to send shipments as promised	Willingness to make rapid adjustments to price, delivery etc
Unilateral price increase without notice	Inviting the purchaser to discuss areas of difference
Insistence on unreasonable length of contract, onerous escalation clauses etc	Giving ample advance notice of pending changes in price, lead times etc

4.13 According to the authors, stroking techniques are more likely to be used in the A quadrant, further strengthening the stability of the relationship. The use of crunch tools, by contrast, may accomplish short-term objectives, but may damage chances of a stable relationship in the future.

5 Managing relationship development and improvement

Why seek relationship growth?

5.1 The relationship lifecycle model suggests that, in the early stages of the cycle, there may be a shift 'along' the relationship spectrum, from arm's length or transactional relationships towards collaboration and partnership. As we saw in Chapter 1, this may be desirable for a buying organisation for a number of reasons.

- The need to gain a strategic foothold in a new market: eg through overseas alliances or sharing of technology and knowledge
- Potential synergies of objectives, culture, technology or brand (eg PC manufacturers promoting the use of 'Intel' microprocessors in their products)
- Potential reductions in supplier selection and transaction costs, through developing regular trading with fewer preferred suppliers
- Potential integration of information systems for data sharing, information flow, expediting and so on – and related efficiencies arising from this integration
- The need for either party (or both) to invest in specially adapted equipment or systems which are non-transferable to other relationships ('asset specificity') – making it desirable to protect the investment by ensuring relationship continuity
- Market risk, and the extent to which more collaborative relationships enhance the security of supply, quality and so on.

Managing the shift towards closer relationship

5.2 Managing the shift towards long-term partnership relations may require the consideration of factors such as the following.

- Monitoring and managing risks of being 'locked into' longer-term ties, given environmental changes. Sourcing requirements may change, or the supplier may become less able to meet them for some reason, say

10

- Improving communication at all levels and points of contact between the organisations
- Implementing or improving performance measurement, in order to ensure that objectives and synergies are being fulfilled – and that there is still commitment to (and potential for) continuous improvement and added value
- Ensuring strategic as well as operational 'fit' between the organisations: that is, they have the same values and long-term objectives (especially in areas such as quality, the environment and CSR)
- Monitoring 'trade-offs' in the objectives of the alliance, to ensure that gains and risks are being shared equitably, and managing stakeholder expectations.

Supply base optimisation

5.3   The 'supplier base' is all the vendors that supply a given purchaser. Supplier bases are often described in terms of their size or range (broad, narrow, single-sourced); location (local, national, international or global); and characteristics (eg diversified or specialised).

5.4   One of the ways positive supplier relationships can be leveraged is by 'broadening supply'. The organisation can manage supply risk by having *more* potential suppliers of a given item or category of purchases, pre-qualified and approved as being able to meet its requirements. If there are supply shortages or disruptions (eg because of political unrest or bad weather in one supplier's area), or unforeseen peaks in demand (creating a need for extra supply), or a supplier failure, the organisation has established relationships with 'back-up' suppliers.

5.5   Another advantage of broadening the supply base is that as circumstances change – for both buyer and supplier – suppliers may become more or less compatible with the buying organisation, and more or less competitive in terms of their offering. Increasing the range of potential suppliers enables the buyer to be more opportunistic: taking advantage of the best available price, trading terms, quality, innovation and flexibility on offer.

5.6   More commonly, however, strong collaborative supplier relationships are used to 'narrow supply', enabling purchases to be concentrated on a smaller group of developed and trusted supply partners. *Supplier base rationalisation* (or optimisation) is concerned with determining roughly how many suppliers the buying firm wants to do business with. We discussed this in Chapter 1.

5.7   From our emphasis on security of supply, you might be able to infer the possible downside risk of reducing the supplier base. A very narrow supplier base opens the buyer to the risks of over-dependence on a single supplier, in the event of supplier failure (eg financial collapse or reputational damage); supply disruption (eg due to strikes, technology breakdown or natural disaster affecting the supplier or *its* suppliers) or the loss of the supplier's goodwill and co-operation. The buyer may also miss out on seeking or utilising new or more competitive suppliers in the wider supply market. There is also – as we have seen with any partnership – the risk that the established suppliers may grow complacent and cease to be competitive.

Supplier tiering

5.8   Supply base optimisation aims to manage the trade-off between (a) the desire to minimise the costs and complexity of managing a large supplier base and (b) the desire to minimise the risks of having a very narrow supplier base. One solution is to establish closer, longer-term partnership relationships with a few trusted, qualified suppliers, and this may impact on the way the supply chain is structured: specifically, in the development of supplier tiering.

5.9   Suppose that a manufacturer wishes to maximise its own part in the value adding process by taking in only a minimum contribution from outside suppliers. For example, the manufacturer buys in parts from a number of suppliers, and assembles them through a number of stages to produce a finished product. The structure of the supply chain in such a case is as illustrated in Figure 10.2.

Figure 10.2 *All manufacturing performed by top-level purchaser*

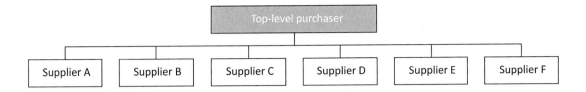

5.10   By contrast, suppose that the manufacturer sees strategic advantage in outsourcing all activities other than the final stages of production. In that case, its direct procurement relationship may be (in simplified terms) with a single supplier or tier of suppliers. Each supplier in the first tier would have an extensive role to fulfil in the manufacture of the final product, making use of 'second-tier' suppliers: Figure 10.3.

Figure 10.3 *Top-level purchaser outsources most manufacturing*

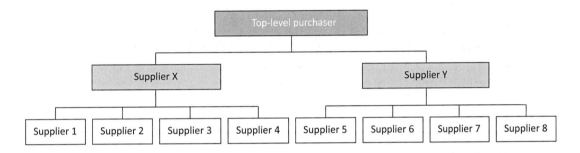

5.11   An organisation might adopt a deliberate policy of tiering its suppliers, so as to reduce the number of first-tier suppliers: the 'vendor/supplier base' with which it has to deal directly. This may be part of a process of supplier rationalisation or supply chain re-structuring, for example. The organisation deals directly only with its first-tier suppliers or 'lead providers': second-tier suppliers deal with a first-tier supplier.

5.12   For example, in a manufacturing operation such as an automobile manufacturer, the top-level purchaser is the 'original equipment manufacturer' (OEM) or assembler. It might have 180 different suppliers with which it deals directly. In order to rationalise its commercial relationships, it might reduce its vendor base to, say, 20 first-tier suppliers (specialist manufacturers of subassemblies). These in turn will organise and manage a second tier of suppliers (component manufacturers, metal finishers and so on) from which they can source required items on the OEM's behalf.

5.13   The relationship between an organisation and its first-tier suppliers or lead providers will obviously be critically important. First-tier suppliers are often expected to collaborate with the top-level purchaser to add value throughout the supply chain (making improvements and eliminating wastes), and pursue innovation in products and processes. With only a small number of first-tier supplier relationships, the top-level purchaser can focus on developing these as long-term, collaborative supply partnerships.

5.14   The impact of supply chain tiering on supplier management in the top-level purchasing organisation may include the following.

- The sourcing, selection and contracting of the first-tier suppliers will be a crucial strategic exercise. It should involve a range of key stakeholders (including senior management, procurement and user functions). Adequate resources and time must be allocated to comprehensive appraisal, selection and negotiation processes. Where competitive sourcing is desirable or necessary (as in the public sector), competition should only be applied as a final stage, following (a) rigorous pre-qualification of shortlisted candidates and (b) negotiation or dialogue to develop collaborative solutions and agreements.

- There will be fewer commercial relationships to source and manage, so the procurement function can direct its attention to managing, developing and improving these key relationships. Indeed, this is essential, since extensive responsibility has been delegated to the first-tier suppliers.
- In order to minimise business and reputational risk, procurement staff will still need to 'drill down' through the tiers in the supply chain: appraising and monitoring policies, systems and performance to ensure that the first-tier supplier's supply chain is being well managed. Priorities for 'drill down' may include risk management; ethical, environmental and labour standards; and quality assurance and compliance.
- The buyer may exercise influence over the first-tier supplier to adopt some of its own existing suppliers as subcontractors or lower-tier suppliers, in order to maintain business relationships and the benefit of relationship-specific investments and adaptations.
- Procurement may be freed up to pursue a more strategic focus and contribution (such as sustainable sourcing, global sourcing or supplier relationship development) with fewer operational tasks and transactions to handle.
- More and better supply chain improvements and innovations may be available from sharing information and collaborating with expert first-tier suppliers.

Implementing partnership sourcing

5.15 Partnership Sourcing Limited have set out a series of steps to guide a buyer in setting up a partnership relationship, and this may act as a good general guide to setting up and managing any long-term supply chain relationship. (A similar process is summarised by Lysons & Farrington.)

Step 1: Which markets and which products and services?
- Identify your supply strategy
- Identify and prioritise services for start-up of partnering
- Develop an action plan

Step 2: Sell the idea
- Sell to management
- Sell to the rest of your organisation
- Sell the idea to potential partners

Step 3: Choose your partners
- Identify candidates
- Review candidates' performance to date
- Define the criteria for selecting partners
- Assess their management's interest in developing partnership relations
- Understand their objectives and strategy
- Select partner(s) for a pilot project: don't attempt to launch too many partnerships at once.

Step 4: Define what you want from the partnership relationship
- Agree the style of relationship
- Agree common objectives (eg reduction in total costs, adoption of total quality management, zero defects, JIT or on-time deliveries, joint research and development, implementation of EDI, inventory reduction etc)
- Agree performance criteria for measuring progress towards objectives (eg service response times, on-time deliveries, stock values, lead times, quality rejects and returns, service levels)
- Agree tangible relationship links (administrative and contact procedures, information sharing, areas of collaboration, allocation of costs and risks)
- Agree to continuous improvement
- Agree exit strategy (potential breaking points eg breach of confidentiality: if a partnership-breaker is reached, either party may withdraw without penalty)

- Commit to a partnering relationship, by drawing up a simple partnership agreement

Step 5: Make your first partnering relationship work
- Tell everyone what you are doing: gain 'buy in' from stakeholders
- Agree monitoring and measuring systems
- Start work and build joint improvement teams
- Build the relationship
- Continuously monitor results against objectives (and quantify gains to the business as a whole)

Step 6: Refine and develop
- Review and audit: identify areas for improvement and development
- Extend the programme to other areas of co-operation (or a longer period)
- Develop new partners for the future

Issues in long-term relationships

5.16 Whatever the structure of a long-term relationship, certain issues will arise over time.

- The relationship lifecycle concept is based on the assumption that all relationships have a beginning, grow to mutually satisfying maturity, decline and finally end. Long-term supplier relationships are likely to decline (grow stagnant or less successful) and eventually be terminated: these processes must be carefully managed, or the relationship intentionally refreshed and renewed.
- Trust is assumed to grow over time, as parties establish a 'track record' of dependability: this is discussed in the following section of this chapter.
- Complacency or 'cosiness' may become an issue over time, as both parties get used to routines and enjoy the security and stability of the relationship. There may be resistance to change, and little incentive to maintain 'sharp' standards of quality, service and cost – given the comparatively low influence of competition. It is essential to set relationship targets for continuous improvement; monitor and review improvement progress; create incentives to keep performance sharp; and ensure that suppliers remain competitive (eg by reviewing the contract every few years), or that some other business case can be made for maintaining the relationship.
- Adaptation and integration are likely to occur over time, as an expression of partnership, and supported by the security of ongoing business. This can create dependency issues, making it difficult for either party to withdraw from the relationship, when it might be necessary or desirable to do so – especially if assets and competencies acquired for the relationship cannot be easily transferred to other suppliers or clients.

6 Managing relationship problems, decline and termination

Factors constraining relationship development

6.1 A number of factors, both within the parties or relationship itself (intrinsic factors) and in the external environment (extrinsic factors), may hinder the progressive development of a relationship, or cause problems within it.

6.2 Intrinsic causes of difference, barriers and conflict in buyer-supplier relationships may include the following.

- Lack of support from senior managers in the organisation, or in the procurement function, for a particular supplier – or for a particular type of relationship (eg reluctance to enter into partnerships, because of the risks involved)
- Conflicts of interest between the two parties. These are often based on issues of price and profit margin: the buyer trying to secure the lowest possible price (or the supplier trying to secure the highest possible price), at the expense of the other party's profits. A variety of other conflicts of

10

interest is possible, however. One party may want an exclusive supply or distribution contract, while the other wants to broaden its supply or distribution base to minimise risk. A buyer may want its suppliers to off-shore production to low-cost-labour countries, while suppliers may not want to shoulder the risk and cost of doing this. And so on.

- An adversarial approach on the part of a buyer or supplier, especially where the other party wants to enter into partnership relations
- Imbalance of power between the parties, and the exploitation of the weaker party by the stronger (or the perception that this is occurring)
- Lack of trust, often arising from (and contributing to) failure to share information or make commitments to the relationship
- Changes of personnel, whether at a senior level (creating changes of policy and loss of relationship champions) or at an operational level (creating loss of established contacts and communication channels)
- Communication breakdown
- Dissatisfaction, conflict and lack of trust arising from repeated failure to meet agreed terms (or expectations): eg a supplier repeatedly delivering late or causing quality problems – or a buyer repeatedly paying suppliers late or taking them to court over minor contract disputes
- Incompatibility of culture and values, processes and procedures or systems and technology
- Commercial factors: eg the risks and costs involved in the relationship; the volume and value of the business to each party (now and in the future); the extent of investment and integration in the relationship; the length of any existing agreement; and the availability of alternative suppliers. These factors will help to determine how committed the firm is to maintaining the relationship (and overcoming distance and barriers): is it easier, safer and more cost-effective to stay in – or to get out?

6.3   Extrinsic or environmental factors also impact on relationships, as we demonstrated in Chapter 8.

Managing relationship decline

6.4   Again, looking at the relationship lifecycle, we have seen that there will be times when internal and external circumstances and requirements change, and a relationship becomes less profitable or value-adding; or one or both of the participants become less committed to it; or problems arise which inject barriers or distance into the relationship. It may then be desirable to shift the relationship from partnership to arm's length (to withdraw resources from an unprofitable relationship) or even adversarial (to squeeze the last available profit from the relationship) in the 'decline' stage. This may also be a responsible and ethical way of withdrawing from a situation of inter-dependency, managing the expectations of stakeholders and allowing both parties to make preparations for the eventual termination of the relationship.

6.5   In 'downgrading' a relationship from partnership to an arm's length or adversarial footing, the buying organisation may need to:

- Set and reinforce pragmatic and objective criteria for purchasing decisions, with well-defined price data and so on. This will help to re-establish – for both buyers and suppliers – a regime of economic and competition-based decision-making and contract award, rather than relying on an assumed ('cosy') preferential relationship.
- Redefine the roles of people previously assigned to manage and administer the partnership
- Set up arm's length purchasing (eg framework agreements or call-off contracts), so that routine or indirect purchasing can be carried out by user or budget-holder departments
- Establish precise price bases and quality requirements for routine purchases, in order to 'de-mystify' the process for user departments, and give clear guidelines for comparison and contract award

Managing and resolving conflict in contractual relationships

6.6 It is worth making the point that conflict is not always negative or destructive in internal and external supply chain relationships. Conflict can be constructive, when its effect is to:

- Clarify issues and power relationships
- Focus attention on the need for improvement and problem-solving
- Bring misunderstandings, disappointed expectations, hostility and resistance out into the open, where they can be dealt with (rather than erupting later...)
- Avoid the risk of 'group think' and complacency by encouraging the testing and challenging of ideas
- Highlight the need for better communication.

6.7 However, conflict can also be destructive, where it encourages defensive or 'spoiling' behaviour; causes resentment; polarises views and creates barriers to communication; absorbs people's attention and energy, at the expense of the task; or escalates into hostility (and even legal disputes) which may permanently damage a relationship.

6.8 The purpose of supplier management and contract management is to facilitate communication, secure co-operation and minimise the risk of relationship problems (especially legal disputes). However, it should be clear that relationships can fail to develop as planned, and that one or more of the parties may fail to meet the terms of an agreement in a range of different circumstances. In such cases, it is sound management to plan ahead for conflict and dispute resolution.

6.9 There are many approaches to the management of conflict, and the suitability of any given approach must be judged according to its relevance to a particular situation. There is no single 'right way'. In some situations, the best outcome may be achieved by compromise; in others, imposition of a win-lose solution may be required; in others, the process of seeking a win-win solution, whatever the eventual outcome, may be helpful – particularly where the parties want to preserve ongoing working relations.

6.10 There are also a number of formal mechanisms for managing and resolving conflicts in contractual relationships, depending on the nature of the relationship (eg the desire to preserve positive working relations), and the nature and 'stage of escalation' of the conflict. These were discussed in detail in Chapter 7.

Relationship breakdown and termination

6.11 No commercial relationship lasts forever, especially in dynamic business environments, where strategic directions and external factors may be constantly changing. 'Terminal' breakdowns in supply relationships may occur for a number of reasons.

- A change in the strategic objectives or circumstances of the buyer or supplier, so that the other party no longer 'fits' its needs. For example, a buying organisation may be forced to modernise its products and streamline its inventory management in line with its competitors, and if its established supplier is unable or unwilling to develop the necessary innovation capability and flexibility, the buyer will need to find another supplier. More simply, a buyer may cease to produce a particular product (because demand for it has dropped or it has become obsolete, say) and may therefore no longer require supplies of materials for that product.
- New suppliers entering the market offering a product, service or terms that the existing supplier cannot match (eg as a result of lower labour costs or technological innovation)
- Conflict, lack of communication or relationship difficulties making the relationship less effective and less worthy of further investment – or indicating that there is no longer commitment (on one side or both) to genuine alliance
- Poor quality or delivery performance by the supplier (especially if failures lead to legal disputes, creating a major rift between buyer and supplier). This may be made worse by complacency about

contract management – and may become 'terminal' if improvement commitments are not agreed and met over time. The same applies to poor conduct by the buyer (eg late or disputed payments, short-notice changes, failure to provide information or breach of confidentiality), making it an undesirable or unprofitable client.

- Economic factors, making the supplier or buyer financially unstable or 'at risk', so that the other party needs to find alternative sources of supply or business for the future
- Changes of management, personnel, culture or systems in the buyer or supplier organisation (perhaps as a result of merger or acquisition), creating fresh incompatibilities which the other party may not be able to resolve.
- Fulfilment of the contract: both parties conclude that they have fulfilled the objectives they wished to achieve when entering the relationship, so it comes to a natural and mutually satisfied end.

6.12 The circumstances and reasons for terminating (or suspending) a supply chain relationship will dictate how the process should be handled. In some cases, the relationship may be mutually terminated or suspended by notice or agreement (eg at the end of a contract period), while other cases may be adversarial or disciplinary in nature (eg in the event of breach of contract or unsatisfactory performance by a supplier, or – within the internal supply chain – misconduct by an employee). In either case, it is useful to manage the termination constructively, with a view to:

- Maintaining the possibility of future relationship
- Learning from the past relationship, in order to improve relationship management in future.

6.13 Termination may not be easy, especially if dependency has developed in a relationship over time. Lysons & Farrington identify a number of key issues.

- *Timing*. Whenever possible, the termination should coincide with expiration of a current agreement or contract. Too much advance warning can lead to poor service in the run-down period, while too little may be unethical.
- *Relationship aspects.* Terminations should be handled constructively and professionally, in order to avoid hostility and reputational damage – and to leave the door open to future business, if appropriate.
- *Legal considerations*. These should be anticipated in drawing up supply contracts, but may need to be negotiated. There may be financial consequences to terminating an agreement. In addition, there may be issues surrounding confidentiality agreements, and the return of assets or intellectual property (eg drawings or designs).
- *Succession issues*. Before terminating a supplier, steps should be taken to secure continuity of supply, by: warning internal parties affected by a change of supplier; investigating and engaging new suppliers; and reflecting on the lessons learned from the terminated relationship in order to improve future agreements (where possible).

6.14 A comprehensive approach to managing termination would include steps such as the following.

- Defining rules and standards of conduct and conformance: clearly defining and communicating what will be construed as a breach, violation or shortfall worthy of terminating or suspending the relationship
- Setting and agreeing remedies or penalties for breach or violation
- Setting out formal procedures for pursuing a grievance or dispute
- Giving adequate time and information for preparation by both parties for any discussion of a complaint
- Opportunities for investigation and explanation (right of reply) of any complaint
- Agreeing methods of slowing or avoiding the escalation of conflict in the event of a dispute: 'cool off' periods, mediation and so on
- Paying attention to relational aspects, with the long-term goal of preserving constructive working relationships where possible
- Giving accurate, balanced, constructive feedback

- Acknowledging the value of existing work done by both parties
- Attacking the problem – not the people
- Setting improvement targets (or other conditions) for renewal or replacement of the contract, so that the door is left open – but the interests of both parties are protected.
- Re-emphasise to all stakeholders the benefits of using free-market competition to reduce costs and improve service quality
- Be prepared to switch suppliers if necessary – effectively terminating or suspending the relationship.

Maintaining post-termination relations

6.15 Depending on the circumstances in which the relationship terminated, it may be appropriate to keep lines of communication open. This is unlikely to be the case if the relationship ended in acrimony, but even so, purchasing and marketing practitioners must be professional in their attitudes to their supply and product markets. It is never appropriate to conduct oneself in a way that shuts down all possibility of future profitable relationships between firms.

6.16 Once a supply contract has terminated, it may still be desirable to maintain contact – or to 'keep the door open' to future dealings, if occasion arises. This is particularly important where the contract has simply been satisfactorily fulfilled: there is every reason to think that both parties will be able to work together effectively and profitably in future. Apart from the possibility of future business, there is also the consideration that buyers wish to stay up to date with developments in the supply market: the more co-operative contacts they preserve, the better they are able to do this.

10

Chapter summary

- It is important to distinguish supplier relationship management (a broader responsibility) from contract management (related to a particular supply contract).
- Suppliers should be pre-qualified and appraised as part of the supplier selection process.
- Carter's 10Cs is a useful framework for supplier appraisal.
- Suppliers may not always welcome an appraisal.
- Supplier motivation is important for gaining commitment and co-operation (beyond the minimal compliance required by the supply contract).
- One motivational technique is to offer suppliers incentives; another is to apply penalties.
- Buyers must assess their relationships with individual suppliers to ensure that they are appropriate in each case.
- Leenders *et al* provide a model for assessing buyer and supplier satisfaction.
- Supply base optimisation is the process of broadening or shrinking the supply base for the best possible leverage of supplier relationships.
- There are often barriers preventing or constraining the development of relationships with suppliers.
- Conflict in supply relations can be constructive. However, destructive conflict must be managed carefully.
- Even when a supply relationship terminates, it may be important to maintain good relations in the aftermath.

Self-test questions

Numbers in brackets refer to the paragraphs where you can check your answers.

1   Explain the implications of the distinction between contract management and supplier relationship management. (1.2)

2   What is the purpose of supplier pre-qualification? (2.1)

3   List Carter's 10Cs. (2.9)

4   Why may suppliers not welcome an appraisal by the buyer? (2.15, Table 10.1)

5   List methods of improving supplier commitment and co-operation. (3.5)

6   Give examples of supplier incentives. (3.7)

7   What aspects will a buyer consider when assessing relationships with suppliers? (4.2)

8   Sketch the purchaser-supplier satisfaction model by Leenders *et al.* (Figure 10.1)

9   Why may it be desirable for a buyer to shift a relationship along the spectrum from transactional to collaborative? (5.1)

10 Why might a buyer introduce a system of supplier tiering? (5.11, 5.12)

11 List the steps involved in implementation of partnership sourcing. (5.15)

12 List possible barriers to the development of closer buyer-supplier relationships. (6.2)

13 In what circumstances may conflict be constructive? (6.6)

14 Why may it be necessary to terminate a buyer-supplier relationship? (6.11)

10

CHAPTER 11

Supplier Performance Management

Assessment criteria and indicative content

4.2 Explain the main techniques for supplier relationship management

- Supplier performance measurement
- Creating targets and assessment of performance

4.3 Explain the main techniques for supplier development

- Approaches to supplier development
- Defining quality assurance and total quality
- Approaches to quality improvement

4.4 Explain techniques for relationship improvement

- Continuous improvement
- The operation of balanced scorecards
- Value stream mapping

Section headings

1 Supplier performance measures
2 Appraising supplier performance
3 Benchmarking and supplier balanced scorecards
4 Quality management and improvement
5 Managing service levels
6 Supplier development

Introduction

In this chapter we gather together the various aspects of the syllabus content that deal with the measurement, management and improvement of supplier performance.

We start with the process of supplier performance measurement, exploring: firstly, the formulation of performance measures and standards (including key performance indicators or KPIs) for suppliers; secondly, methods of monitoring, reviewing and evaluating supplier performance; and, thirdly, particular techniques including benchmarking and scorecards.

We then go on to look at some of the processes of supplier performance management and improvement, focusing on quality management and improvement – and equivalent issues in managing the quality of services.

Finally, we look specifically at supplier development, which embraces a range of approaches to enhance the capacity, capability and performance of suppliers.

1 Supplier performance measures

What is performance measurement?

1.1 Supplier performance measurement is the comparison of a supplier's current performance against:

- *Defined performance criteria* (such as KPIs or service level agreements), to establish whether the aimed-for or agreed level of performance has been achieved
- *Previous performance,* to identify deterioration or improvement trends
- *The performance of other organisations* (suppliers, procurement functions) or standard *benchmarks,* to identify areas where performance falls short of best practice or the practice of competitors, and where there is therefore room for improvement.

1.2 Performance measurement is important because it supports the planning and control of operations and relationship: it is often said that 'what gets measured, gets managed'. It is intended to lead to performance improvement and supplier development, by identifying areas in which suppliers' current performance falls short of desired, competitive or best-practice levels. It is an important tool for communicating with stakeholders about their part in supply chain performance, and how they are doing: performance measures, such as KPIs, can be used to manage, motivate and reward individuals, teams and suppliers.

Key performance indicators (KPIs)

1.3 There are a number of different approaches to setting performance targets and measures, and we will briefly outline some of the main ones here. We begin with key performance indicators.

1.4 KPIs are clear qualitative or quantitative objectives which define adequate performance in key areas (or critical success factors), and against which progress and performance can be measured.

1.5 The process of developing KPIs can be summarised as follows: Figure 11.1.

Figure 11.1 *Developing key performance indicators*

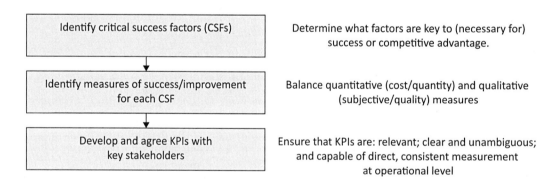

1.6 The point about KPIs is that they state performance goals in a way that is capable of direct, detailed, consistent measurement at operational level, using available data collection systems. Where possible, such goals will be *quantitative:* that is, numerical or statistical. They may, for example, be expressed in terms of cost (eg cost per service delivery, amount of cost savings), time (eg hours per service delivery), quantity of outputs (eg offices cleaned per hour, number of deliveries made on-time-in-full, number of cost reduction initiatives proposed) or other statistics (eg the proportion or ratio of deliveries made on-time-in-full, or the number of customer complaints per review period).

1.7 Some targets, however, will be more *qualitative:* that is, subjective and pertaining to qualities or attributes that cannot readily be quantified. For example, you may want to evaluate customer satisfaction, the effectiveness of the supplier's account management, its flexibility and responsiveness or commitment to quality, or the professionalism of purchasing staff. Even so, KPIs in these areas should be expressed as quantitatively as possible: the proportion of services rated satisfactory or non-satisfactory by customers; the degree of satisfaction expressed by customers (eg using rates scales or points scores); the proportion of requests and proposals responded to, and how quickly; scores on commitment to quality obtained via attitude surveys; number of 'critical incidents' illustrating professional or non-professional conduct; and so on.

1.8 Some of the benefits of using KPIs as performance measures are as follows.

- Increased and improved (results-focused) communication on performance issues
- Motivation to achieve or better the specified performance level (particularly with KPI-linked incentives, rewards or penalties). Motivation is in any case stronger where there are clear targets to aim for.
- Support for collaborative buyer-supplier relations, by enabling integrated or two-way performance measurement (with KPIs on both sides of the relationship)
- The ability directly to compare year on year performance, to identify improvement or deterioration trends
- Focus on key results areas (critical success factors) such as cost reduction and quality improvement
- Clearly defined shared goals, facilitating cross-functional and cross-organisational teamwork and relationships
- Reduced conflict arising from causes such as goal confusion and unclear expectations

1.9 Setting KPIs for *supplier* performance, in particular, may be beneficial in the following areas.

- Setting clear performance criteria and expectations: motivating compliance and improvement
- Managing supply risk: controlling quality, delivery, value for money and so on
- Supporting contract management (to ensure that agreed benefits are obtained)
- Identifying high-performing suppliers for inclusion on approved or preferred supplier lists (which in turn supports efficient buying by user departments)
- Identifying high-performing suppliers with potential for closer partnership relations
- Providing feedback for learning and continuous improvement in the buyer-supplier relationship – both for the supplier, and for the purchasing department

1.10 It is worth noting that KPIs can have some disadvantages as well. The pursuit of individual KPIs can lead to some dysfunctional or sub-optimal behaviour: cutting corners on quality or service to achieve productivity or time targets, say, or units focusing on their own targets at the expense of cross-functional collaboration and co-ordination. Targets will have to be carefully set with these potential problems in mind.

Examples of supplier performance measures

1.11 There are a number of critical success factors in a supplier's performance that a buyer may want to evaluate, and a range of key performance indicators can be selected for each. In an exam, you will need to select or devise those most relevant to the context and (if specified by the question) the type of contract. For a general supply contract, however, sample CSFs and KPIs are suggested in Table 11.1.

Table 11.1 *General KPIs for supplier performance*

SUCCESS FACTORS	SAMPLE KPIs
Price	• Basic purchase price (and/or price compared with other suppliers) • Value or percentage cost reductions (and/or number of cost reduction initiatives proposed and implemented)
Quality and compliance	• Reject, error or wastage rates (or service failures) • Number of customer complaints • Adherence to quality standards (eg ISO 9000) and/or environmental and ethical standards and policies
Delivery	• Frequency of late, incorrect or incomplete delivery • Percentage of on time in full – OTIF – deliveries
Service/relationship	• Competence, congeniality and co-operation of account managers • Promptness in dealing with enquiries and problems • Adherence to agreements on after-sales service
Financial stability	• Ability to meet financial commitments and claims • Ability to maintain quality and delivery
Innovation capability	• Number of innovations proposed or implemented (and/or investment in R&D) • Willingness to collaborate in cross-organisational innovation teams
Technology leverage and compatibility	• Proportion of transactions carried out electronically • Number of technology breakdowns
Overall performance	• Benchmarking against other suppliers • Commitment to continuous improvement (eg number of suggestions proposed and implemented)

Performance measures for services

1.12 Lysons suggests that service levels should be:

- Reasonable (since unnecessarily high service levels may incur higher costs, and may focus service providers' attention on targets to the detriment of overall service)
- Prioritised by the customer (eg as 'most important', 'important' or 'less important')
- Easily monitored (using specific, observable and quantifiable measures)
- Stated in a way that is readily understood by both customer-side and provider-side staff.

1.13 General performance criteria for service levels have been developed as part of an assessment tool called *SERVQUAL* (Zeithaml, Parasuraman & Berry).

- *Tangibles*: appearance of physical facilities, equipment, personnel, communications. For example: does the service provider have smartly-dressed staff and well-maintained equipment? Is its feedback documentation user-friendly?
- *Reliability:* ability to perform the promised service dependably and accurately. For example: is the service always delivered to specification, on time, within budget?
- *Responsiveness*: willingness to help customers and provide prompt service. For example: do service staff respond positively to urgent or non-routine requests?
- *Assurance*: customer confidence in the service provider, based on demonstrated competence, courtesy, credibility and security.
- *Empathy*: customer confidence that the service provider will identify with the customer's needs and expectations in relation to ease of access, communication and co-operation.

1.14 More specifically, key performance indicators (KPIs) can be drawn up to suit the needs of a particular service contract. Using the example of a cleaning service, for example, there might be KPIs covering areas such as the following.

- Time taken to complete designated cleaning tasks
- Thoroughness of cleaning (perhaps specified as amount of dust or number of stains identified in spot checks, or proportion of litter bins left unemptied)

- Number of re-cleans (or customer complaints or requests for re-cleans)
- Customer satisfaction with overall cleaning service (eg on the basis of feedback reports, or specified as number of complaints, or proportion of complaints to approvals).

1.15 Note that you don't want too many KPIs: only those that are indicative measures of performance in areas necessary to achieve critical success factors. Otherwise, it will be too complicated and costly to monitor and measure performance.

2 Appraising supplier performance

2.1 As we saw in Chapter 10, supplier performance appraisal (or vendor rating) can:

- Help identify the highest-quality and best-performing suppliers: assisting decision-making regarding: (a) which suppliers should get specific orders; (b) when a supplier should be retained or removed from a preferred or approved list; (c) which suppliers show potential for more strategic partnership relationships; and (d) how to distribute the spend for an item among several suppliers, to manage risk.
- Suggest how relationships with suppliers can (or need to be) enhanced to improve their performance (eg to evaluate the effectiveness of purchasing's supplier selection and contract management processes)
- Help ensure that suppliers live up to what was promised in their contracts
- Provide suppliers with an incentive to maintain and/or continuously improve performance levels
- Significantly improve supplier performance, by identifying problems which can be tracked and fixed, or areas in which support and development is needed.

Performance monitoring and review

2.2 Performance monitoring (checking progress and performance against defined key performance indicators or KPIs) and review (looking back at performance over a given planning period) may be carried out in various ways.

- *Continuous monitoring* may be possible in some contexts: electronic monitoring tools, for example, allow variance or exception reports to be produced whenever results (eg productivity, costs or on-time-in-full deliveries) deviate from plan, within defined parameters or tolerances.
- More generally, performance may be monitored at key stages of a process, project or contract: for example, at the end of project stages, or production or delivery deadlines.
- *Periodic reviews* are often used: examining results against defined measures or targets at regular and fixed intervals. The purpose of such reviews is generally 'formative': supplying feedback information while it is still relevant for the adjustment of performance or plans. So, for example, a buyer may sample a supplier's process outputs periodically, to check quality and conformance to specification. Buyer-side and supplier-side teams may meet periodically to discuss any issues in contract performance.
- *Post-completion reviews* are often used for projects and contracts, with the purpose of exchanging feedback and learning any lessons for the future.

2.3 There is a wide range of feedback mechanisms for gathering data on supplier performance, and comparing them against relevant performance measures. Which mechanism is used will depend on what kind of quantitative or qualitative data is required, and what aspect of performance is being evaluated. Here are some examples.

- The gathering of feedback from internal and external customers and other stakeholders, using feedback groups, complaint procedures, survey questionnaires and project reviews
- The gathering of performance information through observation, testing (eg quality inspections), and analysis of documentation, transaction records and management reports (eg analysis of inspection reports, complaint and dispute records and so on)
- Budgetary control: monitoring actual costs against budgeted or forecast costs

Figure 11.2 *Vendor rating form*

SUPPLIER:		DATE:	
Summary evaluation, by department	**Good**	**Satisfactory**	**Unsatisfactory**
Purchasing	☐	☐	☐
Receiving	☐	☐	☐
Accounting	☐	☐	☐
Engineering	☐	☐	☐
Quality	☐	☐	☐
	☐	☐	☐
Performance factors			
Purchasing			
Delivers on schedule	☐	☐	☐
Delivers at quoted price	☐	☐	☐
Prices are competitive	☐	☐	☐
Prompt and accurate with routine documents	☐	☐	☐
Anticipates our needs	☐	☐	☐
Helps in emergencies	☐	☐	☐
Does not unfairly exploit a single-source position	☐	☐	☐
Does not request special consideration	☐	☐	☐
Currently supplies price, catalogue and technical information	☐	☐	☐
Furnishes specially requested information promptly	☐	☐	☐
Advises us of potential troubles	☐	☐	☐
Has good labour relations	☐	☐	☐
Delivers without constant follow-up	☐	☐	☐
Replaces rejections promptly	☐	☐	☐
Accepts our terms without exception	☐	☐	☐
Keeps promises	☐	☐	☐
Has sincere desire to serve	☐	☐	☐
Receiving			
Delivers per routing instructions	☐	☐	☐
Has adequate delivery service	☐	☐	☐
Has good packaging	☐	☐	☐
Accounting			
Invoices correctly	☐	☐	☐
Issues credit notes punctually	☐	☐	☐
Does not ask for special financial consideration	☐	☐	☐
Engineering			
Past record on reliability of products	☐	☐	☐
Has technical ability for difficult work	☐	☐	☐
Readily accepts responsibility for latent deficiencies	☐	☐	☐
Provides quick and effective action in emergencies	☐	☐	☐
Furnishes requested data promptly	☐	☐	☐
Quality			
Quality of material	☐	☐	☐
Furnishes certification, affidavits, etc	☐	☐	☐
Replies with corrective action	☐	☐	☐

- Formal performance reviews or appraisals (sometimes called 'vendor rating' exercises): reviewing performance against benchmark standards, KPIs and/or agreed service levels, and feeding back the information for improvement planning
- Contract management, continually monitoring compliance with contract terms
- Regular meetings between buyer and supplier representatives (or project or account managers) to review general progress, or specific issues such as rates or delivery problems, and exchange feedback on 'how things are going'
- Project management: reports and meetings at the end of key project stages or milestones; periodic 'highlight' reports by the project manager; and post-completion review and reporting, with the aim of extracting learning for the next project
- The use of consultants to monitor compliance with quality standards, benchmarks or ethical standards (eg monitoring overseas suppliers' treatment of their workforces)
- The use of technical specialists to monitor supplier performance (eg on construction or IT projects) beyond the expertise of purchasers.

Vendor rating

2.4 Systematic post-contract performance appraisal and evaluation is often referred to as 'vendor rating': a vendor being a person or organisation that currently sells you something, and rating being a way of evaluating or 'scoring' performance. Vendor rating is the measurement of supplier performance using agreed criteria or KPIs.

2.5 One common approach to vendor rating is based on the use of a **supplier performance evaluation form**: a checklist of key performance factors, against which purchasers assess the supplier's performance as good, satisfactory or unsatisfactory: Figure 11.2 (adapted from *Dobler & Burt*). A weighting is applied to each factor, so that the supplier's performance in key performance areas, and overall, can be summarised as good, satisfactory or unsatisfactory. This is comparatively easy to implement, once meaningful checklists have been developed, but it is fairly broad and subjective.

2.6 Another approach is the *factor rating method*, which gives a quantified, numerical score for each key assessment factor. For example, the measure of quality performance might be '100% *minus* percentage of rejects in total deliveries': a supplier whose deliveries contained 3% rejects would score 97% or 0.97 on this measure. Each of the major factors is also given a *weighting*, according to its importance within overall performance, and this is applied to each score, to end up with an overall score or rating: Figure 11.3.

Figure 11.3 *Factor rating method*

Performance factor	Weighting	Score	Supplier rating
Price	0.4	0.94	0.376
Quality	0.4	0.97	0.388
Delivery	0.2	0.72	0.144
Overall evaluation	1.0		0.908

2.7 The supplier in our example has achieved a rating of 0.908 out of a possible 1. This score can be compared with that achieved by other suppliers, and gives a good measure of exactly where each stands in the order of preference. It may also be used year on year, to provide a measure of whether a supplier's performance is improving or declining.

2.8 Of course, neither approach to vendor rating diagnoses the *causes* of any performance shortfalls identified, nor what needs to be done to address them. A vendor rating should therefore be seen within the whole process of performance management: Figure 11.4.

11

Figure 11.4 *Vendor rating*

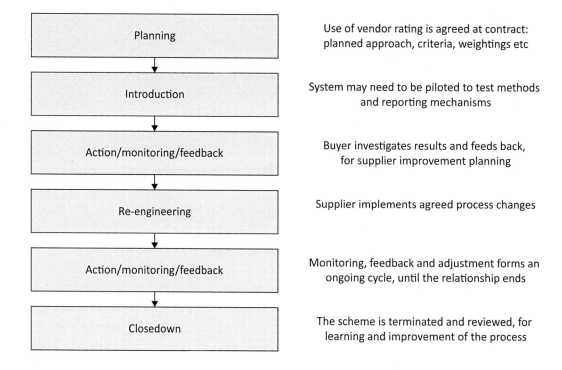

Planning	Use of vendor rating is agreed at contract: planned approach, criteria, weightings etc
Introduction	System may need to be piloted to test methods and reporting mechanisms
Action/monitoring/feedback	Buyer investigates results and feeds back, for supplier improvement planning
Re-engineering	Supplier implements agreed process changes
Action/monitoring/feedback	Monitoring, feedback and adjustment forms an ongoing cycle, until the relationship ends
Closedown	The scheme is terminated and reviewed, for learning and improvement of the process

3 Benchmarking and supplier balanced scorecards

Benchmarks

3.1 A useful definition of benchmarking is: 'Measuring your performance against that of best-in-class companies, determining how the best-in-class achieve these performance levels and using the information as a basis for your own company's targets, strategies and implementation' (Pryor). The aim is to learn both *where* performance needs to be improved and *how* it can be improved, by comparison with excellent practitioners.

3.2 The then DTI (now the Department for Business, Innovation and Skills) described the process of benchmarking as follows.

Benchmarking is the practice of comparing a company's performance against others to stimulate improvements in operating practices. It can be used across almost all of the company's departments and it can also be the comparison of departments or sites within an organisation. It can be used to help clarify where you stand, relative to others, in those practices which matter most in your area of business. The technique can also be used to help companies become as good as, or better than, the best in the world in the most important aspects of their operations.

3.3 Benchmarking can be used to analyse any aspect of organisational performance, such as purchasing, stock control, customer service or relationship management, so it has wide application in buyer-supplier performance measurement. Within purchasing, benchmarks may be selected for prices, inventory levels, delivery times, quality, staff training, use of e-procurement – and so on.

3.4 Benchmarked performance targets and quality standards are likely to be realistic (since other organisations have achieved them), yet challenging (since the benchmarking organisation hasn't *yet* achieved them): the most effective combination for maintaining motivation. At the same time, benchmarking helpfully stimulates more research and feedback-seeking into customer needs and wants, and generates new ideas and insights outside the box of the organisation's accustomed ways of thinking and doing things.

3.5 Bendell, Boulter & Kelly distinguish four types of benchmarking.

- *Internal benchmarking*: comparison with high-performing units in the same organisation. For example, a divisional procurement function might be benchmarked against a higher-performing procurement function in another division.
- *Competitor benchmarking:* comparison with high-performing competitors in key areas which give them their competitive advantage.
- *Functional benchmarking:* comparison with another, high-performing organisation. For example, an electronics manufacturer might benchmark its purchasing against that of a construction company known for effective materials management.
- *Generic benchmarking:* comparison of business processes across functional and industry boundaries. The benchmark may be set by 'excellent' companies, learning organisations, ethical leaders – or exemplars of whatever attribute the firm is interested in.

3.6 The stages in the benchmarking process are shown in Figure 11.5

Figure 11.5 *The benchmarking process*

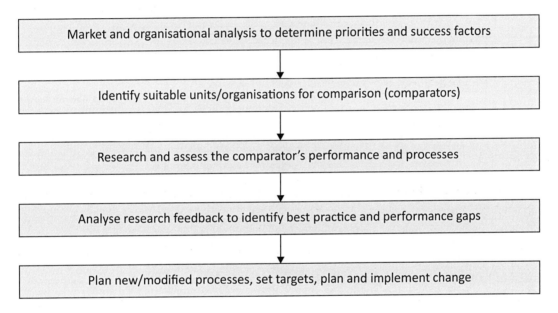

3.7 Whilst benchmarking can make significant contributions to continuous improvement objectives, the following points should also be considered.

- The costs associated with benchmarking projects are somewhat variable in nature, but can be significant. Typical project costs are normally associated with meetings, visits, training, possible consultancy etc and therefore projects must be carefully managed and planned.
- One of the most important requirements of a successful benchmarking project is effective communication. It is important to inform concerned parties about project progress and developments via presentations, reports, analyses, etc. This not only reduces confusion and conflicts, but may also trigger communication and ideas about how perceived best practice can be cascaded within the organisation or supply chain.

Balanced scorecards

3.8 The balanced scorecard model was developed by Kaplan & Norton, who argued that purely financial objectives and performance measures are not enough to control organisations effectively. Indeed, they tend to encourage short-term, limited thinking, because managers are judged by criteria which do not measure the long-term, complex effects of their decisions. Other parameters and perspectives are needed for more balanced performance management.

11

3.9   Kaplan & Norton proposed four key perspectives for a balanced scorecard, focusing on long-term 'enablers' of corporate (and supply chain) success.

- *Financial:* financial performance and the creation of value for shareholders
- *Customers:* how effectively the organisation delivers value to the customer, and develops mutually beneficial relationships with customers and other stakeholders
- *Internal business processes:* how effectively and efficiently value-adding processes are carried out throughout the supply chain
- *Innovation and learning:* the skills and knowledge required to develop distinctive competencies for future competitive advantage and growth.

3.10   This can be depicted as follows: Figure 11.6.

Figure 11.6 *The balanced scorecard*

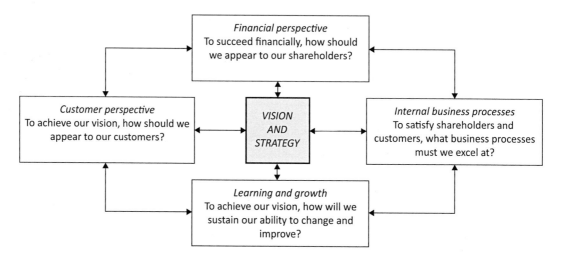

3.11   The 'balance' of the scorecard is thus between: financial and non-financial performance measures; short-term and long-term perspectives; and internal and external focus. This offers strong motivational potential, as a spur to continuous improvement – both for internal units and within the supply chain. Linked buyer and supplier scorecards could be used to integrate strategy, performance measurement and feedback across key supply chain partnerships.

3.12   Working with a balanced scorecard requires identification and description of several factors for each perspective selected.

- The organisation's long-term goals
- The critical success factors (CSFs) in achieving those goals
- The key activities which must be carried out to achieve those success factors
- The key performance indicators (KPIs) which can be used to monitor progress

3.13   To develop KPIs from the **customer perspective,** the organisation must define its target customers and define value from their point of view. Typical indicators may include measures such as customer satisfaction, customer retention and market share.

3.14   From the **internal process** perspective, the task is to identify the key processes the organisation must excel at in order to continue adding value in the eyes of customers and other stakeholders. Having identified these key processes the next step is to develop the most appropriate performance measures with which to track progress. It may be necessary to consider more innovative solutions, rather than concentrating efforts and resources on incremental improvements to existing activities. All internal and external supply chain activities should be considered within this perspective.

3.15   From the **innovation and learning** perspective, the key focus initially should be on the 'enablers' that underpin business success, since people skills, knowledge and learning provide the foundations for all future development. A 'gap analysis' should be carried out to identify shortfalls between the current business infrastructure and that required to achieve future objectives. Performance measures for innovation and learning are then targeted to closing any identified 'gaps'.

3.16   From the **financial perspective**, measures should be designed to indicate the extent to which corporate and supply chain strategies, and the way they are being executed, are achieving improved bottom line results (profitability) and shareholder value. It is no good focusing on improved customer satisfaction, say, if this does not have a measurable effect on sales revenue, profits or market share.

3.17   Having defined performance criteria related to the four business perspectives, it is important not to view purely as a static list of metrics, but rather as a framework for implementing and aligning complex programmes of change, that will constantly evolve over time. The strategic-level scorecard must be cascaded through the organisation, and expressed in, or aligned with, functional and operational plans.

3.18   It should be noted that there are drawbacks and limitations to the balanced scorecard approach in practice. Developing and implementing the scorecard is a complex and time-consuming exercise. It will often imply radical change of management style and organisation culture – for which resources and support may not be available. Commitment from senior management must be genuine and consistent to avoid 'mixed messages' (eg if lip service is paid to the balanced scorecard, but procurement is still judged mainly on its ability to reduce costs...)

Supplier balanced scorecards

3.19   The concept of the scorecard has been extended to supplier enterprises where the associated metrics are commonly referred to as supplier balanced scorecard (SBS). In this form the metrics package is constructed to measure the ongoing supply situation. In order for the supplier to meet ongoing requirements and expectations it is vital to provide them with feedback about their performance. Indeed, many companies allow their suppliers to access this measurement analysis online via the buyer's web pages.

3.20   The models used for this SBS formulation can range from standardised models to those that are bespoke to meet the organisational needs. A typical SBS model by which supplier performance is measured is illustrated in Table 11.2.

Table 11.2 *A supplier balanced scorecard*

Factor	Weighting (%)	Points award	Measurement criterion
Quality	30	1.50	PPM (0.7), reject frequency (0.3)
Delivery	25	1.25	On-time-in-full delivery (1.0)
Support systems	15	0.75	Quality management systems, eg ISO 9000 (1.0)
Commercial	30	1.50	Cost savings (0.7), after-sales support (0.3)
Total	100	5.00	

3.21   The factors and the associated weighting used in the SBS model will vary to accommodate each business requirement. The weighting for each factor used will usually have a direct alignment with the customer's strategic objectives.

3.22   Each supplier's performance is assessed in the following manner.

- For each factor, the total scores for each measurement criterion are summed (max 1.0) and multiplied by the factor weighting
- All the factor scores are totalled and a score out of 5.0 is recorded

- The factor and criterion scores are formulated via conversion tables devised by the customer.
- The resultant final score will enable an overall supplier rating to be established for the supplier.

3.23 The resultant data from the SBS analysis, if used in positive, future-oriented and development-focused dialogue with the supplier, can be used to establish further improvement targets. Where deficiencies of performance are recorded these can be subjected to gap analysis with a view to setting action targets for improvement.

4 Quality management and improvement

Definitions of quality

4.1 'Quality' will mean something different for the purchase of computer equipment, engineering components, building materials, cleaning supplies, accountancy services or catering services. A buyer's definition of quality may therefore focus on a range of different dimensions.

- *Excellence*: the degree or standard of excellence of a product; the design, workmanship and attention to detail put into it; and the extent to which finished products are free from defects.
- *Comparative excellence*: how favourably a product is measured against competitive benchmarks (other products), best practice or standards of excellence
- *Fitness for purpose or use*: that is, the extent to which a product does what it is designed and expected to do; or, more generally, the extent to which it meets the customer's needs.
- *Conformance to requirement or specification*: that is, the product matches the features, attributes, performance and standards set out in a purchase specification. Conformance therefore also implies lack of defects, and therefore reflects on the quality of the supplier's processes.
- *Acceptable quality and value for money*: buyers may be willing to sacrifice some performance and features in order to pay a lower price for a product, as long as it is still fit for purpose.

4.2 For a buyer looking to appraise the quality of a supplier's products or services as part of the contract management process, the most important definitions of 'right quality' are likely to be fitness for purpose and conformance to specification. The BSI definition of quality is: 'the totality of features and characteristics of a product or service that bear on its ability to satisfy a given need.'

4.3 Ideally, a buyer would like to transfer as much of the cost and effort of quality management as possible to the supplier. Instead of just appraising the quality of the supplier's **outputs** (which might not be a reliable measure, if based on process or output sampling at a particular moment in time), the buyer will want to be assured that the supplier *itself* has robust **systems and procedures** in place for monitoring and managing the quality of its outputs.

Costs of quality

4.4 The cost of quality is defined (BS 6143) as: 'The cost of ensuring and assuring quality, as well as the loss incurred when quality is not achieved'.

- The costs of **ensuring and assuring quality** include: *prevention costs* (costs incurred to prevent or reduce defects or failures eg quality circles, specifications, costs of staff training or equipment maintenance) and *appraisal costs* (costs incurred to ascertain conformance to quality requirements eg inspection and testing costs).
- The **loss incurred when quality is not achieved** includes: *internal failure* costs (costs arising from inadequate quality *before* sale to the customer eg scrap and rework costs) and *external failure costs* (costs arising from inadequate quality discovered *after* sale to the customer eg complaints, warranty claims, returns and recalls, loss of goodwill and so on).

4.5 Appraisal and prevention costs can be substantial. Wouldn't it be more cost effective to spend less on such measures, and simply deal with a few defects now and then? Or won't there come a time when the benefits of improving 'that little bit more' will be outweighed by the costs of doing so? The answer generally given these days is: no. The costs of getting quality wrong may well be higher than the costs of getting it right – and the law of diminishing returns may not apply, because there will always be some benefit to improvement. Since the costs of 'getting it wrong' are generally perceived as being higher (and further-reaching) than the costs of 'getting it right', there has generally been an increased emphasis on quality management, with the aim of 'getting it right first time'.

4.6   Although you may come across a wide variety of techniques for managing supply and supplier quality, they generally fall into two basic categories or approaches: reactive detection approaches (finding and fixing problems) such as inspection and quality control (QC); and proactive prevention approaches (stopping problems at source) such as quality assurance (QA) and total quality management.

Quality control

4.7   Quality control is based on the concept of **defect detection**. It embraces a range of techniques and activities used to: monitor a batch of items at each step of the supply and production process; identify items that are defective or do not meet specification; scrap or rework items that do not pass inspection; and pass acceptable items on to the next stage of the process. Various degrees of 'tolerance' may be specified: 100% inspection may be used on critical features where zero defects are required, while sampling may be used on less sensitive features.

4.8   Quality control has certain obvious limitations. A very large number of items has to be inspected to prevent defective items from reaching customers. Quality guru W Edwards Deming argued that this ties up resources – and does not in fact improve quality. Defect tolerances may be unacceptably high due to budget and schedule pressures. The process identifies mistakes which have already incurred design, supply and processing costs: 'locking the door after the horse has bolted'. Inspection activity also tends to be duplicated at each stage of the process – magnifying the inefficiencies.

Quality assurance

4.9   Quality assurance is a more integrated and proactive approach, based on **defect prevention**. It seeks to build quality into every stage of the process from concept and specification onwards. It includes the full range of systematic activities used within a quality management system to 'assure' or give the organisation adequate confidence that items and processes will fulfil its quality requirements. In other words, quality assurance is a matter of 'building in quality' – not 'weeding out defects'.

4.10   Defect prevention systems (such as statistical process control or SPC) were proposed by Deming *(Out of the Crisis)* to identify the potential of a process for producing defective items *before* such items had in fact been produced. Operating processes are monitored and unacceptable variations in output identified as soon as they occur: corrective action is then taken immediately, preventing further defects.

4.11   Crosby *(Quality is Free)* argued that: 'a prudent company makes certain that its products and services are delivered to the customer by a management system that does not condone rework, repair, waste or non-conformance of any sort. These are expensive problems. They must not only be detected and resolved at the earliest moment, they must be prevented from occurring at all.'

4.12   Quality assurance programmes (and certification) may build quality measures and controls into: product designs; the drawing up of materials specifications and contracts; the evaluation and selection of quality-capable and improvement-seeking suppliers; communication and feedback mechanisms with suppliers; supplier training (where required to integrate quality systems); motivation of employees and suppliers to maintain and continually improve levels of performance.

4.13   The concept of approved supplier lists and supplier certification arises from the recognition that the quality management systems of a supplier and buyer are really part of the same process. If the buying organisation can be assured that the supplier has already done all the quality control required to supply 'the right quality' inputs, it won't have to duplicate the effort by monitoring or re-inspecting everything on delivery: it can merely check, from time to time, that the supplier's quality management systems are working as they should, by sampling outputs or inspecting procedures and documentation. Integration may be as simple as getting a 'quality guarantee' from suppliers – or there may be detailed formal systems for responsibility sharing, in areas such as specification, inspection, process control, training, reporting and adjustment.

Quality management

4.14   The term quality management is given to the various processes used to ensure that the right quality inputs and outputs are secured: that products and services are fit for purpose and conform to specification; and that continuous quality improvements are obtained over time. Quality management thus includes both quality control and quality assurance.

4.15   A **quality management system** (QMS) can be defined as: 'A set of co-ordinated activities to direct and control an organisation in order to continually improve the effectiveness and efficiency of its performance'. The main purpose of a QMS is to define and manage processes for systematic quality assurance.

4.16   A QMS is designed to ensure that:

- An organisation's customers can have confidence in its ability reliably to deliver products and services which meet their needs and expectations
- The organisation's quality objectives are consistently and efficiently achieved, through improved process control and reduced wastage
- Staff competence, training and morale are enhanced, through clear expectations and process requirements
- Quality gains, once achieved, are maintained over time: learning and good practices do not 'slip' for lack of documentation, adoption and consistency.

4.17   There are several international standards for measuring and certifying quality management systems of various types, including the ISO 9000 standard developed by the International Organisation for Standardisation (ISO). Organisations can use the framework to plan or evaluate their own QMS, or can seek third party assessment and accreditation.

Total quality management (TQM)

4.18   The term 'total quality management' (TQM) is used to refer to a radical approach to quality management, as a business philosophy. TQM is an orientation to quality in which quality values and aspirations are applied to the management of all resources and relationships within the firm – and throughout the supply chain – in order to seek continuous improvement and excellence in all aspects of performance.

4.19   Laurie Mullins (*Management and Organisational Behaviour*) synthesises various definitions of TQM as expressing: 'a way of life for an organisation as a whole, committed to total customer satisfaction through a continuous process of improvement, and the contribution and involvement of people'. From the buyer's point of view, the provision of 'the right' quality inputs is only one part of a total quality picture, which also embraces excellent supply chains; continuous collaborative improvement; cross-functional co-operation on quality; and so on.

4.20   Some of the key principles and values of a TQM approach can be summarised as follows.

- *Get it right first time*. Quality should be designed into products, services and processes, with the aim of achieving zero defects. Taking into account all the costs of poor quality, no proportion of defects can be considered 'optimal' or tolerable.

- *Quality chains*. The quality chain extends from suppliers through to consumers, via the 'internal supply chain' (supplier and customer units representing the flow of work within the organisation). The work of each link in this chain impacts on the next one, and will eventually affect the quality provided to the consumer.
- *Quality culture*. Quality is a 'way of life': a key cultural value in the organisation, which must be expressed and modelled by senior management, and supported and reinforced by recruitment, training, appraisal and reward systems.
- *Total involvement*. Every person within an organisation potentially has an impact on quality, and it is the responsibility of everyone to get quality right.
- *Quality through people*. Commitment, communication, awareness and problem-solving are more important in securing quality than mere systems.
- *Team-based management*. Teams must be empowered and equipped to take action necessary to correct problems, propose and implement improvements, and respond flexibly and fast to customer needs. This requires high-quality, multi-directional communication.
- *Process alignment*. Business processes should be deliberately designed and modified so that every activity is geared to the same end: meeting the customer's wants and needs. Where this is not the case, there may be the need for radical change programmes such as business process re-engineering (BPR).
- *Quality management systems*. Attention is focused on getting processes right. Quality systems should be thoroughly documented in company quality manuals, departmental procedures manuals and detailed work instructions and specifications.
- *Continuous improvement*. Quality improvement is not seen a 'one-off' exercise. By seeking to improve continuously, organisations stay open to new opportunities and approaches, and encourage learning and flexibility at all levels. In contrast to radical, 'discontinuous' or 'blank slate' change approaches such as BPR, continuous improvement may operate by small-step or incremental changes.
- *Sharing best practice*. Quality circles, networks or matrix structures, benchmarking, accreditation and certification schemes and supply chain networking are used to share quality data, techniques and standards.

4.21 Total quality management may sound like such a good thing that you wonder why every firm isn't implementing it. Here are a few suggestions as to why this is the case.

- TQM can prove limited in practice. The initiative may be poorly introduced or managed, and therefore ineffective. Short-term benefits of introducing TQM may wear off over time, as people get complacent or bored.
- TQM can be disruptive, if it is introduced with a 'blitz' approach – leaving people unsure about what to do, or what to do next. The extent and trauma of the change required should not be underestimated.
- TQM is time-consuming, costly and difficult to introduce, implement and 'settle in' – particularly in large, bureaucratic organisations which may resist new cultural values such as customer focus and employee involvement.

Continuous improvement (*kaizen*)

4.22 Quality management involves the ongoing and continual examination and improvement of existing processes: 'getting it more right, next time'. This process is sometimes referred by its Japanese name of *kaizen*: 'a Japanese concept of a total quality approach based on continual evolutionary change with considerable responsibility given to employees within certain fixed boundaries' (Mullins).

4.23 *Kaizen* looks for uninterrupted, ongoing incremental change: there is always room for improvement, for example by eliminating wastes (non value-adding activities) or making small adjustments to equipment, materials or team behaviour. A basic cyclical approach to *kaizen* may be depicted as follows: Figure 11.7. You may recognise it as a variant of the Plan-Do-Check-Act (PDCA) approach to continuous process improvement.

11

Figure 11.7 *Continuous cycle of improvement*

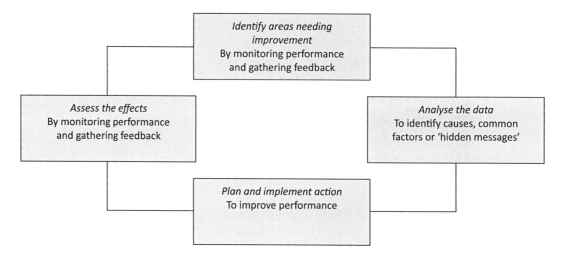

Quality circles

4.24   One technique for continuous improvement, utilised as part of TQM, is the use of 'quality circles': voluntary-participation teams of employees from different levels and functions in an organisation (or representatives from the supply chain), which meet regularly to discuss issues relating to quality, share best practice and recommend improvements.

4.25   Quality circles may or may not have significant responsibility for making, implementing or monitoring the progress of their recommendations. Even as discussion groups, however, they can have significant benefits: harnessing the expertise of different functions and levels of the organisation; overcoming resistance to quality management and creating quality 'champions'; improving communication and information-sharing on quality issues; and general support for a quality culture.

Six Sigma methodology

4.26   Six Sigma is a disciplined application of statistical problem-solving tools to identify and quantify waste and indicate steps for improvement. It uses a broad DMAIC methodology (Define, Measure, Analyse, Improve, Control) in order to:

- Identify and prioritise characteristics that are critical to quality (CTQ) for customers
- Define detailed performance standards and tolerances for key variables
- Statistically measure true process capability, using metrics such as number of defects per number of outputs and probabilities of process success or failure
- Control defects and variations in the vital few factors (aiming for zero defects)
- Involve management and staff in the process, to create a quality-focused learning culture.

Continuous improvement agreements

4.27   Commitment to continuous improvement – with performance measures and targets for improvement (reviewed and updated periodically) – may be built into long-term supply contracts, relationship charters or partnership agreements.

Improving supply chain performance

4.28   More generally, in an exam, you may be asked to suggest potential improvements in the overall management of a company's supply chain (even though, in practice, such strategic improvements would usually be planned and implemented at a more senior level in an organisation).

4.29　At the level of the overall supply chain, performance improvements may be obtained in a wide variety of ways. (In an exam, take care to select and recommend those that are applicable to the specific context of the question, especially in case studies.) Here are some examples, gathered from across our syllabus coverage so far.

- Improving procedures and criteria for supplier evaluation and selection
- Introducing or developing IT or ICT systems and applications: for example, track-and-trace systems to monitor deliveries and stock movements (eg using barcoding or radio frequency identification) or the integration of inventory control and transactions systems with suppliers (eg via EDI systems)
- The planning of logistics and storage and distribution networks to increase efficiency
- Training in contract and supplier relationship management disciplines for buying staff – and perhaps also the account managers of supply chain partners
- Increasing the flow and transparency of information between supply chain partners (eg via open book costing, collaborative planning, cross-organisational project teams, regular meetings and so on)
- Applying techniques for more accurate demand forecasting, enabling more efficient production and logistics planning and lower inventory
- Applying detailed KPIs and performance monitoring and measurement mechanisms such as contract management and vendor rating (for high-priority suppliers, especially if currently underperforming). These may include specific improvement targets for cost reduction, inventory control and so on.
- Rationalising or optimising the supply base, focusing resources on a few core suppliers (especially for strategic purchases), while retaining enough suppliers to secure supply and choice or competition
- Progressively removing waste (non value-adding) operations and activities from the supply process across the supply chain: a process called 'supply chain optimisation'. This is an important element in 'lean' and 'just in time' (JIT) supply, which focus on removing waste, particularly in the form of unnecessary inventory. The preference is to collaborate more closely with fewer suppliers, to enable fast, responsive delivery of small quantities of supplies, as and when they are needed.
- Negotiating continuous improvement agreements and KPIs for year-on-year performance gains
- Introducing early supplier involvement (ESI) to improve new product development and specification (as discussed earlier)
- Implementing supplier development programmes to support suppliers in improving their performance or capabilities (discussed in Section 6 of this chapter).

5　Managing service levels

5.1　A service may be defined as 'any activity or benefit that one party can offer to another that is essentially intangible and does not result in ownership of anything' (Kotler). Some obvious examples include call-centre, cleaning, transport and logistics, and IT services: something is 'done for you', but there is no transfer of ownership of anything as part of the service transaction. (It is also worth remembering that some form of service is part of the 'bundle of benefits' you acquire when you purchase materials and goods: sales service, customer service, delivery, after-sales care, warranties and so on.)

5.2　When it comes to specifying requirements and managing performance, services present buyers with problems additional to those that arise in purchasing materials or manufactured goods.

- Goods are tangible: they can be inspected, measured, weighed and tested to check quality and compliance with specification. Services are *intangible:* specifying service levels – and subsequently checking whether or how far they have been achieved – is therefore fraught with difficulty (as we will see later).
- Goods emerging from a manufacturing process generally have a high degree of uniformity, which also simplifies their evaluation. Services are *variable:* every separate instance of service provision is unique, because the personnel and circumstances are different. It is hard to standardise requirements.
- The exact purpose for which a tangible product is used will usually be known, and its suitability can therefore be assessed objectively. It is harder to assess the many factors involved in providing a

11

service: what weight should be placed on the friendliness or smart appearance of the supplier's staff, say, compared with the efficiency with which they get the job done?

5.3 It is harder to draft accurate specifications and performance measures for services than for goods, because of their intangible nature – and yet this makes it even more important. Otherwise buyer and supplier could argue interminably as to whether the service was exactly what was asked for, or of an adequate standard. An advertising agency or architect might submit a design which meets all the client's stated criteria in regard to aims, inclusions, style and budget – but the client may still find it is not what he wanted or 'had in mind'. Who, if anyone, is at fault – and who pays for the second attempt?

5.4 The more work that can be done at the pre-contract stage, the better. This means agreeing service levels, schedules and the basis for charges in as much detail as possible before the contract is signed: disputes often stem from differing expectations on the part of buyer and supplier.

5.5 Supplier management is also an important ingredient in successful service buying. Often the level of service agreed upon is expressed in terms which are difficult to measure: it is not like purchasing steel rods, which indisputably are – or are not – of the diameter or length specified. It is vital that from the earliest stages, the supplier is made aware of exactly what the buyer regards as satisfactory performance and exactly what will be regarded as unsatisfactory. This is where service level agreements come in.

Service level agreements

5.6 Service level agreements (SLAs) are formal statements of performance requirements, specifying the nature and level of service to be provided by a service supplier. The purpose of a service level specification and agreement is to define the customer's service level needs and secure the commitment of the supplier to meeting those needs: this can then be used as a yardstick against which to measure the supplier's subsequent performance, conformance (meeting standards) and compliance (fulfilling agreed terms).

5.7 The main benefits of effective SLAs, as summarised by Lysons & Farrington, are as follows.

- The clear identification of customers and providers, in relation to specific services
- The focusing of attention on what services actually involve and achieve
- Identification of the real service requirements of the customer, and potential for costs to be reduced by cutting services or levels of service that (a) are unnecessary and (b) do not add value
- Better customer awareness of what services they receive, what they are entitled to expect, and what additional services or levels of service a provider can offer
- Better customer awareness of what a service or level of service costs, for realistic cost-benefit evaluation
- Support for the ongoing monitoring and periodic review of services and service levels
- Support for problem solving and improvement planning, by facilitating customers in reporting failure to meet service levels
- The fostering of better understanding and trust between providers and customers.

5.8 SLAs are therefore a useful tool for client-supplier communication and relationship management; expectations and conflict management; cost management; and performance monitoring, review and evaluation.

5.9 The basic elements of an SLA are as follows.

- What services are included (and not included, or included only on request and at additional cost)
- Standards or levels of service (such as response times, speed and attributes of quality service)
- The allocation of responsibility for activities, risks and costs
- How services and service levels will be monitored and reviewed, what measures of evaluation will be used, and how problems (if any) will be addressed
- How complaints and disputes will be managed

- When and how the agreement will be reviewed and revised

Of course, these elements will be adapted to the specific nature of the service contract.

Mechanisms for monitoring service levels

5.10 A wide range of techniques is available for monitoring – keeping an eye on – service provision and service levels, and feeding back the data in order to identify 'service gaps' which need to be addressed. Depending on the nature of the service and the data collection mechanisms in place, examples of such techniques include the following.

- *Observation and experience*: that is, seeing and experiencing the service. It may be obvious, for example, that an office has (or has not) been cleaned to a promised standard, or that a commitment to deliver goods on time has (or has not) been met. Customers may log or report service failures as and when they occur.
- *Spot checks and sample testing*: performance may be periodically tested or measured in some way. In the case of our cleaning service, a 'spot check' would involve an unannounced inspection of the offices with a checklist of measures (bins emptied, windows clear, toilets disinfected, carpets vacuumed), while 'sampling testing' might involve analysing the number of dust particles present in selected areas of the carpet, say.
- *Business results and indirect indicators:* services have a purpose – so good or poor quality service has a knock-on effect on customers' activities. For example, feedback from the customers' customers might indicate dissatisfaction with the cleanliness of the premises, late transport deliveries, or lack of courtesy by call centre staff.
- *Customer and user feedback:* customers and users of the service should periodically be invited to complete feedback surveys on the quality of the service they have received. In addition, mechanisms should be in place to facilitate customers and users in making complaints, to notify the service manager (and/or the service provider) promptly of specific service failures.
- *Electronic performance monitoring:* in some cases, service performance can be monitored using measuring or tracking devices. Examples include clocking-in-clocking-off devices to record hours worked; 'black box' journey recorders used by transport providers to track delays and routes; and computer programmes recording the number of transactions processed, telephone calls made or taken, cost and schedule variances from plans; and so on.
- *Self-assessment by the service provider*: service providers may require reports by their own staff or supervisors. This may range from a checklist signed off by the cleaners' supervisor at the end of a shift (with notes on where service could not be satisfactorily provided, and why, where relevant), to periodic, systematic self-review reports. (How did we do? How could we do better? What do we need from the customer to support improvement?)
- *Collaborative performance review.* Periodically, all the above information should be gathered and shared by customer and service provider, with a view to evaluating the success of the service contract.

5.11 Whichever method of monitoring and review is used, the information will have to be fed back to service or account managers on both sides, who will in turn disseminate the information to those responsible for performance.

Service quality gaps

5.12 The performance data will be measured against the SLA, KPIs or other benchmark targets (eg quality standards), and 'gaps' will be identified where the perceived service level falls short of the target level: the SERVQUAL tool, for example, measures stakeholder perceptions of a provider's service quality against that of an acknowledged 'excellence' (or benchmark) organisation. Identified gaps will then be used to develop targets and actions for improvement.

5.13 It is worth remembering that 'service quality gaps' may be perceptual – as well as actual – shortfalls.

11

There may be a gap between what is specified and what is *delivered:* that is, a shortfall which the service level agreement will entitle the customer to have addressed. However, there may also be a gap between what users or consumers expect and what service managers *think* they expect (and lay down in SLAs): the service may fall short of specification – but be quite acceptable to users, and *vice versa.* The service level agreement and KPIs may themselves need adjusting, so that service quality isn't over-specified (wasting resources) or underspecified (causing user and provider dissatisfaction).

5.14 As Lysons and Farrington point out, the services and service levels enjoyed and expected by customers do not necessarily correspond to (a) what they really need, (b) what really adds value or (c) what the service provider is capable of offering. This complicates the picture, because 'maintaining service levels' may in fact be wasteful and inefficient (if high levels of service, at high cost, do not add value), or – on the other hand – may miss opportunities for improvement (if specified services or service levels ignore value-adding capabilities of the service provider).

6   Supplier development

Objectives of supplier development

6.1 Supplier development may be defined as: 'Any activity that a buyer undertakes to improve a supplier's performance and/or capabilities to meet the buyer's short-term or long-term supply needs'.

6.2 Hartley & Choi identify two overall objectives for organisations engaging in supply development programmes.

- Raising supplier competence to a specified level (eg in terms of reduced costs, or improved quality or delivery performance). *Results-oriented* development programmes therefore focus on solving specific performance issues: the buyer supports the supplier in making step-by-step technical changes, to achieve pre-determined improvements.
- Supporting suppliers in self-sustaining required performance standards, through a process of continuous improvement. *Process-oriented* development programmes therefore focus on increasing the supplier's ability to make their *own* process and performance improvements, without ongoing direct intervention by the buyer. The buyer supports the supplier in learning and using problem-solving and change management techniques. The process of *kaizen* or continuous improvement (mentioned earlier as part of TQM) is an important aspect of this kind of supplier development.

Responsibilities for supplier development and improvement

6.3 Supplier development programmes will often involve cross-functional representatives from both buyer and supplier organisations, perhaps working in a project team or problem-solving task force. In addition, there will probably be multiple contact points in both organisations, for ongoing monitoring and management. Another common practice is the temporary transfer of staff: supplier staff may be seconded to the buyer organisation to learn, or buyer staff may be seconded to the supplier to advise or train, say.

6.4 Supplier development is another area in which executive sponsorship is essential. A senior-level manager should oversee the progress of specific supplier development initiatives, especially those of a strategic or partnership nature. The executive sponsor will be the primary driver of the supplier development initiative, and the co-ordinator and enabler of cross-functional collaboration: his senior position allows him to mobilise resources and apply influence across functional boundaries.

Directive and facilitative approaches

6.5 There are two generic approaches to supplier development programmes.

- Directive – suppliers are directed, regulated via specification of targets, goals etc. In some senses this can be viewed as a 'telling' or 'command and control' approach.

- Facilitative – buyers and suppliers engage collaboratively in learning, teamwork and improvement planning, to achieve continuous improvement, best-practice sharing, collaborative learning and a 'win-win' orientation.

6.6   Both strategies can be used by purchasing as components of the 'supplier development toolkit'. For example, in the initial stages of supplier development programmes a more directive, structured approach might be advisable to ensure understanding and alignment of development goals for both parties. As the development programme matures and trust increases then the bias of the relationship may move to a more facilitative, emergent approach.

6.7   Before it is decided which approach purchasing will use they firstly need to identify the degree of influence the company has with the suppliers concerned: there is little point in expending significant organisational resources where there is minimal scope to manage or influence the existing marketplace. How important is the buyer's business to the supplier? What is the degree of buying influence in the relationship due to the perceived importance of the business to the supplier?

6.8   Generally, buyers will only be able to make demands where they are perceived by the supplier as key clients and/or where a positive business relationship already exists. Table 11.3 summarises possible buyer considerations.

Table 11.3 *The importance of buyer influence*

DEGREE OF BUYER INFLUENCE	POTENTIAL BUYER ACTIONS
High	Very demanding via directive and/or facilitative control
Moderate	Target key areas of improvement only
Low	• Seek alternative sourcing • Concentrate on developing supplier awareness

A supplier development programme

6.9   A nine-stage approach to implementing a supplier development programme is suggested by Lysons & Farrington: Figure 11.8.

6.10   If you had to pick five steps to describe this process (which might be more realistic for discussion in an exam), you might boil the programme down to: identifying critical products; appraising supplier performance and identifying performance gaps; forming a cross-functional SD team; negotiating improvements and deadlines; and monitoring performance.

Figure 11.8 *The stages in a supplier development (SD) programme*

1 *Identify critical products for development*	For example, using Kraljic's matrix, discussed in Chapter 4: mainly strategic or bottleneck products
2 *Identify critical suppliers for development*	Identifying suppliers who have the capability to meet present and future needs, with the potential for leverage
3 *Appraise supplier performance*	As discussed earlier
4 *Determine performance gaps*	The gap between present and desired supplier performance (eg quality achieved versus quality required, or level of purchaser relationship compared with the expectations of both parties)
5 *Form cross-functional SD team*	To appraise suppliers, identify gaps and negotiate and collaborate with suppliers on improvements
6 *Meet with supplier's top management*	To clarify mutual expectations and build trust
7 *Agree how perceived gaps can be bridged*	Using a range of possible approaches, discussed in detail below
8 *Set deadlines for achieving improvements*	Reasonable, jointly agreed and strictly enforced
9 *Monitor improvements*	For example, via follow-up visits, supplier evaluation and performance feedback.

Approaches to supplier development

6.11 A wide variety of approaches may be used to bridge perceived performance or relationship gaps. Here are some examples.

- Enhancing working relationships (eg by improved communication systems and routines)
- Clarifying or increasing performance goals and measures (eg KPIs for improvements in waste reduction or delivery lead times), and associated incentives and penalties to motivate improvements
- Seconding purchaser's staff to the supplier (or *vice versa*) for training, coaching, consultancy, support or liaison
- Providing capital (eg to help finance a new development project or the acquisition of new plant and equipment)
- Providing progress payments during the development of a project or product, to support the supplier's cashflow
- Loaning machinery, equipment or IT hardware. CIPS guidance cites some practical examples including: a buyer providing electronic terminals to suppliers, so that buyers can use purchasing cards; a buyer paying

for a supplier's manufacturing processes to be updated, in return for discounted supplies in future; and a buyer giving an outsource supplier the machinery previously used to perform the activity in-house.

- Granting access to IT and ICT systems and information (eg extranets and databases, inventory systems, computer aided design capability and so on)
- Using the purchaser's bargaining power to obtain materials or equipment for the supplier at a discount
- Offering training for the supplier's staff in relevant areas (eg technical aspects of the requirement, or benchmarked best practice)
- Providing help or consultancy on value analysis (waste reduction) programmes, costing or other areas of expertise
- Encouraging the formation of supplier forums or a supplier association (*kyoryoku kai* in Japanese, since this is a feature of large Japanese manufacturing). These bring key suppliers together on a regular basis to share information, expertise and best practice, and to encourage joint problem-solving and improvement planning. According to Hines, they may facilitate the flow of information across the supplier network; improve the skills of suppliers and encourage best practice; keep suppliers in touch with market developments; help smaller suppliers lacking specialist resources (eg for training); and increase the length and strength of business relationships.

Costs and benefits of supplier development activities

6.12 Bearing in mind the expense and effort that may be involved in supplier development, buyers will expect to make significant gains from: sharing in the specialist knowledge of the supplier; taking advantage of the supplier's capabilities to support the outsourcing of non-core activities; or improving supplier and supply chain performance to achieve better quality, delivery or cost. Like other forms of collaborative relationship, however, the aim is for benefits to accrue to both sides.

6.13 The benefits and costs of development activities, from both the buyer's and the supplier's perspective, are summarised in Table 11.4.

Table 11.4 *Costs and benefits of supplier development activities*

BUYER'S PERSPECTIVE

COSTS	BENEFITS
Cost of management time in researching, identifying and negotiating opportunities	Support for outsourcing strategies
Cost of development activities and resources: risk of over-investment in a supply relationship which may not last or prove compatible	Improved products and services: time-to-market, quality, price, delivery – supporting increased sales and profitability
Costs of ongoing relationship management (where required)	Streamlining systems and processes: reduced waste, process efficiencies, cost reduction
Risks of sharing information and intellectual property	Gaining discounts or other benefits as a quid pro quo for development

SUPPLIER'S PERSPECTIVE

COSTS	BENEFITS
Cost of management time in researching, identifying and negotiating opportunities	Support for production and process efficiencies and cost savings, leading to greater profitability
Cost of development: risk of over-investment and over-dependence, if customer turns out to be too demanding or unprofitable	Improvements in customer service and satisfaction, leading to retained or increased business
Costs of ongoing relationship management (where required)	Improved capacity and service levels, leading to additional sales to other customers
Risks of sharing information and intellectual property	Direct gains in knowledge and resources provided by the customer
Cost of discounts or exclusivity agreements given as quid pro quo	Enhanced learning and flexibility: skills for problem-solving and continuous improvement

11

Performance measures and supplier development

6.14   Performance measurement (discussed earlier) is an important part of supplier development, because both parties will want to:

- Select the right partners to work with: buyers will undertake development activities only with suppliers capable of improvement and leverage
- Measure the gains from the cost and effort put in. Both parties will want a 'before and after' picture of performance to reassure themselves that the activities were effective and justified
- Agree on objectives and a programme of activities that benefit them both.

Chapter summary

- Supplier performance can be measured against defined criteria, or previous performance, or standard benchmarks.
- There are many benefits of using KPIs as performance measures, though there are also some drawbacks.
- Vendor rating is the systematic post-contract appraisal and evaluation of supplier performance.
- Benchmarking is the process of measuring performance against that of best-in-class firms or other appropriate comparators.
- Kaplan and Norton's balanced scorecard emphasises that performance should be measured along more than one dimension (ie not just financial performance).
- The costs of quality include ensuring and assuring quality, as well as the loss incurred when quality is not achieved.
- Quality control is based on defect detection; quality assurance is based on defect avoidance.
- Total quality management is a radical approach to quality management as a business philosophy.
- One aspect of quality management is continuous improvement (*kaizen*).
- There are particular difficulties in measuring service performance that go beyond those involved in purchasing materials or manufactured goods.
- Supplier development refers to activities that a buyer undertakes to improve a supplier's performance so as to benefit the buyer.
- Supplier development programmes may be either directive or facilitative.

Self-test questions

Numbers in brackets refer to the paragraphs where you can check your answers.

1   What is a key performance indicator? (1.4)

2   What are the benefits of using KPIs? (1.8)

3   List methods of gaining feedback on supplier performance. (2.3)

4   Describe the factor rating method of vendor rating. (2.6)

5   Define 'benchmarking'. (3.1, 3.2)

6   What are the four perspectives in Kaplan and Norton's balanced scorecard? (3.9)

7   Define 'cost of quality'. Give examples of the cost elements included in it. (4.4)

8   Distinguish between quality control and quality assurance. (4.7, 4.9)

9   List key principles of TQM. (4.20)

10   Give reasons why it is more difficult to evaluate services than manufactured goods. (5.2)

11   List basic elements of a service level agreement. (5.9)

12   What are the overall objectives of supplier development? (6.2)

13   List possible approaches to supplier development. (6.11)

14   Give possible costs and benefits of supplier development from a buyer's perspective. (6.12, 6.13, Table 11.4)

Subject Index